Studies in Rhetorics and Feminisms

Series Editors, Cheryl Glenn and Shirley Wilson Logan

⧽⧼

Educating the New Southern Woman: Speech, Writing, and Race at the Public Women's Colleges, 1884–1945

David Gold and Catherine L. Hobbs

Southern Illinois University Press
Carbondale

17   16   15   14   4   3   2   1

Publication has been partially supported by subvention from
the University of Oklahoma and the University of Michigan.

Library of Congress Cataloging-in-Publication Data
Gold, David, [date]
Educating the new Southern woman : speech, writing, and
race at the public women's colleges, 1884–1945 / David Gold,
Catherine L Hobbs.
    pages.   cm. — (Studies in Rhetorics and Feminisms)
Includes bibliographical references and index.
    ISBN-13: 978-0-8093-3285-4 (pbk.)
    ISBN-10: 0-8093-3285-X (paperback)
    ISBN-13: 978-0-8093-3286-1 (ebook)
1. Women—Education—Southern States—History. 2. En-
glish language—Rhetoric—Study and teaching—Southern
States—History. 3. Report writing—Study and teaching
(Higher)—Southern States—History. 4. Rhetoric—Southern
States—History. 5. Education, Higher—Southern States—
History. I. Hobbs, Catherine. II. Title.
LA230.5.S6G65 2013
371.8220975—dc23   2013016639

Contents

Acknowledgments

MANY PEOPLE HAD A HAND in making this book possible. We would like to thank Studies in Rhetorics and Feminisms series editors Cheryl Glenn and Shirley Wilson Logan for their support and assistance in developing this project and our anonymous reviewers for their cogent feedback and advice; this book has been strengthened through their joint efforts. Southern Illinois University Press editor-in-chief Karl Kageff and the press staff made the editing and production process smooth. The Spencer Foundation provided a generous research grant that allowed us to conduct the initial archival research for this project; we also received crucial support from our home institutions.

Our archival history would not have been possible without extensive local support at our sites of study, and we would like to acknowledge the kind assistance of the archives, special collections, oral history, and library circulation staffs at Florida State University, Georgia College and State University, Mississippi University for Women, Texas Woman's University, the University of Montevallo in Alabama, the University of North Carolina at Greensboro, the University of Science and Arts of Oklahoma, and Winthrop University in South Carolina. We are particularly grateful to Burt Altman, Ann Barton, Nancy Davis Bray, Kelly Brown, Bridget Pieschel, Robin Jeanne Sellers, and Gina P. White.

Liz Rohan provided the initial introduction that got our project started, and Sharon Crowley and other table members offered early encouragement at the Rhetoric Society of America Research Network when our manuscript consisted of a one-page bulleted list of questions. Aubrey Schiavone provided valuable copyediting and proofreading assistance. We'd also like to thank our friends and colleagues who kept asking us, "So when is your book coming out?" with the full expectation that it would; your confidence kept us going. Finally, David would like to thank his wife, Priscilla Hohmann, for her unwavering faith and confidence, and Catherine would like to thank her father, Dan S. Hobbs, for his historical work at the University of Science and Arts of Oklahoma that provided inspiration and direction for the book.

An earlier version of chapter 5 appeared as "Students Writing Race at Southern Public Women's Colleges, 1884–1945," *History of Education Quarterly* 50.2 (2010): 182–203; material used courtesy of the journal, the History of Education Society, and Blackwell Publishing.

add Cheryl Glenn

⊰⊱   *lit. review
outline*

Introduction: Peculiar Institutions

UNTIL QUITE RECENTLY, much of the significant work treating women's higher education in America in the late nineteenth and early twentieth centuries centered on single-sex private liberal arts colleges in the Northeast. When the first wave of revisionist and feminist scholars in the history of rhetoric began examining these institutions and their wider cultural environs to better understand the development of women's rhetorical education, they sometimes found gendered rhetorical spaces that limited women's opportunities for self-expression, both written and oral, and circumscribed their participation in civic life (Connors; N. Johnson; Smith-Rosenberg; Wagner). Even at elite women's colleges, administrators and faculty members at times subjected women to a rigid current-traditional rhetoric, disparaged student writing, and discouraged women's public speaking and political participation (J. Campbell; Conway; Simmons).

★ look into these people

Over the last decade, scholars have increasingly begun to complicate these earlier histories by examining a broader range of institutions, taking into account local institutional and regional circumstances as they speak to larger national trends, and recognizing pedagogical practices as dialogic rather than monologic. Susan Kates and Jessica Enoch have examined pioneering progressive women educators at previously underexamined sites of instruction, Kathryn Fitzgerald and Beth Ann Rothermel have studied women's rhetorical education at coeducational normal colleges; Shirley Wilson Logan and Jacqueline Jones Royster have examined African American

1

women's rhetorical education and activities, and Anne Ruggles Gere, Wendy B. Sharer, and others have analyzed how women used literacy in social and civic organizations. Our view of the Seven Sisters is also changing; in recent years, Lisa S. Mastrangelo, Julie Garbus, and Suzanne Bordelon (*Feminist Legacy*) have demonstrated the presence of robust rhetorical programs at, respectively, Mount Holyoke, Wellesley, and Vassar, challenging the notion that these schools were replicating, in reductive fashion, current-traditional models fostered by elite male institutions.

We still, however, lack a full accounting of the diversity of women's educational experiences in the era, particularly in the South, and particularly in state-supported institutions, where changing expectations of women's public and professional roles created new institutional contexts for emerging national trends.

To address this research need, we in this volume examine rhetorical education—reading, writing, and speech instruction—at a chain of eight public colleges in the South founded originally for white women: Mississippi State College for Women (1884), Georgia State College for Women (1889), North Carolina College for Women (1891), Winthrop College in South Carolina (1891), Alabama College for Women (1896), Texas State College for Women (1901), Florida State College for Women (1905), and Oklahoma College for Women (1908).[1] These schools served as crucial centers of women's education in their states, particularly where other opportunities for public higher education were restricted. As these schools developed, their combined yearly enrollments would come to exceed that of the Seven Sisters colleges (see table 1.3 in chapter 1); using enrollment figures from catalogues and other sources, we estimate that they collectively educated approximately one hundred thousand women before World War II. We treat the period from the founding of the first of these schools through 1945, when social changes following the war greatly expanded educational opportunities for women, signaling the beginning of a decline for single-sex institutions.

Despite their importance, surprisingly little work has been done on these schools.[2] This may be in part because their identities as women's colleges were largely subsumed in the wake of coeducation. Though all are still in operation as public coeducational colleges, only two, Mississippi University for Women and Texas Woman's University, retain a reference to their original mission in their names (see table 0.1).[3]

Established by state legislatures primarily as industrial-vocational colleges, often meant to perform a complementary function to that of state men's A&M schools, these schools soon evolved into hybrid institutions offering liberal arts, vocational education, and teacher training. All shared

Table 0.1

Current names and focus of former public women's colleges

Formerly	Currently	Focus
Alabama Coll. for Women	U of Montevallo	Public liberal arts U*
Florida State Coll. for Women	Florida State U	Comprehensive public U
Georgia State Coll. for Women	Georgia College and State U	Public liberal arts U*
Mississippi State Coll. for Women	Mississippi U for Women	Comprehensive public U
North Carolina Coll. for Women	U of North Carolina at Greensboro	Comprehensive public U
Oklahoma Coll. for Women	U of Science and Arts of Oklahoma	Public liberal arts U*
Texas State Coll. for Women	Texas Woman's U	Comprehensive public U
Winthrop Coll. (South Carolina)	Winthrop U	Comprehensive public U

*Members of the Council of Public Liberal Arts Colleges, whose members seek to provide small-college liberal arts education in a public setting.

a mission of educating women for new public and professional roles in a rapidly changing and modernizing South and serving an economically and socially diverse constituency. Together, they illuminate a number of trends and tensions in the post–Civil War and Progressive eras, including the shift from an agrarian society to an industrial one; the land-grant impetus and the democratization of education; the industrial and vocational education movement; the advent of women's clubs and domestic science as social and political forces; the women's rights movement; the national public debate over how best to educate and train women for a new social and economic order; and shifting definitions of regional, American, female, and white identity.

These trends often played out differently in the South than elsewhere. For example, though arguably less progressive on race and more conflicted on suffrage than their northern counterparts, southern women used women's clubs to expand the traditional domestic domain of women into the public sphere and exert powerful political influence on educational affairs. As opposed to the coeducational ideal promulgated in midwestern land-grant institutions and normal schools, in the South, separatist institutions for men and women were part of a larger cultural ideal that both limited and extended women's educational opportunities. Industrial and vocational education also took on special meaning in the South, where the Civil War had resulted in economic distress and left many "surplus women" who needed to work; as such, vocational education was often seen as liberating, while the old liberal arts ideal was sometimes associated with an elitist and outdated antebellum ideology. Over time, the liberal arts would strengthen and even come to dominate in some of these colleges, but most never lost their broad vocational purpose.

Combining the ideals of public education *and* women's education in a uniquely southern context, these schools fostered approaches to pedagogy and women's public roles that are worth studying. Because these southern state-supported colleges emerged at the end of the nineteenth century when the nation's oratorical culture was waning but still extant, especially as part of the southern feminine ideal, their curricula all began with rhetoric, elocution or expression, and written composition in various disciplinary configurations, however uneasy. Extracurricular activities in all eight colleges included a blend of debate, oratory, theater, and literary and lyceum activities that amplified the opportunities for these young women to practice rhetorical arts. At Oklahoma College for Women, for example, students received a special strain of southern feminine rhetorical education that was perhaps less threatening to men because it framed oratory as expression, a performative fine art closely allied with drama and dance, and thus safely within the limits of traditional feminine roles. Nonetheless, this training did prepare these women for teaching and leadership in the still-developing young state of Oklahoma. Florida State College for Women has been criticized for its numerous paternalistic and patriarchal features. Yet despite tight restrictions on campus life, students were able to create an effective rhetorical space in the classroom and through their campus writing, which commonly treated issues of public import and at times took positions that challenged the conservative religious and political orthodoxy within the state. At Texas State College for Women, students modeled themselves on tough Texas clubwomen, deftly employing their traditional role as caretakers of the home to argue for expanded women's participation in politics, science, and public health. At each of the campuses in our study—though to varying degrees—women discussed and debated not only suffrage and women's rights and roles, but issues such as socialism, the peace movement, fascism, one-world government, and the "race" question. The presence of such discussion suggests campuses more responsive to changing social dynamics than has previously been credited.

An Incomplete Picture

As numerous historians of the South have noted, among the lingering burdens of southern history—and historiography—are persistent public misperceptions of the South, which has long been portrayed as other to an enlightened North, nonrepresentative of the American experience and thus

easily dismissed.[4] Such perceptions have extended to scholarly treatments
of education. Notes Amy McCandless,

> Southern women and Southern colleges have shared many of the "bur-
> dens" of Southern history. The image of the South as a poverty-stricken,
> guilt-ridden, and benighted region has tinged portraits of its people
> and institutions for generations. Southern women have been dismissed
> as "belles" more concerned with marital prospects than with mental
> accomplishments, and Southern colleges as bastions of "good ole boys"
> more interested in booze than in books. Southern women's colleges
> have been characterized as mere "finishing schools" for the wealthy,
> and Southern black colleges as outmoded "trade schools" for the poor.
> More often than not the term "educated Southerner" has been viewed
> as an oxymoron. (*Past in the Present* 14)

Even today, negative portrayals of the anti-intellectual southern sorority
girl or her slouching, baseball cap–wearing brother loom large in the public
rhetoric of complaint against college students. In the late nineteenth and
early twentieth centuries, women attending southern women's colleges also
had to contend with negative stereotypes, many generated from within the
region. Faculty and administration members, meanwhile, fought to overcome
lingering perceptions that education for women—and women themselves—
should ideally be largely ornamental.

Established to respond to the needs of their states and placed in often
rural and removed settings, the southern public women's colleges are local
institutions, and their histories reflect many regional concerns. But they
originated in the tumultuous post–Civil War environment across the South
and also interacted with progressive educational movements and ideas from
elite colleges across the nation and the industrial education movement in
Europe. They attracted good faculty members and administrators, trained
from across the nation, who networked with their peers at other colleges,
both inside and outside the system, and were conscious of their roles as educators in distinctly public *and* women's institutions operating in a distinct
regional milieu. The parallel origins, charters, goals, and reciprocal relations
of the southern public women's colleges are why we treat them as a single
phenomenon, despite institutional differences.

We consider it important to emphasize that faculty and administrators of
these colleges largely viewed themselves as modern, forward-looking educators and kept up with the latest educational trends. For example, the opening
of Johns Hopkins University in 1876 is usually said to mark the turn to the
modern, disciplinary, German university from the old character-building
college. Two decades later, in its first year of operation as a "normal and

industrial college," Winthrop hired a Johns Hopkins Ph.D., James Pinckney Kinard, to teach English language, literature, and civics.[5] Graduates of two progressive Boston schools of elocution, the Emerson College of Oratory (now Emerson College) and the School of Expression (now Curry College), filled the ranks of speech and oratory faculty at these schools through the 1930s. The colleges were also able to hire graduates of the nation's finest colleges, especially women. Women graduates desiring college teaching often had nowhere else to go, as few were chosen for faculty positions in men's or mixed colleges, so even these small and rural colleges could have their pick. Such women often provided strong models of resistance and individual agency for their students. Anna Forbes Liddell, one of the first women to earn a Ph.D. from the University of North Carolina, in 1924, taught at Florida State College for Women from 1926 to 1962, most of that time as chair of philosophy. A publicly active woman who lived long enough to fight for both suffrage and the Equal Rights Amendment, she was a central figure on campus.[6] Said Daisy Flory, a 1937 graduate, "One can hardly deny that many FSCW customs . . . might have had disastrous and narrowing effects but for the free and fiery spirit of Forbes Liddell and other strong and liberated women" (qtd. in Stern 50).

In the early-twentieth-century American South, the very formation of a "normal and industrial" college (or often just "industrial girls' school") was a forward-looking notion, designed particularly to help young women in a region still economically devastated and with many Civil War widows and other displaced citizens and too few able-bodied men. Mississippi State College for Women, the earliest, and a model for the other schools, created a hybrid of liberal arts, normal, and industrial education for its young white women.[7] By turns across the South, various factions, including progressive educators' and teachers' associations, the Grange and other farmers' organizations, and public-spirited women's clubs pressured state legislatures to provide higher education for their states' white daughters. These schools early functioned as substitute A&M schools for white women, and they typically had orchards, dairies, farms, and a variety of industrial arts, including telegraphy, stenography, photography, designing, engraving, bookkeeping, dress design, and other arts. Industrial training originally copied German and European models, and faculty early on traveled to study European institutions. Home economics curricula developed by the first decade of the twentieth century, with the Smith-Lever and Smith-Hughes Acts appropriating federal funds for home demonstration and rural educational projects. These schools received federal funding, although in some cases, such as with Winthrop in South Carolina and Texas State College for Women, the money was administered through their respective state's men's A&M college.

Changing Ideals

Though all the southern public women's colleges were established as "modern" colleges, they were also all created in a transitioning new South still tied to old South traditions. Socially, if not academically, they combined the social life and women's culture of private women's colleges in the Northeast with the old character-building function and religious tenor of southern female seminaries, a pattern that held sway for many decades, and indeed long after northern women's colleges had relaxed certain restrictions. Students were sequestered behind high fences and gates, uniforms and chapel attendance were mandatory, and presidential power, although usually benign, dominated everywhere. Towns bid for these colleges and offered them financial and community support, and the colleges in turn added value to these communities, which took pride in their "girls"; the "blue line" of uniformed young women heading off to church each Sunday was a common theme in these pleasant towns. Students were not necessarily expected to be, as one turn-of-the-twentieth-century Wellesley student complained, "a lady first and a college girl afterwards" (qtd. in J. Campbell, "Freshman" 117); for most of them, too much was economically at stake. However, they were expected to maintain feminine ideals even as those ideals were being simultaneously reinforced and undermined by their educational experiences. From the start, then, forces existed in these eight colleges pulling two ways—forward toward "modern" emergent national notions of education and culture in the U.S. and the attendant promise of an industrialized and reunified new South, and back again to visions of magnolias and violets, plantation life, and the putatively gentler agrarian time of the old South. These competing tropes oscillated and intertwined in unexpected ways in the young women's literary work, school pageants and rituals, and life choices.

Higher education thus was—and remains—a double-edged sword. Women could accept it passively as a reinforcement of the status quo, or they could focus on the empowerment and choices it offered them, changing not only their own lives but the lives of those around them. As McCandless explains of her own broad survey of women's education in the twentieth-century South: "For some women, the culture of deference and dependence that pervaded southern institutions did, unfortunately, stifle aspirations and reinforce the status quo. For others, however, higher education provided the wherewithal for them to expand their intellectual and social horizons, to understand their regional heritage, to ameliorate its worse aspects, and to build on its best elements" (*Past in the Present* 14). In this book, we seek to understand the nature of rhetorical training at the public colleges for women in the South in the late nineteenth and early twentieth centuries. To what extent did these schools constrain and expand women's opportunities for self-expression, professional development, and participation in public life? How did these schools resemble and differ from that of private women's and coeducational colleges elsewhere? Can general conclusions about these schools as a serial phenomenon be reached, or must each be assessed according to its local institutional circumstances?

In chapter 1, "Making Modern Girls: The Ideals of the Southern Public Colleges for Women," we examine the development of higher education for women in the South in the late nineteenth and early twentieth centuries and trace the establishment and evolution of the public women's colleges. In particular, we explore tensions between old and new South conceptions of white female identity as they played out through the lens of education. As the South struggled to rebuild after the Civil War, new cultural mandates for women emerged, challenging antebellum conceptions of gender identity. The public women's colleges were established as a response to these changes, at once looking backward toward a protectionist ideology regarding young white "girls" and forward toward an increasing consensus that new educational and economic opportunities were required for the coming "new woman" of the South. Instructors and administrators often had to contend with legislators, parents, and populaces with varying conceptions of the purposes of education and the proper public and professional roles of women. We argue that the southern public women's colleges both made use of and reacted against traditional tropes of femininity as they negotiated a place for themselves and their students in the emerging new South.

In chapter 2, "Effective Literacy: Writing Instruction and Student Writing," we examine writing instruction at the schools, setting faculty and departmental goals and methods against larger institutional, professional, and cultural contexts. We complement this inquiry by further considering how students publicly represented themselves through writing. We argue that the public women's colleges created a robust climate of expression that complicates our understanding of both the development of writing instruction in American colleges and the rhetorical constraints and opportunities experienced by women in this era. In particular, faculty took part in a wide range of contemporary pedagogical conversations as they struggled to develop locally appropriate curricula. While writing instructors often emphasized the correctness in expression associated with reductive current-traditional approaches, they simultaneously promoted a social view of writing, encouraging students to write in public forums and treat topics of contemporary import. More often than not, the colleges promoted what Catherine Hobbs has termed an "effective literacy," one that allows its user to effect change in both her life and society (1).

In chapter 3, "Evolution of Expression: Speech Arts and Public Speaking," we examine oratorical education offered at the public women's colleges. Though the colleges differed in the strength of their speech education offerings, some having independent departments, some subsuming instruction under English, all offered extracurricular activities through literary societies, competitive debate, and drama that helped women develop their abilities to speak in public; and all recognized the importance of training future teachers to speak. Indeed, the early intertwining of elocutionary arts with reading and teacher-training programs gave oral instruction a long life in these institutions. Before the professional field of speech developed, elocutionary "parlor rhetorics" were brought in from the domestic arena and public platform to the academic environment, where they helped shape the curricula for women's speech and drama activities for decades to come. These elocutionary rhetorics helped women learn to present themselves in public and became a solid foundation for graduates who entered careers or engaged in civic activities requiring public speech. We argue that it would not be possible to understand the peculiar features of these women's colleges—their styles of oratory and expression, rituals, Greek dances, theatrical forms, pageants, military drill teams, and Swedish gymnastics—without understanding their origins in a feminized elocutionary theory and practice that scholars have often overlooked or dismissed.

In chapter 4, "Useful Careers: Professional Training for Women of the New South," we examine the various ways the public women's colleges prepared women to succeed in available occupations in the region. We also consider how women made use of their education in rhetoric and writing as they considered and made their career choices. We begin with historical background about the development of industrial education before addressing the three major areas of professional education emphasized by the public women's colleges—business and industry, teaching, and home economics. Industrialism came slowly to the South, and was just gaining ground by the late nineteenth century when the earliest of the public women's colleges opened. In these colleges' post–Civil War settings, industrialism was a double-edged sword, seen as tinged with northern values at the same time as the jobs it promised were sorely needed. Although the colleges all turned more toward the liberal arts over time, their mission to educate and train women for work was never lost, and all emphasized preparation for careers in business, the schools, industry, and home economics, as well as nursing, government service, and other fields. This vocational mission distinguished the colleges from other women's institutions and shaped their development in important and subtle ways.

In chapter 5, "The Absent Presence of Race," we examine the role of race at these schools, which were established as both separatist and segregated institutions for white women. Scholars have long debated the complicity of southern white women after the Civil War in contributing to a "culture of segregation" (J. Johnson, "Drill" 527) promulgated by racialized constructions of southern, American, and female identity. To what extent were students at the public women's colleges complicit in this process, and what role, if any, did the colleges play in breaking down racial divisions and promoting interracial understanding? We argue that although students adopted many tropes of Lost Cause rhetoric, they were also more willing than many contemporary elite white women writers to temper their romanticizing of the old South, which they recognized as lacking in opportunities for women. Though we find a continuum of racial attitudes both within and across campuses, with paternalism and essentialism even in sympathetic treatments, we also find students sometimes ahead of community norms in advocating for more equitable treatment of African Americans, reflecting both emerging themes of study in literature and sociology and the examples of local campus authorities.

In our conclusion, "A Continuing Legacy," we consider the legacy of the public women's colleges as it speaks to both the history of women's education and contemporary challenges in the teaching of rhetoric and writing. Though all these schools remain extant, most as comprehensive public universities, they began transitioning into coeducational institutions following World War II. Yet the primary reason for which they were established—to educate young women of modest economic means for public and professional roles in a rapidly changing society—remains a critical concern for contemporary instructors. How do we balance liberal arts education with professional training? How do we devise appropriate curricula for our local campus constituencies? How do we negotiate with publics holding views on education at variance with our own? And how do we find room for the instruction in reading, writing, *and* speaking our students will need? Though the histories of the public women's colleges do not provide simple answers to these questions, they do suggest the power of locally responsive curricula to meet student needs and the remarkable adaptability of students in responding to institutional ideologies.

Research Design

Historical scholarship in rhetoric and writing studies is increasingly recognizing the value of archival sources and archival methodologies as well as the need to theorize and detail their use (Donahue and Moon; Kirsch and Rohan; L'Eplattenier; Ramsey, Sharer, L'Eplattenier, and Mastrangelo). At the same time, historiographers are often reluctant to detail their *own* methods and methodologies in their published work. Historian John Lewis Gaddis terms this an "anti-Pompidou Center aesthetic"; historians, he notes, "don't like to display ductwork" (92). Gaddis suggests this reluctance might be born of disciplinary insecurity. Working largely inductively, and in narrative form, "we mumble when the social scientists tell us we aren't really doing science ... [and] grumble at the postmodernists who claim that what we're writing is only fiction. But we don't respond effectively to either argument" (92). In her recent "An Argument for Archival Research Methods," Barbara E. L'Eplattenier calls for rhetoric and composition scholars to "begin incorporating more explicit discussions of our primary research methods into our historical research" in order to "make the invisible work of historical research visible" (68–69). Here we would like to take up that call.

Although we draw from many published sources, our study is primarily an archival history. As such, it examines the institutional archives at each of our eight sites, studying material such as catalogues, course syllabi, lecture notes, textbooks, manuscript collections, and administrative records. As we are especially interested in student experiences, we also examine materials such as class essays, course notes, diaries, school newspapers, literary journals, yearbooks, and oral histories, comparing institutional self-representations with the experiences reported by instructors and students. We also make use of external archival resources, such as the records of professional societies, state and federal educational reports and legislative records, and contemporary academic journals, magazines, and newspapers. We supplement this material with sources culled from full-text subscription databases such as JSTOR, Communication and Mass Media Complete, ERIC, and ProQuest Historical Newspapers, and web-based search tools such as Google Books, Google Scholar, the Internet Archive, and WorldCat. Finally, we set our research against contemporary scholarship in the history of women's education, rhetoric and writing studies, and southern history.

In conducting our research, we have been challenged to balance institutional self-representations with the experiences reported by instructors and students. College bulletins and institutional documents, which predominate in our archives, present an authorized narrative, though these documents elide the diversity of individual experiences in these institutions. Student writing in yearbooks, literary magazines, and newspapers provide insight into student experiences, though these writings are meant for public display and moreover represent a small fraction of the number of students at these institutions. We uncovered little in the way of private journals from faculty or students, but scrapbooks and some interviews with older alumnae were helpful in filling the gap between private experience and public representation. Together these sources provide us with a sense of what constituted authorized discourse at these schools—as well as a rich base for exploration.

We find that the young women in these schools were intensely public, in part perhaps because of the intensely public nature of their education. In these schools' earliest days, students used to small-town and rural life were literally crowded into dorms and communal dining halls. Institutional authorities—conscious of their duties in loco parentis, fearful of scandal, and perhaps seeking to shake students from their ostensibly agrarian cultures into modern industrial time—scheduled their lives to the hilt with religious services, mealtimes, extracurricular activities, classes, and study activities. No wonder there was little time for reflection in private journals. More so than their male-only and coed counterparts, the southern public colleges for women experienced intense scrutiny by political authorities, religious leaders, women's clubs, newspaper editors, parents, and anyone else concerned with the state of young white southern womanhood, the health of which these schools were charged with—and sometimes accused of corrupting. Students at these colleges through the World War II era were intensely conscious of their roles as southern women in the public eye.

Our work takes a microhistorical approach, looking at local institutional sites both as local cultures and as lenses for illuminating national trends.[8] Descriptions of general context are complicated by the individual agency of faculty and students, who do not always act according to the dominant cultural context they are immersed in. We thus hope our specific case studies can complement, complicate, and challenge the conclusions reached by more general histories. We are particularly inspired by rhetoric and composition historians such as Thomas P. Miller (*Formation*) and Winifred Bryan Horner, whose work on the development of English literature in Scottish public schools reminds us that educational sites that, at first glance, may appear to be at the cultural margins may actually be a fount of innovative pedagogical practices. Our work differs from some earlier historiography in rhetorical education, however, in its theoretical assumptions. In contrast with scholars such as Robert J. Connors, Sharon Crowley, and James A. Berlin, who sometimes take a more deterministic view of the relationship between ideology and pedagogy, we assume a more fluid and complex interaction, preferring to see teachers and students as potential agents and active shapers of their educational experiences and to "acknowledge the mixed goals and hybrid forms that most often mark classroom practice" (Gold, "Remapping" 22).

In writing our histories, we have been sensitive to postmodern critiques of knowledge that underscore the epistemological biases underlying any scholarly inquiry and suggest the limitations of any form of historical representation. Though we do not share Michel Foucault, Hayden White, or Alun Munslow's pessimism regarding historiography, we are informed by their skepticism. As scholars, we are limited not only by the interpretive frames we bring to historical evidence but also by the evidence itself; in conducting our research at these schools we were continually reminded of the partial and contingent nature of archives and the conclusions we draw from them. As an increasing number of rhetoric and composition scholars are acknowledging, we cannot hope to recover "a unified narrative of the discipline" (Moon 3) or get the story "exactly right" (Glenn and Enoch 11).

In recent years, as historians have taken up the challenge of postmodern critiques of historiography, they largely have come down, as we do, on the side of referentiality. That is, though history requires imperfect, ideologically bound human historians, it also requires empirical support, in the form of evidence, often drawn from archives. Historical narratives might share tropes with literary narratives, but they are not fictions. As Peter Burke notes in the introduction to the second edition of *New Perspectives on Historical Writing*, "historians have long been aware of the difficulty of defining the extent to which evidence can be trusted and the extent to which historians fill in the gaps with the help of their imagination" (20).

Throughout the researching and writing of this manuscript, we have been particularly conscious of the generative effect of interpretive differences in attempting to negotiate our own. We came to this project through shared goals: a commitment to recovering women's histories, an interest in interrogating received historical narratives, and a desire to portray the richness and complexity of southern voices while avoiding the romanticism, presentism, and simple binaries that sometimes characterize representations of the South. Yet we also brought to this project differing life experiences, professional histories, scholarly questions, ideological frames, and blind spots. Two guiding principles have kept us moving forward. The first is an acknowledgment that complete consensus is impossible. Information technology experts sometimes speak of the importance of "rough consensus and running code." The phrase, coined by Internet pioneer David Clark to describe the process used to develop Internet standards and protocols and adopted as a manifesto in internetworking circles, can serve as a heuristic for decision making in any nonhierarchical environment with open-ended projects, indeed, as a model for developing disciplinary knowledge. As described by science and technology historian Andrew L. Russell, *rough consensus* refers to the need for a high, though not unanimous, level of support; "a proposal must answer to criticisms, but need not be held up if supported by a vast majority of the group." *Running code* refers to the importance of creating working models, usually developed out of "discussion and testing" rather than trying to work from a fixed theoretical model (55). In practical terms, agreement on broad principles matters more than disagreement on more narrow points. While the process can lead to a stifling of unorthodox or even counterhegemonic readings and a blurring of difference, as we each try to conform to an emerging shared consensus, it can also *allow* for such readings, as we acknowledge that we need not always be in complete agreement.

Closely tied to this principle is sensitivity to the recursiveness of the collaborative research process. Empirical researchers sometimes make a distinction between discovery and verification modes. In the first, one knows little and works inductively to find patterns; in the latter, one works deductively to test hypotheses. In comparing what he terms "positivist" and "constructivist" forms of inquiry, Egon G. Guba argues that an emphasis on verification as the real work of science discounts the importance of discovery and that we should instead see these modes as part of a "continuum of inquiry" (23). Indeed, our work in this volume has often proceeded in this fashion. Our individual observations lead to the suggestion of a pattern, tested by the other, which often leads to new discoveries, and so on. We have continually challenged each other, when confronted with a difference in interpretation, to return to the archive for further elaboration.

Of course, even with these guideposts in mind, negotiating difference remains a difficult and delicate process. While we have largely agreed on our readings of individual artifacts, we have had at times lengthy exchanges over the relative weight to give a particular artifact. Though we are confident about the conclusions we have reached, we are aware that another set of scholars with a different terministic screen might emerge from these same archives with a counterreading. We welcome, encourage, and indeed call for more such work. The schools in our study represent significant, overlooked centers of women's education for the period. First, they educated large numbers of students, having substantial regional impact. Second, as public institutions, these schools were pivotal centers in debates over the goal of women's education and public roles. Third, as southern institutions, they represent a distinct and often-dismissed regional culture and history. Finally, much historiography on white southern women has focused on elite women, but the institutions in our study were designed for women of a broad range of economic circumstances. By examining these previously unexplored but important institutional sites, we will gain a richer and more complex history of the experiences of a more generally representative and overlooked group of women in American higher education. We will have a better understanding of not only how women learned to read, write, and speak in American colleges, but also what they did with their education both within and outside of cultural boundaries in their lives beyond college.

1

Making Modern Girls:
The Ideals of the Southern Public Colleges for Women

THE FEATURES SECTION of the 1930 Florida State College for Women yearbook is bookended by two striking photos (depicted on cover). Virginia Bailey, voted "most modern girl," sits in the cockpit of a fixed-wing biplane, wearing a leather bomber jacket, aviator's cap, and goggles. It's easy to envision this woman flying in a few years as a Women's Air Service Pilot. And though the photo is obviously posed, her relaxed, open-mouthed smile gives it the air of a candid and contemporary snapshot. This is indeed the modern era.

At the other end is Virginia Anderson, the campus's "old fashioned girl." Her photo has been taken in a lush garden before the entrance to a grand plantation home, complete with white Doric columns and a shady magnolia tree. She stands quietly, hands cupped in front, her smile revealing no teeth, wearing a layered floor-length white dress, the picture of demure purity. It's an intentionally antebellum image.[1] Yet looking again, we see that her dress, though redolent of a bygone era, is a modern cut. The ruffled top sits entirely off the shoulders. The waist is natural—no whalebones here—and the tiers of the skirt sit not on hoops but gracefully fall, following the natural line of her hips and legs. And her hair is a flattering and modern bob.

Perhaps Miss Anderson is not so old fashioned after all?

Not many years prior, her hair alone would have been considered scandalous.[2] The first bob reportedly appeared on campus in 1919; by 1924, 69 percent of students wore their hair short, despite the efforts of campus authorities to dissuade them (Sellers 153). Long-serving English professor and dean of the college William G. Dodd, who arrived in 1910, later somewhat wistfully recalled the gentler, more prescriptive "feminine decorum" of the school's earliest days, compared to the discarding of tradition that followed World War I. For those prewar women, wrote Dodd, "'Victorian' was not a dirty word. They would have been utterly astounded if someone had told them that a change would come, and soon, where a young woman could still be a lady and bob her hair and leave off most of her unmentionables" (Dodd, "Old Times" n. pag.). If Miss Anderson in dishabille represents a moment where antebellum sensibilities meet the modern era, it is not *the* moment, of course, but one of many. From the college's start—as with each of the schools in our study—these elements were in tension. Indeed, this continued interplay between old and new South conceptions of female identity would be a prominent—if not defining—feature in the development of the southern public colleges for women.

In this chapter, we examine the development of higher education for women in the South in the late nineteenth and early twentieth centuries and trace the establishment and evolution of the public women's colleges. In particular, we explore tensions between old and new South conceptions of white female identity as they played out through the lens of education. As the South struggled to rebuild after the Civil War, new cultural mandates for women emerged, challenging antebellum conceptions of gender identity. The public women's colleges were established as a response to these changes, looking at once backward toward a protectionist ideology regarding young white "girls" and forward toward an increasing consensus that new educational and economic opportunities were required for the coming "new woman" of the South.[3] Instructors and administrators often had to contend with legislators, parents, and populaces with varying conceptions of the purposes of education and the proper public and professional roles of women. We argue that the schools both made use of and reacted against traditional tropes of femininity as they negotiated a place for themselves and their students in a changing region.

Changing Ideals for White Southern Womanhood

The movement of southern women's work into the public realm was a revolution that began after the Civil War. This did not mean that southern women, especially women in small landholding, tenant, and lower-class households, did not previously work. Their labor, however, was largely subsumed into family farm and household economic production.[4] But the creation and flourishing of the southern public women's colleges was both a sign of and one cause of this revolution in the increasing visibility and valuing of women's work. Though largely agreeing on the dire economic conditions after the war that led many previously domestic women to seek employment outside the home, scholars disagree about the extent to which this changed social ideals for white women. These conflicting accounts, as Jane Turner Censer reminds us, underscore the necessity of acknowledging the South as a place of "nuances and complexity" (2).

Censer's own archival work among the papers of three generations of elite women in North Carolina and Virginia after the war supports the conclusions about changing ideals for women drawn by Anne Firor Scott's classic *The Southern Lady,* although Scott's thesis applies best to Censer's later generations in the nineteenth century. Scott influentially argued that the war helped emancipate women, though she has since been criticized by scholars for overgeneralizing the extent of postwar socioeconomic and cultural change, in particular the willingness of postwar white women to abandon antebellum ideologies of gender and race (Faust, *Mothers of Invention*; Whites; Rable; Fox-Genovese; Lebsock). (We treat themes of race and identity in more detail in chapter 5.) Censer suggests that some of the conflict between Scott and her critics can be reconciled by examining the behavior of women after the war on a generational basis. In doing so, she finds that "notions of proper behavior and the characteristics of the ideal woman were in flux." Through the 1870s and 1880s, an increasing number of southern women "promulgated an ethic that emphasized 'nondependence'" in both their private and public writing (6–7). By the century's end, and in particular among those women born after 1850 and thus with no little or no adult memory of antebellum life, Censer finds an increasing polarization between "a revived image of the 'southern belle' and that of the emancipated new woman. . . . Even white women who argued for traditional female roles at the same time claimed new, prominent positions for themselves in hereditary and memorial societies, while others turned toward women's rights and more political forms of activism" (9). Although Censer studies elite southern women, this polarization or paradox appears among many of the middle- and lower-middle-class women who sought higher education for vocational purposes at the public women's colleges. Indeed, paradox is the primary trope of much scholarship on white southern women.

As described by Scott, among the first scholars to explore the difference between the ideal and the reality of southern womanhood, the antebellum southern ideal for women held them to be submissive, passive, physically weak, and dependent on male protection and guidance to make it through life. A creature of intuition and sentiment rather than reason and intellect, the southern lady was innocent, sympathetic, nurturing, self-denying, and silent in suffering. Though possessing an ability to "create a magic spell" over any man near her, her natural piety made her a "natural teacher, and a wise counselor to her husband and children" (4–5). Many southern women took these ideals seriously and tried to live up to them.

Medieval imagery was important in maintaining this romanticized ideal, especially the conception of the "Lady" of medieval chivalry as portrayed in books like Castiglione's *The Courtier,* a sixteenth-century etiquette book (A. Scott 15), and popularized by nineteenth-century romances such as Walter Scott's 1819 *Ivanhoe*, whose celebration of feudalism Mark Twain only half-facetiously blamed for southern backwardness, slavery, and the Civil War.[5] Twain was largely concerned with the ill-effects of "chivalry silliness" (378) on male codes of honor. But, as Christie Anne Farnham argues, the image of the southern lady, which merged "separate spheres ideology . . . with notions drawn from chivalry and a glorification of myths of Anglo-Saxon culture," provided both a romanticization of and justification for slavery and white domination (2). Borrowing from an "idealized vision of knights in shining armor, ladies fair, and serfs paying homage to their betters," elite southerners modeled themselves and their society after an imagined "English squirarchy" (30), with slaves substituting for serfs. This affiliation with the medieval carried on after the war and well into the twentieth century; it was manifest in the southern public colleges for women in studies in medieval literature, adulation for Sir Walter Scott, and the oft-repeated Medieval Pageant at Winthrop College, as well as May poles, May queens, and associated symbols and rituals. Paradoxically, this ideal existed at the same time these women students were striving to become "nondependent" and self-consciously modern.[6]

If the antebellum southern ideal held that a woman was, as one early-twentieth-century critic of it complained, a "frail vessel of charm and spirituality . . . [un]sullied by activities in the market place" (Threlkeld 35), the reality of course was different. For independent yeoman farm and small business families, women's work often folded invisibly into that of men, who were praised for running farms and endeavors independently.[7] Lower-class women had always done domestic work, alongside their farm or textile-mill wage labor, and even elite women worked as housekeepers, household managers, hostesses, and agricultural workers. With tasks that included providing child care and medical care, spinning, weaving, sewing, milking, gardening, caring for poultry, hog butchering, and making yeast, lard, and soap (A. Scott 30–31), few had time to be the leisured belles of mythology.

After the war, women of all classes embraced such tasks—and more—from necessity. Household help could now walk away, and even in families with some resources, the house staff was smaller. At all class levels throughout the

South, men were a valued but scarce commodity; in the states in our study, the male proportion of the white population declined from 51.4 percent in 1860 to 49.6 percent in 1870.[8] Throughout the South, at least a quarter million men died from battle, disease, or internment.[9] With so many men dead or disabled and the economy disrupted, white widows could not easily remarry, and their daughters might never wed. Women at all class levels faced the reality that they might have to provide their own living and work independently, perhaps for the rest of their lives. In this atmosphere, women took pride in their domestic skills, ushering in a new emphasis on domesticity. But women also turned to education, clerical work, and writing, as well as becoming active in churches and women's organizations. These trends would find full flower in the home economics and women's club movements of the late nineteenth and early twentieth centuries. These movements, while embracing many tropes of traditionally private women's sphere activities, also moved them into the public arena, providing some southern women with their first taste of economic and political power.

One response to these changes was to further idealize woman and fetishize the southern belle and lady. But the traditional ideal was by now even further from the reality. "The days of knight-errantry have passed," wrote one Georgia woman to the *Atlanta Constitution* in 1889 in support of the establishment of a women's college. "Women are now forced to work, oftentimes at man's work, to earn a living. Orphanage and widowhood occur every day. To deny these women suitable education . . . is cruel and oppressive, especially when they are allowed no voice in the legislation which determines their fate" ("Vital Question" 15). Women were just trying to make a living, doing anything and everything to make money, whether it be school, agriculture, sewing, or working in expanding industries. On the threshold of the founding of the public women's colleges, women were moving rapidly into various types of manual, factory, and professional work. This new economic reality would create a demand for and help shape women's public higher education in the coming years.

Higher Education for Women in the South

Though emerging out of the new South economic order, the southern public women's colleges also developed in the context of antebellum educational ideals for women. In *The Education of the Southern Belle*, Christie Anne Farnham notes that while elite southern women had traditionally enjoyed the possibility of higher education, such education was intended to create value in young southern women by serving as a marker of elite social status. Because it was not designed to enable women to compete with men for jobs, it was not seen as threatening. In contrast with the North, where by mid-nineteenth century, women were beginning to earn money through teaching and other limited careers—thus reaping criticism from men—in the South, elite families wanted their daughters to have some collegiate education to mark their social status and make them more eligible for marriage as more "fascinating" belles.[10]

As a result, writes Farnham, the South "far outdistanced the rest of the nation in the founding of female colleges" (18). The first of these, Georgia Female College, now Wesleyan College, was chartered in 1836 and opened in 1839; it has been estimated that by the 1850s, thirty-two of thirty-nine chartered female colleges nationally were in the South, in every state but Florida (Farnham 18). Most of these schools, or seminaries as they were often called, took up the model of Massachusetts's Mount Holyoke Female Seminary (1837, chartered as a college in 1888), offering a combination of liberal and "feminine" arts. Students studied Latin and Greek, French and English, language and literature, music and art, hygiene and domestic science. These schools also took on a distinctly southern cast. The classical tradition, at its peak in 1825 but already beginning to fade, retained its force in a region that took as its model the English landed class rather than the American industrial one.[11] Competing models of femininity, based in part on ostensible economic and cultural differences between North and South, also clashed. While the southern agrarian ideal allowed for and even celebrated youthful frivolity, northern educators who eventually populated southern women's schools promoted a middle-class ethic of "sober seriousness of purpose . . . self-discipline and orderliness." Neither side won out entirely. Notes Farnham, students "took what resonated to the requirements of Southern culture and modified it to the necessities of the Southern belle" (145).

Such schools would come to be criticized by progressive educators in both the North and South for perpetuating antiquated models of femininity and leaving women unprepared for the exigencies of modern life.[12] Yet as Farnham argues, these schools also planted the seeds for the future development of women's education in the South: "To dismiss antebellum female colleges . . . as merely seminaries with high sounding titles would be to ignore the pioneering efforts of a generation of educators and women students" (28). These schools helped legitimize fine arts as a subject of study. They taught history, rhetoric, and literature courses similar to that offered in men's colleges. Farnham's work is significant historically to our project for describing this culture and for showing that higher education for women was a traditional part of southern culture and not alien to southern ideals. Moreover, by describing how "basically conservative agendas produced an advance in women's education" (7), she speaks to the importance of separating institutional ideologies from actual classroom practices in understanding educational

developments. As we will describe, the public women's colleges, as they developed, far exceeded the expectations and imaginations of the legislative
bodies that sometimes only begrudgingly brought them into existence.

This historical background also helps us understand some of the conflicts
that arose over the curricula of the public colleges for women, chartered
originally in a different environment for a wider class of women than was
typical of many private women's colleges in the North or South. We do not
mean to suggest that such schools were not themselves diverse, or did not
serve students of the emerging middle class, or remained static in their curricular offerings. Among the Seven Sisters, Barnard was famously open to
Jewish students long before its peers (Horowitz 258).[13] At Mount Holyoke,
founder Mary Lyon, an advocate for expanding educational opportunity to
women of modest means, established a cooperative labor system for students
to reduce expenses, for many years after her death, tuition and board at the
school remained substantially less than at the other Seven Sisters schools
(Porterfield; Turpin). The Wellesley and Vassar campuses, both ostensibly
domains of "highly privileged" students (Bordelon, *Feminist Legacy* 10), were
energized by the presence of, respectively, Vida Scudder and Gertrude Buck.
Scudder, a socialist reformer and herself a Smith graduate, took sheltered
students who "had grown up shielded from the unsightly poor" and sought
to "jolt [them] out of complacency" by introducing them to settlement work
(Garbus, "Service Learning" 551–52). Buck, who had studied with rhetorician
Fred Newton Scott at the University of Michigan, promoted argumentation and debate as a means of encouraging civic participation, in particular,
Progressive-era "concerns related to furthering social justice" (Bordelon,
Feminist Legacy 159).[14] Buck's colleague, English chair Laura Johnson Wylie,
along with other instructors associated with Vassar and Bryn Mawr, participated in the progressive and politically charged Bryn Mawr Summer School
for Women Workers (Hollis). Indeed, arguably, faculty at the Seven Sisters
colleges in the reform-minded North had more freedom to be politically
active than their colleagues at the southern public women's colleges, where
campuses were under significant legislative scrutiny and oversight.

Nor is it our goal here to set up the Seven Sisters as a contrastive foil to the
public women's colleges. But we do think it worth pointing out that, though
as women's colleges they shared similar goals and features—in particular,
the desire to offer an education both equal to and distinct from that received
by men—they collectively emerged out of differing historical exigencies. It is
this latter background that we wish to explore in this volume. By the time of
the founding of the public women's colleges, the Seven Sisters were largely
established and stable institutions, with substantially greater budgets and
endowments. Moreover, their models had primarily been northern men's

liberal arts colleges and private female seminaries. Though their graduates would eventually go on to work in similar numbers to those of the public women's colleges, their orientation was not initially vocational.[15] Like their private counterparts, the public women's colleges all promoted, as per Smith's early catalogue copy, "intellectual culture," "social refinement," and even "true Christian life" (*Catalogue 1879–80* 12). Yet while Smith could promise that it was "not intended to fit woman for a particular sphere or profession, but to perfect . . . her intellect, that she may be better qualified to enjoy and do well her work in life, whatever work that may be" (*Catalogue 1879–80* 1), the public women's colleges were explicit about their intent to train students for both domestic and professional spheres—and devoted much effort to delineating what fields of work, exactly, their graduates would be prepared for.[16] (We will take up professional training further in chapter 4.)

Compared to other areas of the country, the region that gave birth to the public women's colleges was poorer, was less educated,[17] had greater class stratification, and generally offered fewer opportunities to women. The public women's colleges were explicitly founded to serve women of modest economic means—typically with no other opportunity to attend college—and tuition, board, and other and expenses were kept low; at a time when the Seven Sisters colleges were among the most expensive in the nation ("Comparative Expenses"; "Increase in Faculty Pay"), the southern public women's colleges were among the least expensive, with total costs averaging about one-third of that of their northern peers (see table 1.1).[18]

Perhaps not surprisingly, funding was also modest. Through the first quarter of the twentieth century, the schools' yearly catalogues, board of regent reports, and other documents are filled with both pleas to their respective legislatures to increase their economic support and accountings of their remarkable achievements on shoestring budgets, especially in regard to job placement of graduates. In its 1918 *Report of the Board of Trustees*, South Carolina's Winthrop noted that its annual budget was a fraction of that of Smith, Vassar, and Wellesley's, though it was educating about as many students (26–27).[19] In its 1919 *Report*, it noted that the salaries of its female department heads compared unfavorably not just to those of faculty at the state's other public colleges, but also to those of train brakemen, campus carpenters, window cleaners in New York, and the college's own recent graduates working as secretaries and stenographers (14).

Although the high purpose of making the public women's colleges equal to that of men's was proclaimed in every case, the question became, which colleges would be their models? Would it be the antebellum southern female seminary with its emphasis on what now was widely called "ornamental"

Table 1.1

Estimated minimum expenses for resident students at
Seven Sisters and public women's colleges, 1925–26

School	Total ($)
Barnard	800
Bryn Mawr	770
Mount Holyoke	900
Radcliffe	813
Smith	970
Wellesley	1,000
Vassar	1,000
Average	893
Alabama	3?6
Florida	237
Georgia	227
Mississippi	225
North Carolina	301
Oklahoma	350
South Carolina	235
Texas	1?5
Average	291

Source: American Council on Education, *American Universities and Colleges*. Totals include tuition, required annual fees, board, and least-expensive room options. Because of differences among colleges, figures should be taken as rough estimates of fee calculations, but in each case we have attempted to provide the minimal annual expenses reported by the college.

education? Elite men's colleges of the Northeast and their Seven Sisters correlates, with their emphasis on the liberal arts? The new agricultural and mechanical colleges with their industrial and vocational education geared toward careers? The states initially favored narrow industrial and vocational models, whereas many women held onto models of traditional elite education. At the same time, students and faculty were keenly aware of the need for "practical" training. Against this background, the southern public women's colleges would become hybrids, with teacher education widely featured. Founded as industrial and normal colleges, their faculty and students turned them gradually toward the liberal arts, and eventually into comprehensive universities as time went on. Throughout this book, we seek to understand the history of the public women's colleges against the backdrop of their particular time and place—an industrializing and modernizing "new" South seeking opportunities for its daughters in a rapidly changing world, and yet uncertain about those changes.

The Rise of the Southern Public Women's Colleges

The public women's colleges were created during a period of expanding but still-limited higher educational opportunities for southern women (see table 1.2). At the time of the founding of their respective women's colleges, three of the eight states in our study, South Carolina, North Carolina, and Georgia, restricted enrollment at the white state flagship to men, while Florida, in consolidating its system in 1905 and establishing its women's college, eliminated coeducation at the flagship University of Florida.

Table 1.2
Availability of public higher education for women in
southern states with public women's colleges

State	White women's founded	White flagship fully coed*	White A&M fully coed*	Black land-grant fully coed*
Mississippi	1884	1882	1930	1895
Georgia	1889	1918	1968	1890
North Carolina	1891	1963	1963	1891
South Carolina	1891	1894	1955	1896
Alabama	1896	1895	1892	1873
Texas	1901	1883	1971	1876
Florida	1905	1947	N/A	1887
Oklahoma	1908	1890	1890	1897

N/A, not applicable.
* Earliest date that women were fully admitted to all programs without restrictions.

Even after the legal establishment of public coeducation, the state flagships tended to discourage women from attending through various combinations of enrollment limitations, behavior restrictions, housing discrimination, and informal hostility.[20] Although the University of Mississippi became coeducational in 1882, there would be intermittent legislative calls for abolishing coeducation over the next two decades; it would take the opening of a female dormitory and the appointment of a dean of women in 1903 to "symbolize . . . the acceptance of coeducation as a legitimate function of the state university" (Sansing, *University of Mississippi* 159). The University of South Carolina did not build a women's dormitory until 1924 (*Catalogue 1924–25* 21, 31), by which time women made up 28 percent of the regular session student body, and women faced restrictions on dress and dorm life through the 1960s.[21] The University of North Carolina allowed limited enrollment of women in graduate programs beginning in 1897, and local freshman in 1917, but did not provide campus housing for women until 1925. Even as the university slowly lifted restrictions on the entrance of women, they were segregated in campus activities and subject to gender-specific regulations on campus life even more rigid than the typical women's college; in 1951–52, female students made up only one-seventh of the student body but accounted for more than half of disciplinary cases, almost all for returning to the dorm late or failing to sign out (Dean 14–15). Women would not be admitted to all undergraduate programs until 1963 and would not obtain equal access to housing until the passage of Title IX in 1972. With the exception of the western border states of Texas and Oklahoma, whose flagships were coed from the start and early on had robust female enrollments, female enrollment at these schools tended to be low or limited to specific degree programs through the 1940s.

At state A&M colleges, restrictions on women were even more severe. Of the seven states with extant white A&M colleges at the time of the founding of their respective women's colleges, five, Georgia, Mississippi, South Carolina, North Carolina, and Texas, were male only; Oklahoma founded its A&M in 1890 as coeducational; Alabama's became coed in 1892, a few years before the establishment of its women's college.[22] The white state A&Ms were also late in allowing women students. Mississippi would not become fully coeducational until 1930, and four of the schools, South Carolina, Georgia, North Carolina, and Texas, would not become fully coeducational until the second half of the twentieth century.[23] Given these restrictions, the public women's colleges played a crucial role in educating the white women of their states.

The first of the colleges to be founded was Mississippi State College for Women (MSCW), chartered by the legislature as the Industrial Institute and College for the Education of White Girls of Mississippi in the Arts and Sciences in 1884, and opened in Columbus, a town of just under four thousand people, in 1885. Like most of the other public colleges for women across the South, MSCW became a reality because women themselves willed and worked it into being. On at least five occasions between 1856 and 1882, advocates managed to get a bill before the legislature—one passed in 1872 but was repealed the following year for lack of funding—before succeeding. Early women advocates for the school included educator Sallie Eola Reneau, who fought for two decades for a women's college that would offer "the indigent as well as the opulent . . . the imperishable riches of a well-cultivated mind" (qtd. in Pieschel and Pieschel 4), and Annie Coleman Peyton, who along with other leading women waged a public campaign, eventually gaining the support of the state Democratic Party, the state Grange, and black Republican legislators.[24]

The narrow vote to establish the college—it passed by only one vote in the Senate and two in the House (Orr, *State-Supported* 39)—and its first charter demonstrate the interplay in the South between antebellum and Progressive-era notions of education and appropriate gender roles. As such, the original charter promised a hybrid of liberal arts, normal, and vocational-industrial training:

> The object of the school should be the giving of education in the arts and sciences, in normal school systems, in kindergarten instruction, in telegraphy, in stenography, and photography; also in drawing, painting, designing, and engraving in their industrial applications; also in fancy, practical, and general needlework; also in bookkeeping, and such other practical industries as may, from time to time, be suggested to the trustees by experience or tend to promote the general object of the institution, to wit, fitting girls for the practical industries of the age. (qtd. in Pieschel and Pieschel 8)

The founding of Mississippi State College for Women largely set the pattern for the establishment of the other southern public women's colleges, with various combinations of progressive educators and newspaper editors, populist farm-advocacy groups, and women's clubs and professional organizations joining together to lobby state legislatures to create hybrid industrial–liberal arts institutions designed to serve a broad range of female students. In Georgia, the wife of a state legislator, Susan Milton Atkinson, inspired by Mississippi's example, encouraged her husband to introduce a bill establishing a women's college.[25] She publicly solicited the aid of the state's women in her campaign, who in turn petitioned newspapers and the legislature for support, leading to the bill's eventual passage. In Texas, women were also at the vanguard of efforts to establish a women's college. Though the flagship University of Texas had been coeducational from the start, the state's white A&M school was not. When efforts by the Grange to establish a parallel women's school failed before the legislature in 1891, public-minded clubwomen[26] took up the cause, and legislation to create the college passed in 1901; in similar fashion to Mississippi, it took tie-breaking votes by the leaders of both the House and the Senate. In contrast to Texas, in Alabama, the effort was nearly single-handedly led by one woman, Julia Strudwick Tutwiler, a progressive educator and reformer who campaigned at her own expense for many years.[27]

In North Carolina, which had no public schools of higher education open to white women, efforts to establish a coeducational state teacher's college were spearheaded in 1886 by two young graduates of the University of North Carolina, Charles Duncan McIver and Edwin Anderson Alderman, who soon gained the support of the Farmers Alliance and various women's groups. Public education for women, however, was apparently an easier sell than *coeducation*, and after two failed attempts before the legislature, a revised bill chartering a college for women passed in 1891 (Trelease 4–6). The one exception to the general pattern of publicly fought campaigns was Florida State College for Women, which was created with apparently little forethought in 1905 when the state consolidated its higher education system, ending coeducation at the then University of Florida and Florida State College and establishing two single-sex colleges for white students in their place.

Though each of these schools varied in their initial curricular emphasis, all blended vocational, liberal arts, and, eventually, teacher training. Texas State College for Women was open to "all white girls of good moral character . . . who have a knowledge of the common school subjects, who wish to acquire a higher education which includes a thorough practical training for life" (*Catalogue 1903–4* 10). The 1891 act establishing South Carolina's Winthrop College promoted as the school's objects "(1) to give to young women such education as shall fit them for teaching; (2) to give instruction to young women in stenography, typewriting, telegraphy, bookkeeping, [industrial] drawing . . . designing, engraving, sewing, dressmaking, millinery, art needlework, cooking, housekeeping, and such other industrial arts as may be suitable to their sex and conducive to their support and usefulness" (South Carolina, *Acts and Joint Resolutions* 1104).[28] Although Florida State College for Women ambitiously promoted itself from the start as a liberal arts college, "not a normal and industrial school," seeking to provide the state's women "the same opportunities for culture and for professional training" as its men (*Catalogue 1906–7* 10), it too offered vocational subjects in catering to its student body.

Though the emphasis on domestic training might appear retrograde to contemporary eyes, it is important to note that these schools had been established to explicitly fill a need not met by the private antebellum seminary.[29] At the same time, campus officials had to honor traditional ideals regarding their state's young white daughters, especially given the sometimes shaky initial legislative support for their institutions. In numerous examples of early catalogue copy and other communications, college leaders explicitly strive to find a balance between old South traditions and new South needs. In an 1887 report to the board of trustees, Mississippi State College for Women president Richard W. Jones assured board members, "We are not teaching women to demand the 'rights' of men nor to invade the sphere of men" but rather offering the "high training" of the mind, taste, and morals "which fits her for the ways of modest usefulness" (qtd. in Maynes 252). In 1903, at the opening ceremonies of Texas State College for Women, regent Clarence Ousley declared, "In this institution, the young ladies will be taught to be

useful as well as ornamental" (qtd. in "Launching of College" 1). His remarks
were echoed by President Hosea Baker Abernethy of Oklahoma College for
Women (OCW) on that school's opening day: "It is the purpose of this institution to elevate and dignify the industrial as well as literary studies and
the fine arts. We want to teach the girls to be as well prepared for and to
take just as much pride in preparing and serving a meal as they would in
playing well on the piano" (qtd. in D. Hobbs 25). Abernethy, a Mississippian,
no doubt had the example of that state's public women's college in mind. As
Dan S. Hobbs comments, "The president thus identified the institutional
DNA which made up the course of study at the original college: the liberal
arts and sciences, the fine arts, and the learning of useful occupations" (25).

Though these colleges sometimes struggled at first, they soon filled an important niche in their states. Designed as they were for women who would be
expected to work—at the very least until marriage—all attracted significant
numbers of students of modest means. At Texas State College for Women
in 1904–5, 38 percent of students were children of farmers, and 19 percent
were fatherless or orphans (*Catalogue 1905* 52). At North Carolina College
for Women in 1896–97, 22 percent of students were fatherless, and approximately one-third were paying their own way without parental help (Trelease
38); as late as 1915–16, 20 percent were fatherless, and 23 percent were paying
their own way (*Catalogue 1915–16* 163–65). Florida State College for Women's
Alumnae News reported in November 1931 that 54 percent of seniors paid for
part or all of their schooling through work, loans, or scholarships (5), while
Oklahoma College for Women's campus newspaper reported in 1927 that
60 percent of fine arts students worked (*Trend* 19 May 1927 1). At Winthrop
in South Carolina, early board of trustees reports noted the percentage of
students who "could not have attended any other college if Winthrop had
not brought education within their reach" (*Report of the Board of Trustees
1902* 869); this ranged between 50 and 60 percent from 1898 to 1903, a number mirrored at North Carolina during its first two decades, where roughly
60 percent of students yearly reported that they would have attended no
other school in the state had they not gone to the women's college. As James
L. Leloudis notes of North Carolina's early students, "Most had grown up
in middling households that provided the relative luxury of uninterrupted
school attendance. . . . But few had known truly privileged lives. . . . Women
like these came . . . seeking opportunity and firm footing in a turbulent and
challenging world" (*Schooling* 94).

For those students at the public women's colleges who received parental
assistance, minimal or free tuition and low living expenses kept the schools
in reach of families with modest incomes. The schools, moreover, promoted
economy among their charges; for example, encouraging students to make

their own uniforms, discouraging travel home, or allowing students to do their own laundry to save on fees. The colleges' strict regulation of students' off-campus activities likely kept indulgences in check, as did a common policy of requesting that parents send money in care of the college, which would monitor students' accounts on their behalf. "This is not a society school," declared the Texas State College for Women, "and it is the policy of the Faculty not only to discourage needless expenditures, but to forbid conspicuous evidences of extravagance" (*Catalogue 1914* 42).

Those students who financed all or part of their education typically did so through some combination of modest scholarships, loans, and work; common jobs included serving in the dining hall, cleaning the dorms, working in the laundry, doing light secretarial or clerical work, working as faculty or staff assistants, babysitting for faculty children, and, less often, working in local shops or offices. In the colleges' earliest years, a number of full-time students had worked previously as teachers and may have had some savings, while other working teachers attended summer sessions to obtain teaching certificates, normal degrees, or other credentials.

In their earliest years, the schools functioned largely as junior colleges, offering various levels of work, including college preparatory classes. Universal primary and secondary education were still developing in the South, and it was understood that not all students would be equally ready to do collegiate work. The colleges' "normal" or teacher preparation courses occupied a transitional slot, with states typically requiring two or three years of training and the passing of a state exam for certification, though not necessarily four full years of college work.

The schools quickly became training centers for teachers, who were much in demand, and prior to official accreditation most relied on their reputations for producing qualified graduates in having their diplomas "recognized" by various colleges and state departments of education for the purposes of transferring credits or teaching. Florida State College for Women had its diplomas qualify for teacher certification by New York and Pennsylvania in 1913 and, after raising entrance requirements to four years of high school, became the first of the colleges to be accredited by the Association of Colleges and Secondary Schools of the Southern States (now the Southern Association of Colleges and Schools, or SACS), in 1915 (Sellers 38–39). Texas State College for Women was recognized by the state as a "first class" college and awarded its first bachelor's degrees in 1915 and was accredited by SACS in 1923. By 1925, all of the southern public colleges for women had received accreditation by their primary regional agencies.[30] As these schools developed into full-fledged four-year colleges and then comprehensive universities, their original vocational functions became subsumed. The process of the various schools shifting to liberal arts study from the original industrial/technical emphasis is often reflected in their changing names. Typical is Alabama: founded in 1896 as the Alabama Girls' Industrial School, in 1911 it became the Alabama Girls' Technical Institute, then in 1919 the Alabama Technical Institute and College for Women, before becoming Alabama College, the State College for Women in 1923, typically shortened to Alabama College for Women or simply Alabama College (see the appendix for a complete list of name changes). With accreditation came increased growth and expansion. In 1925, the eight southern public women's colleges enrolled a combined total of 9,392 students, exceeding the Seven Sisters colleges, and by 1940 enrolled 13,403 students, resulting in some of the largest women's colleges in the nation (see table 1.3).

Table 1.3
Enrollment comparison, southern public women's colleges and Seven Sisters colleges

School	1918	1925	1940
Alabama	491	425	902
Florida	486	1,208	2,048
Georgia	815	1,062	1,544
Mississippi	933	1,238	1,170
North Carolina	271	1,485	2,047
Oklahoma	121	734	1,096
South Carolina	946	1,448	1,741
Texas	1,247	1,792	2,855
Total	5,310	9,392	13,403
Barnard	697	947	985
Bryn Mawr	489	398	635
Mt. Holyoke	858	992	1,094
Radcliffe	618	625	1,000
Smith	2,103	2,080	2,085
Vassar	1,129	1,150	1,200
Wellesley	1,612	1,583	1,506
Total	7,506	7,775	8,505

Sources: U.S. Bureau of Education, *Biennial Survey of Education, 1916–18*, vol. 3 (743–853), vol. 4 (94–99); *World Almanac and Book of Facts, 1926* (385–91), *1941* (529–37). Winthrop's (South Carolina) figures for 1917–18 taken from Winthrop College, *Report of the Board of Trustees, 1918* (8).

Coeducation and the Decline of Women's Colleges

During the first half of the twentieth century, the number of female college students dramatically increased, from approximately eighty-five thousand in 1900 to nearly 806,000 in 1950. However, this rise was exceeded by a surge in male enrollment, so that the *proportion* of college students who were women actually declined from a peak of 47.3 percent in 1920 to 28.9 percent in 1948 (National Center for Education Statistics, *Digest 2008* 277–78).[31] In an era where women remained minorities on coeducational campus, women's colleges continued to play an important role; as late as 1940, they enrolled 17.8 percent of all female college students. The absolute number of women's colleges remained relatively stable through the first half of the twentieth century, entering into steep decline only after 1960. In 1900, there were 141 colleges for women in the United States, of which 128 were dedicated single-sex institutions and thirteen coordinate colleges to men's institutions; the number rose to 276 in 1945, then fell back to 250 in 1960. By 1976, however, only 125 colleges identified themselves primarily as women's colleges, and by 2009, only forty-eight remained (see table 1.4).[32]

In the second half of the twentieth century, the increasing availability of coeducation reduced the apparent need for dedicated women's colleges.[33]

Table 1.4

Women's enrollment in college (all levels), 1879–80 through 2009–10

Year	No. in college*	Percentage of total students*	No. in women's colleges†	Percentage in women's colleges†
1879–80	37,845	32.7	15,700	41.5
1899–1900	85,338	35.9	24,400	28.6
1919–20	282,942	47.3	52,900	18.7
1939–40	600,953	40.2	106,900	17.8
1956–57	1,006,754	34.5	98,300	9.8
1980–81	6,222,521	51.4	105,185	1.7
1999–2000	8,300,578	56.1	93,488	1.1
2009–10	11,658,207	57.1	93,739	0.8

* *Source*: National Center for Education Statistics, *Digest 2010* (290–91).

† *Sources*: 1879–80 through 1956–57, Newcomer (49); 1980–81, Touchton and Davis (185); 1999–2000, National Center for Education Statistics, *Digest 2001* (258); 2009–10, National Center for Education Statistics, *Digest 2010* (357).

† Calculated by the authors. Due to rounding and varying methods for counting/estimating enrollment, our percentages differ slightly from those calculated by Newcomer.

While many women's colleges struggled during this period, eventually becoming coeducational, merging with their affiliated men's schools, or even closing in the face of stagnant or declining enrollment, the southern public women's colleges did not face an across-the-board decline. Rather, the switch to coeducation mirrored larger national educational trends, as states responded to increased enrollment pressures following World War II, women's rights activities and antidiscrimination legislation during 1960s and 1970s, and court rulings during the 1980s and 1990s.

The first of the southern public women's colleges to become coeducational was Florida State College for Women in 1947, now Florida State University. While the college had maintained consistent growth, the state legislature, responding to increased enrollment pressure on the male-only University of Florida (UF) from the recently passed G.I. bill, voted to make both schools coeducational. The change happened with little controversy. Talk of coeducation had been in the air for about a decade, and many students and faculty were amenable to it; a 1945 poll found that 53 percent of FSCW students favored coeducation at both colleges and another 39 percent at UF only (Sellers 265–66), suggesting support for coeducation as a right but also continued support for the choice of single-sex education.[34] The potential loss of the women's college was likely tempered by the gain of full coeducation at the state flagship. Students might also have been tantalized by the promise of newfound freedom that coeducation might bring; when a limited number of male students were permitted on campus in anticipation of full coeducation, the administration's "tolerant attitude" toward them "astounded the female students," who began to demand similar treatment for themselves (Sellers 269–70).

Between 1956 and 1975, five of the remaining colleges became coeducational, four because of declining or stagnant enrollment.[35] At Alabama College for Women, historically the smallest of the eight schools, enrollment, never large, had declined from 902 in 1940 to 524 in 1955, and the college decided it could best survive as a coed liberal arts institution; the move was a successful one, and by 1960, enrollment had nearly doubled to 1,022. It continues today as the University of Montevallo, having found its niche as the state's designated public liberal arts college, with approximately twenty-five hundred students in a small college environment.[36] In a similar vein, facing declining enrollment, Oklahoma (from 1,096 in 1940 to 678 in 1965) and Georgia (from 1,544 in 1940 to 897 in 1965) went coeducational in 1965 and 1967; they were eventually redesignated as public liberal arts colleges, now the University of Science and Arts of Oklahoma and Georgia College and State University. Winthrop College in South Carolina, now Winthrop University, struggling to maintain enrollment in the 1970s, went coeducational in 1975 with the support of students, faculty, and administrators.

At North Carolina College for Women, in contrast, enrollment remained strong (from 2,047 in 1940 to 2,566 in 1960), though campus authorities did fear a sloughing off due to the increasing expansion of coeducational opportunity at the state flagship. In 1963, however, the legislature, facing pressure to improve the state's college graduation rate and prepare for an expected influx of baby boom students, voted to reorganize the state university system, in the process making it fully coeducational. The formerly male-only University of North Carolina was renamed the University of North Carolina at Chapel Hill, and the women's college the University of North Carolina at Greensboro.[37] Though there were some concerns about the loss of independence and the watering down of the school's mission, most students and faculty eventually supported the change (Trelease 281–84).

In the climate of the Civil Rights era, coeducation seemed an almost inevitable part of increasing gender equality. At the two colleges that persisted the longest as women's schools, however, the switch to coeducation was charged. The battles for coeducation at Mississippi and Texas suggest the strength of these schools in inspiring their communities, but also, perhaps, fallout from some of the failed promises of the Civil Rights era; women fighting for the continuation of single-sex education were motivated in part by the realization that coeducation and desegregation had had only limited effect in eliminating sexism and racism.

Mississippi State College for Women, now Mississippi University for Women, continued to grow after World War II, from 1,170 students in 1940 to 2,241 in 1965 to 3,010 in 1976. It became coeducational in 1982, following a lawsuit by a male registered nurse, Joe Hogan, seeking admission to the baccalaureate nursing program. By 1989, seven years after coeducation, the number of female students had declined to 1,588, but by 1993, overall enrollment had begun to recover, and in 2008, the school enrolled 2,365 students, 83 percent of whom were women.

At Texas State College for Women, now Texas Woman's University, the first men were admitted into some health science programs in 1972, under antidiscrimination provisions of the Health Services Act, then into graduate programs in 1973 under Title IX of the Higher Education Act. Men were not admitted into undergraduate programs until 1994, following a vocal protest by a male student, Steven Serling, who had been accepted into the nursing program but wanted the option of enrolling in other degree programs. At this time, Shannon Faulkner's lawsuit against the Citadel was making national news, and the board of regents, under public scrutiny, the threat of legal action, and pressure from the legislature, voted to make Texas Woman's University coeducational shortly before the end of the fall semester, leading to the first general division male enrollees in the spring 1995 semester. The decision was initially controversial on campus, leading to public protests by students and faculty, censure by the national alumnae association, and a lawsuit against the board (Sahlin 122–29; McCandless, "Separate" 114–17).[38]

Though coeducation closed a chapter in women's education, it did not end the legacy of separatism. With the exception of Florida, the former southern public colleges for women continue to have larger than average female enrollment (see table 1.5). South Carolina's Winthrop, Alabama, and North Carolina are all over two-thirds female, and Texas and Mississippi, the last schools to become coeducational, are respectively 93 and 83 percent female and remain part of the Women's College Coalition. In their new guise, these still-public, formerly women's colleges continue to play a role in educating the young women of their states.

Table 1.5
Proportion of female and male undergraduates
at former public women's colleges

School and year of coeducation	Female (%)	Male (%)
Texas (1994)	93	7
Mississippi (1982)	83	17
South Carolina (1975)	69	31
Alabama (1956)	67	33
North Carolina (1964)	67	33
Oklahoma (1965)	64	36
Georgia (1967)	59	41
Florida (1947)	55	45
2008 U.S. average	57	43

Source: Fall 2008 women's colleges data from *Peterson's*; U.S. average from National Center for Education Statistics, *Digest 2010* (291).

2

Effective Literacy: Writing Instruction and Student Writing

UNTIL RECENTLY, SCHOLARSHIP on women's rhetorical education in the late nineteenth and early twentieth centuries has tended to emphasize rhetorical constraints on women's expression. Within the last decade, however, scholarly emphasis has shifted from examining how women's voices have been historically marginalized to better understanding how women negotiated—and at times extended—the spaces available to them. At the same time, the increasing acceptance of women's histories as a topic of inquiry and feminist historiography as a mode of inquiry has allowed scholars to be less concerned with finding heroes and villains and better able to see historical subjects within their own cultural contexts. Within the larger field of rhetorical history, a loosening of the hold of epistemological taxonomies and the deterministic force of ideology advanced by earlier histories has made it easier for scholars to acknowledge the complexity of motives shared by writing instructors in the late nineteenth and early twentieth centuries as well as the agency of students engaged with rhetorical curricula. Finally, the spread of site-specific microhistories has encouraged scholars to attend to local historical contingencies in writing histories.

In this spirit, we examine in this chapter writing instruction at the public women's colleges, setting faculty and departmental goals and methods against larger institutional, professional, and cultural contexts. We complement this inquiry by further considering how students publicly represented themselves through writing, taking into account Kathryn Fitzgerald's

reminder that student writing does not simply reproduce institutional ideology, but can negotiate with, contribute to, and even counter it, allowing
students to "explore, extend, and sometimes circumscribe their own communal identities" (274). We argue that the public women's colleges created
a robust climate of expression that complicates our field's understanding of
both the development of writing instruction in American colleges and the
rhetorical constraints and opportunities experienced by women in the late
nineteenth and early twentieth centuries. While writing instructors often
emphasized correctness in expression, they simultaneously promoted what
James A. Berlin termed a social view of writing. To the extent that classes un-
critically reproduced bourgeois subjectivity, they also encouraged students'
self-confidence as writers and promoted writing in public forums. More often
than not, the public women's colleges thus fostered what Catherine Hobbs
has termed an "effective literacy," one that "enables the user to act to effect
change, in her own life and in society" (1).

Numerous factors contributed to this climate of expression, including
the professional and vocational orientation of the schools, particularly their
emphasis on teacher training; their place in the public eye as places of educational experimentation; their high percentage of female faculty; the importance to campus life of literary societies, which promoted interpretive
reading and public debates; and the importance of campus publications such
as student newspapers and literary journals. Within English departments,
the influence of teachers of speech and graduates of schools of education
also helped foster an interest in social problems and civic life. Faculty were
frequently engaged in critical pedagogical questions of the day, and students
too had an interest in professional and public life.

We also address criticism that the schools perpetuated a lingering antebellum atmosphere that imposed antiquated and reductive models of femininity
on students. As Linda K. Kerber has noted, women's spheres were "socially
constructed both *for* and *by* women" (18), and southern women have been
particularly adept at negotiating their own definitions of femininity that
resist easy classification. Certainly, many patriarchal and paternalistic features can be found in the founding, mission, and day-to-day administration
of the public women's colleges, and students' dress, daily schedules, and
off-campus activities were strictly regulated at most campuses well into the
1930s. Despite the restrictions on campus life, students were often able to
create an effective rhetorical space through their campus writing, which
commonly treated issues of public import and at times took positions counter
to reigning orthodoxies within the state or even engaged in direct challenges
to campus authorities. By examining what students and faculty themselves
said, rather than simply what has been said about them, a picture emerges

of campuses much livelier and more responsive to changing social dynamics than has previously been credited.

Early-Twentieth-Century Writing Instruction

Writing instruction in early-twentieth-century American colleges, argues Berlin, fell into three camps: current-traditional rhetoric, emphasizing utilitarian ends of writing; the rhetoric of liberal culture, emphasizing literary interpretation and self expression; and the rhetoric of public discourse, emphasizing engagement with social and political issues (*Rhetoric and Reality* 35–36). For Berlin, these competing rhetorics were grounded not merely in aesthetic, procedural, or even ideological differences, but mutually exclusive epistemologies: objectivist, which locates truth in the external world, discoverable through empirical observation; subjectivist, which locates it in the individual, discoverable through experience or insight; and transactional, which locates it in the interactions between elements in a rhetorical situation, discoverable through rhetorical acts (6–19).

Through two historiographic monographs and numerous articles tracing the evolution of writing studies in American colleges from the early nineteenth to the late twentieth century, Berlin employed a range of terminologies to describe various pedagogies at particular points in time, but he remained consistent in seeing pedagogy through the lens of epistemology.[1] The influence of this insight on writing studies was powerful. Through his taxonomies, Berlin helped give shape to what had previously seemed to be a fragmented intellectual history, providing composition scholars with a framework with which to study the history of school and college writing. Moreover, his application of postmodern theories of knowledge making encouraged composition scholars to recognize the role of ideology in pedagogy, strengthening the theoretical underpinnings of their work. Finally, building on the work begun by scholars such as Arthur N. Applebee, Donald C. Stewart, and Edward P. J. Corbett, Berlin further helped to legitimize historiography as a field of inquiry within composition studies and strengthen composition's ties to rhetoric, increasing the discursive room for crucial works such as Susan C. Jarratt's reclaiming of the epistemic possibilities of Sophistic rhetoric (*Rereading the Sophists*) and Sharon Crowley's explorations of the role of invention (*Methodical Memory*) and ideology (*Composition in the University*) in composition studies, as well as later recovery work by numerous scholars.

While his taxonomies retain an attractive and powerful hold on our field, scholars in recent years have begun to challenge and complicate his findings, both by questioning his overarching categorizations and the teleological line he drew between ideology and pedagogy (Hawk; Paine; Sánchez) and by extending disciplinary inquiries into a more diverse and representative range of institutions (Donahue and Moon; Enoch; Kates; Schultz). Work-ing from this line of inquiry, David Gold has argued that an overly narrow application of Berlin's schema to pedagogical practices "may actually limit our understanding of those practices," suggesting, for example, that "what we have dismissed as current-traditional rhetoric" may in fact represent "a complex of interwoven practices, both conservative and radical, liberatory and disciplining, and subject to wide-ranging local and institutional varia-tions" (*Rhetoric at the Margins* 5).

To be fair, Berlin's critics have sometimes challenged our collective mem-ory of Berlin, rather than Berlin himself. Though current-traditional rhetoric may have been by default the dominant method of overburdened and un-dertheorized instructors, as charged by Berlin, Connors, and Crowley, it was not—as these same scholars acknowledge to varying degrees—unchanging and monolithic. Indeed, as Connors takes pains to point out, the emergence of "composition-rhetoric" (his preferred term) in the late nineteenth century occurred in response to "pressing social problems demand[ing] solutions" (11), most notably a widely perceived literacy crisis at a moment of cultural flux.

In Kenneth Burke's famous dictum, "A way of seeing is also a way of not seeing" (*Permanence and Change* 49); our field's focus on Berlin's seductive metanarratives has tended to deflect attention away from his careful readings of historical texts. The lively debates in the pages of early-twentieth-century composition journals that Berlin reports on in *Rhetoric and Reality* suggest a period of intensely contested pedagogical theories—and, we believe, in-termixing ones. These various strands of pedagogical practice were com-pelling to teachers because they met exigencies they faced and embodied values they shared: that is, wanting to transmit culture, wanting to develop students' individual capacities to succeed in that culture, and wanting to offer students the tools to critique that culture. Indeed, the lines traced by Berlin's historical taxonomies and Richard Fulkerson in his periodic surveys of the contemporary field suggest the continued relevance of these ends to contemporary rhetoric and writing scholars.[2]

If we treat Berlin's taxonomies as representing less mutually exclusive, competing, and zero-sum epistemologies or ideologies but rather, following Perelman and Olbrechts-Tyteca, as particularly ordered hierarchies of values, many of their tensions and contradictions dissolve. Under an epistemological model, one cannot hold mutually exclusive positions in relation to knowl-edge making, and each position implies a specific ideological end; under a values model, one can hold to intertwining and even seemingly incompatible ends. It may also be helpful here to invoke the work of William G. Perry, whose stage-model theory of intellectual development received a brief term of attention from composition scholars in the late 1980s and early 1990s (see Bizzell; Slattery). Though Perry is sometimes read as positing three mutually exclusive stages of development, from dualism to relativism to commitment, categories that map neatly onto current-traditional, expressivist, and epistemic rhetoric, it may be more valuable, as Davida Charney, John H. Newman, and Mike Palmquist have suggested, to see these positions as "parallel epistemological styles that can mix in varying concentrations," depending on the topic at hand (303).[3]

What emerges for us as primary in our readings of teachers' self-depictions of their pedagogies is a sense of their struggle to balance curricula. Those faculty members at the public women's colleges who have left a record of their teaching practices—through catalogue and course descriptions, journal articles, class notes, and other writings—suggest teachers immersed in and engaged with the philosophical struggles of their day and attempting to reconcile and synthesize *multiple* theories, aims, and ends. For example, in Florida State College for Women English professor Samuel M. Tucker's 1905 address at the Southern Educational Association annual meeting, he explicitly calls for colleges and high schools to offer a balanced combination of utilitarian training, liberal culture, and education for democracy, seeing each as a necessary check on and supplement to the other.

Following on the heels of Harvard's 1892 *Report of the Committee on Composition and Rhetoric*, which decried the writing skills of its entering freshmen (Adams, Godkin, and Quincy), and the National Education Association's 1894 *Report of the Committee of Ten*, which called for uniform standards of high school instruction, Tucker speaks directly to a moment of crisis in education, when expanding student populations and emergent college subjects are presenting challenges to traditional curricula.[4] Following Paul Henry Hanus, he prefers to not dwell on the oft-debated distinctions between "preparation for college" and "preparation for life," but rather on the goals that any system of education should provide. His language suggests a painstaking attempt to address advocates of each camp.[5]

Concerned with narrow college entrance requirements that are "too academic, bookish, and remote from life, to afford any actual preparation for its duties" (128), Tucker argues that, "while urging the necessity for broader culture in our public schools . . . we must not fail to recognize the equally great necessity for a training specifically utilitarian" (131). Concerned with "corruption in politics and dishonesty in business," he argues that "the business of the public high school is not merely to teach the student to make a living, but to train him to be a citizen and patriot" (132). Concerned with students too narrowly focused on money making, he argues that "we should encourage something even beyond utilitarian training and the education of the young citizen. . . . The last and great duty is our obligation to encourage

. . . a greater breadth of general culture. . . . a knowledge of the best things that have been said and done in the world" (133). Tucker ultimately hopes for high schools to broaden their curricula and for colleges to recognize the value of all the forms of training high schools offer. Since college entrance requirements drive high school curricula, it is crucial that colleges support public schools, the "college of the people" (130).

Despite his attempts at reconciliation, it is perhaps telling that during the discussion session that followed, Tucker received a blistering attack in response by William R. Webb, founder of the Webb School in central Tennessee, an elite classical liberal arts preparatory school for boys, who declared to applause that "there is no such thing as high culture in English literature, without a knowledge of the classics" and "protest[ed] . . . for the sake of the South . . . against putting into a course of study so many things that you absolutely sap the juice out of youth in fitting them either for life or for college" (qtd. in Tucker 136). Old ways die hard. Of course Webb was training elite young men for private colleges such as Vanderbilt; Tucker was teaching public college women in a state in which, he argued, too few students would have the opportunity to attend college if the strict demands of traditional entrance requirements held sway (130).[6]

Faculty Approaches in the Women's Colleges

Though English departments at the public women's colleges tended to be heavily weighted toward the teaching of literature, the distinctly pragmatic mission of the schools meant that instructors of writing had to keep in mind professional and public ends. In schools explicitly founded to help women secure positions in a rapidly changing social and economic order, pure proponents of liberal culture were not a dominant force. The small size of these schools also meant that subjects which might have split off in larger institutions—speech, journalism, and drama—were subsumed under English at most campuses into the 1930s and at some into the 1940s, meaning that departments had to pay at least lip service to rhetorical production, even if they emphasized literary reception. At all of these schools, literary societies, which served as centers of student social life through the 1930s, and student publications, including literary journals, newspapers, and yearbooks, were sponsored or supervised by English faculty, further contributing to intersections between curricular and extracurricular activities; it was not unusual for faculty to assign essays with publication in mind or to use student publications as a source for in-class critique. Moreover, small department sizes combined with the near-universal freshman composition requirement meant that a relatively large proportion of faculty members taught composition. Finally, the mission of training teachers, at times explicitly built into the schools' program requirements, also encouraged English department heads at these schools to consider the ends of their curricula.

At all the southern public women's colleges, explicit consideration of institutional goals was a dominant theme; administrators and supporters frequently had to publicly defend their schools' mission and compete with larger, more established institutions for state support. It is perhaps not surprising then that this sense of urgency would filter down to the department level. Indeed, at those campuses in which administrators had formal connections to English, rhetorical instruction tended to be the most comprehensive and forward looking. At Florida State College for Women, William G. Dodd, who served (1910–44) as both English chair and dean of the college, valued composition and was an early supporter of the discipline's social turn. At Texas State College for Women, President Louis H. Hubbard (1926–50), a former English teacher and self-described "progressive and imaginative" composition instructor (95), saw English as central to all college subjects and supported both broad-based liberal arts and vocational education. At Georgia State College for Women, William T. Wynn, who served (1925–46) as English chair and dean of arts and sciences, modernized the English curriculum, introducing courses in speech, journalism, and modern literature. At North Carolina College for Women, William C. Smith served (1900–1941) as English chair and dean of arts and sciences, leading chapel exercises and arranging for speakers. All of these men were involved in curricular development at the college level and recognized the importance of balancing liberal arts and vocational education.[7]

Given these contingencies, it is perhaps not surprising that English department mission statements frequently embodied the full range of instructional approaches Berlin finds as competing for dominance in early-twentieth-century colleges. The earliest writing curricula, from the 1890s to the 1910s, explicitly sought to balance utilitarian and "cultural" ends, reflecting the hybrid nature of the schools' ends and wider public debates over the goals of a college education. By the 1920s, following trends in progressive education led by teachers' colleges, most campuses evidence an increased emphasis on the social and civic purposes of writing, reflecting conversations within pedagogically oriented professional organizations such as the National Council of Teachers of English (NCTE) and the National Education Association (NEA). Though attention to prescriptive norms is always a curricular feature, it is not until the mid-1930s, as these schools both grew in size and came increasingly under the jurisdiction of state university systems, that prescription takes on a centralized role, with schools attempting to systematize instruction for growing student bodies with divergent ranges of preparation. Perhaps as a reaction to this trend, increasing dissatisfaction with traditional teaching methods led some faculty members to experiment with new teaching strategies.

Prescriptivism and Personal Connections

There is certainly evidence of current-traditional pedagogy at these schools. Florida State College for Women English professor Hazel Allison Stevenson's (1920–56) 1951 "Facing the Problem in Upperclass English" reads almost like a parody of current-traditionalism, its epistemology positivist, its aesthetic formalist, its pedagogy mechanistic and prescriptivist. "The average student," she declares, "cannot write good simple English. This is . . . the dark corner from which we in English avert our eyes as we mutter faint excuses to our colleagues in other departments" (32). Her terminology throughout suggests an uncritical acceptance of her colleagues' classification of composition as a utilitarian "tool subject"—despite longstanding NCTE concern over this very possibility—and an understanding of good writing "habits" primarily as hewing to mechanical conventions.

Toward a solution, she details a prescriptivist remedial composition program for upperclassmen, instituted at the school in 1943 with the blessing of the faculty senate, that employs a deficit model of evaluation and a clinical model of repair then in vogue (see Berlin, *Rhetoric and Reality* 64–65; see also Masters). All students take a "Junior English Examination"; rather than receiving a "general grade," which might allow, say, a poor speller "to continue his way through life offending the eyes of the literate" (34), they are graded on four discrete categories—usage, spelling, punctuation, and "general writing"—and assigned appropriate remedial sections. Faculty also receive preprinted cards by which they can assign to the clinic any student they deem "deficient" in one or more categories. While Stevenson acknowledges this program may appear narrow, she insists it encourages high standards within those channels throughout the university: "No student passes because he has a flair for self-expression, regardless of accuracy" (34). This approach is quite similar to one adopted at Alabama College for Women in 1935, which tested students in five categories—reading comprehension, fundamentals of composition, fundamentals of speech, literary information, and literary aptitude—and assigned them into appropriate sections and "laboratories" for deficit correction (Orr, "Curriculum Revision" 183).

Alabama College for Women's Leah Dennis (1927–49) had a somewhat cynical view of the prospects of "convert[ing] ignorant youth into writers of flawless prose" ("Guide to Errors" 16). Her 1941 review of John C. Hodges's new *Harbrace Handbook of English*, a soon-to-be enormously popular usage guide organized by pattern of error, suggests that she sees the teaching of composition as a duty largely occupied by hunting unrelentingly for student "blunders." Teaching students to correct their errors requires that teachers anticipate "all the mistakes possible" and employ instructional methods that are "exact, and fool-proof." In this regard, though she supports Hodges's intentions, she finds his execution somewhat lacking: "Some statements are incomplete, some too sweeping, some actually erroneous. The reviewer is certain that 'common sense and reasonable care' . . . are *not* sufficient to make clear the subtleties of sequence of tenses to students unaccustomed to hearing standard speech" (17). Hodges, it appears, does not go far enough.

Yet this emphasis on prescriptivism must be weighed against instructor goals, student desires, and interpersonal relationships among faculty and students, as well as wider cultural contexts. Again and again, faculty in the women's colleges remark on the importance of interpersonal connections with students. This may have been driven in part by the tight community life, single-sex environment, and focused mission, as well as an awareness on the part of instructors that they were training future teachers themselves. Reflecting in 1938 on the "enormous array" of theories and practices instructors sometimes felt compelled to offer, Alabama College for Women English chair A. W. Vaughan declared that "the first essential of good teaching is to establish a sympathetic learning relation between pupils and teacher. . . . [I]t is impossible to cover all the ranges of information. . . . But it *is* possible for the alert and understanding teacher to share her life, the best of it, with her pupils, to share their lives in some measure, and to help them share their best with one another. English teaching can be an adventure in comradeship. It will be if the teacher herself is essentially a learner rather than a teacher" (29).

Such sympathetic relations were not uncommon. Stevenson's prescriptivism was matched by her determined, almost sunny optimism about the prospect of improving student writing. Dennis, despite her somewhat sardonic, world-weary pose was a popular teacher, in part perhaps because of her extracurricular leadership organizing literary-themed social events such as contests and masquerades. Moreover, she was somewhat open-minded about changes in usage; a philological study of the history of the progressive tense in English has her imagining a day when colloquial or proscribed forms such as "Don't be stepping all over my feet" might be acceptable ("Progressive Tense" 865). At Texas State College for Women, strict prescriptivist teachers such as Lucy Fay and Etta M. Lacy, who emphasized the importance of speaking well to their students' future personal and professional lives, were dearly loved by their students for the concern they showed them. Fay wanted students to "never act timid," and Lacy's insistence on grammatical precision had rhetorical intent; she wanted her students' meaning to be clear when they spoke and wrote (Gold, *Rhetoric at the Margins* 89–90). At all these schools, the faculty voices we have recovered suggest that even the most seemingly cynical and prescriptivist instructor demonstrates an ethos of care.

Alabama speech professor Claudia E. Crumpton's efforts at improving student speech might be regarded today as short-sighted or naïve—she expresses some surprise that students would retain their life-long speech habits and "defects" even after "regular explanation and drill" ("Better Speech Week" 570)—and even damaging, rejecting students' language rights and disciplining their subjectivities through an objectivist view of usage and the imposition of dominant discourse norms. Yet at a time of more limited access to broadcast media and a more overt country-city divide, a rural student seeking wider social, cultural, and economic opportunity might welcome hearing pronounced aloud by an educated speaker words that she had previously seen only in print. Crumpton saw speech improvement as a community enterprise, involving student and faculty alike; indeed, at Better Speech Week, which she instituted at Alabama in 1916 and then helped make a national event through the NCTE, discussion included "that most difficult, delicate problem—the faculty's English." After the event, she noted, "several teachers and officers questioned me about certain expressions and invited me to examine their notices on the bulletin boards" (570).[8]

Institutional Differences

Curricular developments at these schools demonstrate the importance of individual faculty members in key roles. At Florida State College for Women, two long-serving key administrators, President Edward Conradi (1909–41) and English chair and dean of the college William G. Dodd (1910–44), contributed to both curricular stability and growth. As president, Conradi was adamant that faculty not simply be committed scholars but teachers with a "human touch." In a 1929 address to the graduating class, he declared that professors who "hold that it is unbecoming . . . to manifest friendship toward a student. . . . should resign and start on a quest for the island of Robinson Crusoe, if it is still uninhabited" (Conradi 3). Dodd, meanwhile, believed in hiring good teachers and getting out of their way. "I won't even tell you what kind of textbooks to use," he told twenty-six-year-old English instructor Sarah Herndon in 1928. "You're completely free" (qtd. in Herndon 2). Though neither Conradi nor Dodd were initially women's education advocates, both were shaped by their interaction with female students and faculty and became fierce defenders of their institution.

In the English department, a confluence of competing forces combined to shape instruction, reminding us that we cannot easily draw clean causal lines between ideology and pedagogy, fit instruction into neat epistemological categories, or rely solely on freshman composition courses for evidence of rhetorical instruction. The disciplinary fragmentation marked by the founding of such organizations as the National Council of Teachers of English (1911), the American Association of Teachers of Journalism (1912, now the Association for Education in Journalism and Mass Communication), and the National Association of Academic Teachers of Public Speaking (1914, now the National Communication Association) was delayed at Florida, where speech, debate, journalism, and drama courses remained linked to English through the 1930s. Students were thus exposed to a wide range of pedagogical approaches.

Under Dodd, writing instruction at the college combined a current-traditional emphasis on correctness with an early and long-sustained turn to the social. Dodd took a broad view of English studies, recognizing composition's historically central role, which he saw as "on the whole the most valuable work the English Department is called upon to do" (*Some Objects* 11). While he accepted the Romantic view that literature was a product of genius and thus dependent on innate talent, he saw composition as a learnable skill, quoting with approval James Weber Linn's assertion in *The Essentials of English Composition* that "the craft of writing can be learned by anyone, like carpentry or dancing" (qtd. in *Some Objects* 9).[9] Dodd maintained a keen interest in pedagogy. As early as 1914, he applauded the growing recognition within the "field of Composition"—whose discussions he took seriously—that "clear expression" was not enough: "The college Composition course must not only train the student in clear expression, but must at the same time teach him to think for himself. . . . English Composition should do more than cultivate facile expression in the student; it should do its part toward enabling him to take his place in the world of men and women who are producing ideas" (*Some Objects* 9).

The 1928–29 Florida catalogue demonstrates Dodd's influence and the intertwining strands of instruction in the department. While freshman composition retains its current-traditional cast, "designed to secure correct and easy expression," sophomore composition shows the influence of socially oriented rhetorics, with the writing and discussion of "familiar, informative, [and] critical" essays "dealing with various aspects of modern life" (114). Literature courses retain a belletristic focus, teaching students literary history and cultivating taste. Yet, as evidenced by essays published in the campus literary journal—which frequently served as a public venue for classroom assignments—the young women in these courses were encouraged to position themselves as critics, capable of passing judgment on established authors.

Spoken English and drama courses at Florida also offered students a chance to engage as rhetors. Dodd believed that "oral composition" was an important part of study in English, and the college's tacit mission in training teachers ensured the popularity of such courses. Most early graduates became teachers, and as late as 1930, 57 percent of first-year students listed teaching as their first career choice (Andrews 8). Teachers had to be not only well read but able to lead reading and speak in public. Oratory, which at the school's founding was required each year, developed from an initial elocution model into a comprehensive speech and communication program. By the 1920s, in addition to traditional offerings in diction and literary interpretation, the school offered a three-year sequence in public speaking, with an emphasis on argumentation and debate. Students studied "arguments, fallacies, sources, and drawing of briefs," "psychology of audience behavior," "applications of principles of persuasion and suggestion," and "criticism of great orators" and participated in formal team debate (*Catalogue 1928–29* 117–18).

Another important influence in the English department was journalism head Earl Vance, who taught from 1928 to 1974 and was for many years one of the school's most widely published faculty members. Vance embodied what Berlin called the social turn in rhetoric; indeed, in *Rhetoric and Reality*, Berlin cited Vance's 1937 description of his composition course, in which students were asked to interrogate the social conditions of their hometown, as the "most ambitious report of a course based on a rhetoric of public discourse" he had found (85; see also Vance, "Integrating"). In 1931, Vance introduced the school's first course in nonfiction prose, with contemporary magazines the primary texts: "The object of the course is primarily to assist the student in understanding her own time either as a cultural background or with a view to writing about it" (*Catalogue 1930–31* 128). Vance embraced the notion of writing as a productive art, eschewing both universal principles and mere instrumental ends and calling for "as much training in rhetoric as can be crowded in" ("Training" 743). While he valued practical newspaper experience—for many years students set copy and produced the newspaper themselves at the offices of the *Tallahassee Democrat*—he also believed that it was not enough, if it were to lead the student only to unquestioningly accept and replicate the worst aspects of professional discourse. Experience at the "average American newspaper," he argued, "can only familiarize one with certain routine practices of the newspaper office and turn him out knowing what he calls 'the newspaper game,' to him a neat little trade requiring adeptness at certain stupid and stereotyped phraseology. . . . If journalism is to justify its place in the curriculum of American colleges, it must be something more than a trade" ("Training" 741–42).

In a well-received 1945 *Virginia Quarterly Review* article, Vance condemned corporatized journalism and media consolidation for providing freedom of the press only to press owners and the business interests that supported them. He hoped that schools could serve as a check on this power by explicitly teaching as part of general education the "nature, operation, and effect of the press" as a social institution ("Freedom" 353). As such, he encouraged journalistic skepticism and critical thinking. Said student Mary Alice Hunt, "If you were dogmatic about anything, saying 'this is so!' [he'd] say, 'Why is it so? What makes you believe that?' He made you think. You had to back up what you said" (6). Vance made use of peer review as well; Hunt recalled that "every feature [she] wrote was critiqued the following week" in class (3). Though Vance's hopes for the power of journalism education to transform the business of journalism may have been over-optimistic, his explicit desire to make students critics of their own discourse practices— and discourse communities—foreshadows the instructional goals of many contemporary composition scholars.

In contrast to Florida, Georgia State College for Women long had perhaps the most narrow writing curriculum, due in part to both the somewhat conservative nature of its early administration and, through the 1920s, high faculty turnover in the English department. Unlike Mississippi State College for Women's English department, which benefitted from the long tenure of Pauline Van de Graaf Orr (1884–1913), who repeatedly stressed the importance of composition to administrators (Kohn), Georgia's suffered from a lack of stable leadership. In its first thirty years, few English faculty members stayed more than five years; for this reason perhaps, literary societies and student publications, central features of campus life at the other public women's colleges from the start, did not get established until the 1920s.

As the second of the public women's colleges to be founded in 1889 and located in a conservative, Deep South state—albeit one in transition—GSCW embodied the tensions between both liberal arts and industrial training and old and new South views of women's roles. As Robin O. Harris notes in her informal history of the school's alumni association, while the state's men's technical college, the Georgia Institute of Technology (1885), was founded as a relatively unconflicted answer to new South needs, the women's "had a heavier load to bear." Georgia State College for Women "was often caught between a mission for the future, and a social status quo regarding the 'proper' role of women" (4). The 1889 act establishing the college promised to "fit and prepare girls for occupations which are consistent with feminine refinement and modesty" (Georgia, *Acts and Resolutions* 13), and for four decades, the school's catalogue retained, almost unchanged, a four-part statement of its purpose, "to prepare the young women of Georgia: 1. To do intelligent work as teachers.... 2. To earn their own livelihood by the practice of some one or other of those industrial arts suitable for women.... 3. To exert an uplifting and refining influence on family and society by means of cultured intellect.... [and] 4. To be skillful and expert in those domestic arts that lie at the foundation of all successful housekeeping and homemaking" (*Catalogue 1929–31* 51–52).

Georgia's first president, J. Harris Chappell (1891–1905), was an ardent supporter of career development for women who took pride in his graduates' record in obtaining jobs; the college, he declared, was "a progressive and aggressive step forward in women's education" (*Catalogue 1892–93* 10).[10] However, he remained ambivalent about women's expanding public roles, and his yearly commencement addresses are filled with exhortations for the school's graduating young women to seek a higher spiritual path and quietly fulfill their womanly duty and destiny. They should "bring about regeneration and reform, not by making speeches, not by delivering lectures, not by running over the country shrieking for the ballot, not by writing articles for the newspapers, not by voting, but by purifying the spring at its very source, in the school room, in the family, in the home" (*Catalogue 1893–94* 80). The college's second president, Marvin M. Parks (1905–26), who greatly expanded the college, was more forward looking. Though criticized for enforcing strict Victorian codes of conduct and dress, he also imagined an expansion of women's opportunities through education, albeit through a gender-specific lens. In his 1913 report to the state Department of Education—which for years afterward served in slightly edited form as the foreword to the catalogue—he declared that the Georgia State College for Women was "distinctly a woman's college. . . . It believes that women have interests and ambitions and spheres of usefulness peculiarly their own; it believes there are fields of work for women which call for new courses of study. It believes that all the Sciences and Arts should be made to contribute to an improvement of the home, the school, the farm, the child, and society" (Georgia, *Forty-First Annual Report* 167).

Early English courses at Georgia embodied a split between the study of literature for cultural purposes and composition for utilitarian ones. The 1908–9 *Catalogue* outlined three goals for English instruction: (1) "to give every student ability to organize her thoughts logically and compactly, and to give them adequate expression in simple, clear, correct, and effective English"; (2) "to put students in possession of the true attitude to literature," so that they may see how "the ideal truths of life are revealed . . . to the end that man's soul may be elevated"; and (3) "to give the students . . . an understanding of the problems of teaching English to children" (26). These three ends persisted, with minor changes, through the 1925–26 *Catalogue*: (1) "to give mastery of the language as a tool, in both oral and written forms"; (2) "to provide a deep, rich, human culture through the study of literature"; and (3) "to equip students, both in the language and the literature, to become successful teachers of English" (100).

In the school's earliest years, when enrollment and faculty sizes were modest, freshman and sophomore English classes combined belletristic literary study, formal grammar instruction, and composition, which was based on theme writing taught with the aid of a rhetoric. Instruction in the latter tended to be a somewhat ad hoc affair, with frequent turnover of texts, including Virginia Waddy's *Elements of Composition and Rhetoric*, emphasizing sentence construction through a study of syntax and figures of style; John Scott Clark's *A Practical Rhetoric*, also emphasizing form and style; Fred Newton Scott and Joseph Villiers Denney's *Elementary English Composition* and *Composition-Rhetoric*; Edwin Herbert Lewis's *A Second Manual of Composition*, emphasizing the modes of writing; Edwin C. Woolley's *Handbook of Composition*, emphasizing "rules" of grammar and writing; and Robert Herrick and Lindsay Todd Damon's *Composition and Rhetoric for Schools*. With the exception of Herrick and Damon and Scott and Denney, these texts give little or no attention to purposes in writing, composing processes, or argument, but rather reduce composition to primarily a study of usage and arrangement—literally the *composition* of sentences—and stylistic figures. By 1920, composition instruction, systematized into a two-semester sequence during the brief tenure of English chair John Walter Good (1918–24), had acquired a solidly current-traditional cast, emphasizing the logical arrangement of ideas and correctness in expression primarily through narration and description. Echoing the rhetorical goals of influential textbook authors such as Harvard's Adams Sherman Hill (*Principles of Rhetoric*, 1878) and Barrett Wendell (*English Composition*, 1891), students were taught to "think clearly, definitely, and orderly, and to express their thoughts and feelings correctly, forcefully, and elegantly, orally and in writing" (*Catalogue 1918–20* 103).

The department modernized considerably with the arrival of William T. Wynn in 1925, who established courses in contemporary literature and journalism and encouraged the establishment of the school's newspaper (*Colonnade*, 1925), yearbook (*Spectrum*, 1926), and literary journal (*Corinthian*, 1927). Wynn also made use of local resources, encouraging students to submit articles to area newspapers and arranging for them to edit once-a-year editions of the *Macon Telegraph* and the Milledgeville *Union Recorder* (Hair, Bonner, and Dawson 149; Curl 83). Wynn himself published several editions of a streamlined grammar handbook, in which he tries to maintain a middle ground between traditionalists insisting on teaching grammar through Latin and more forward-looking instructors holding that students "grow unconsciously into the correct use of [the] mother tongue" (7). He also attempts to apply his understanding of modern theories of learning; for example, including only correct examples of usage in the text.

Though his approach is largely conventional, his books are notable for their eclectic model sentences meant to interest students by doing double duty conveying mini-lessons in history, science, religion, and literature:

- In the Philippine Islands, a territory of the United States, there are more than a quarter of a million people who are followers of Mohammed.
- Cardinal Newman was becalmed in the Straits of Bonifacio when he wrote the hymn, "Lead Kindly Light."
- There are three members of the Barrymore family who are among the finest actors on the American stage.
- James Russell Lowell, a famous American poet, was suspended from Harvard because he did not attend chapel. (19)

Wynn's text reads almost like a self-improvement or self-education manual, particularly with its absence of incorrect examples. Despite his forward-thinking approach to language and literature, he does not appear to have tinkered much with the composition model established by his predecessor. The 1935 course focused on "making language effective, and therefore emphasizes accurate wording, well contrived sentences, and sound organization of ideas," with the second semester emphasizing the modes of narration and description and "extensive analysis of models of the best prose style" (*Catalogue 1935–36* 76); this description remained essentially unchanged through 1945. During this time period, the school also briefly added a remedial composition course for students failing a placement test, perhaps as part of a systemization of requirements after the school became part of the new University System of Georgia in 1932.

A key figure in the English department during Wynn's tenure at Georgia was Katherine Kirkwood Scott (1922–58), who would become one of the school's longest-serving and influential teachers. Her teaching practices suggest that even as curricula become established, they are not necessarily fixed in place, nor can course descriptions tell the entire story. Just as Wynn, enamored of modernity and seeking to develop pedagogies appropriate for "this day of the airplane, radio, [and] automobile" (7), did his best to make his grammar handbook interesting to students, Scott too sought to embrace modern methods, even as she remained in many ways a staunch defender of southern traditions.[11] Born in Milledgeville in 1894, Scott attended Georgia State College for Women, receiving a normal diploma in 1913, after which she attended Columbia University's Teachers College, receiving a bachelor's degree in 1916 and a master's in 1921 (the latter earned while teaching at a girls' school in Savannah). She joined the English department at GSCW in 1922, remaining until 1958. A popular and influential teacher, Scott was highly involved in the life of both the college and the town.

Through her writings as both a professor and student, Scott emerges as a reflective, ideologically flexible teacher, conservative in principle yet interested in pedagogical innovation, and sensitive to local needs in curricular development. The influence of progressive educational theories can be seen in a 1930 article she wrote for the *Georgia Education Journal* entitled "Inductive Teaching of English." She holds to the teaching of grammar but faults poor grammar instruction that separates it from actual composition, no doubt recalling her own experience as a freshman at the women's college, where she likely studied Woolley's *Handbook of Composition*, which treats composing almost exclusively through the lens of prescriptive usage rules.[12] In the "average American classroom," she writes, students "are not shown that grammar is a part of talking and writing. It is diagramming, parts of speech, parsing, and often those who can most glibly rattle off the rules . . . are those who make the most atrocious mistakes in their own speech" (19). Words, she argues, "only mean something in connection with other words" (21).

Scott argues that instead of traditional methods, which start with the deductive memorization of abstract rules, teachers should use induction, following the by-then "truism" of progressive pedagogy of moving from known to unknown, concrete to abstract, making use of knowledge students already possess.[13] In teaching, say, the concept of "subject," teachers should begin not with an abstract definition—"that part of a sentence which names"—but by having students simply name things they see in the classroom, then discussing what naming does, then asking what the naming part of a sentence might do, then offering some sample sentences and asking students to identify the "naming parts." By this means, students can more readily grasp the abstract concept that sentences as well as people may have names ("Inductive Teaching" 20). Though she has internalized progressive principles, she departs from them in that her goals in language study are less social than belletristic, hoping to inspire students to appreciate language, love literature, and want to write well.

In 1940, Scott received a year's leave to study again at Teachers College. In "My Emerged Opinions," written for a class on new curricular trends, she tests the progressive theories she is learning in light of her previous educational and teaching experience, seeking a synthesis between old and new. Aligning herself with the "old order" of educators who hold to a subject-driven curriculum and finding progressive educators often confused and occasionally hypocritical, she worries that the child-centered "experience" curriculum currently in vogue might, in the wrong hands, be intellectually thin or descend into undisciplined chaos. Having returned to Teachers College to learn how to create a core curriculum for future high school teachers, she finds herself "after three months of reading and listening . . . almost as much at sea as ever" (2).

Yet she finds much to admire in progressive educational theory, considering it a welcome contrast to the traditional teaching of her childhood, with its emphasis on recitation and rote learning and "aloofness from the realities of life" ("My Emerged" 8). She lauds numerous progressive educational goals, particularly the development of independent thinking and creativity, and she agrees with Teachers College faculty member Lois Coffey Mossman's assertion that school curricula must "put meaning and significance into daily life" (qtd. in "My Emerged" 8).[14] One of Scott's greatest regrets in her own educational experience was that it left her and many other women "ignoran[t] of the laws, social and political trends, and even . . . current events" (8–9). Ultimately, she rejects either ideological extreme, arguing that what ultimately matters is not theory, but good teaching: "Certainly, the child is the one to be taught not the subject matter, but I also think the *child* is the one to be taught, not somebody's personal theory of education" (6–7). Either curricular approach, she argues, subject- or experience-based, can be successful if one keeps these principles in mind. In her balanced approach, Scott consciously tries to find a pedagogy suitable for both herself and her students.

Even before returning to Columbia, Scott was showing the influence of the social turn in composition. In an unpublished 1935 essay, "Creative Composition," she berates "lazy, ill prepared, or overworked teachers" who assign apparently purposeless themes that students rightfully regard as "useless bits of drudgery." In the past, she argues, such work might have been justified for its value as "mental exercise," but no longer: contemporary writing pedagogy demands subjects with both "intrinsic value" and relevance to students' lives (1).[15] Toward this end, she describes a model composition course developed at Georgia and used both in freshman classes and in the college's model high school. The course resembles in intention Earl Vance's "integrated" composition course at Florida. Though it employs numerous conventional features, such as weekly themes and a rhetoric handbook emphasizing arrangement, the course is organized around a topic of contemporary interest—regional writing from North America—and goes beyond the traditional modes to have students write a wide range of genres, including "paraphrases, outlines, letters, book reviews, playlets, diaries, stories . . . essays, and descriptions" (1), with the end goal of producing a class magazine of student work. Each week, the instructor selects essays to be given over to an editorial committee elected by the class, striving to have each student's work represented at least once during the semester. The editors are advised to "disregard grades," as a mechanically careless paper "might have a freshness and charm [that] a more perfectly spelt and punctuated theme might lack" ("Creative Composition" 2). The last two weeks of the term are devoted to publishing the magazine, with students responsible for all aspects of editing and production. Though Scott acknowledges "many defects" in the course, she asserts its value in providing exigence for writing, ever the bane of composition classes, even rhetorically situated ones today: "It was of interest to the pupils to see their work used, and to feel that a purpose and a plan underlay the whole thing" (2).

Although Scott does not explicitly acknowledge it, a key to the success of this class was its grounding in the community. Completed magazines were placed on display in the classroom, and students from previous classes returned at the start of the following semester to introduce the project and inspire the new students. The magazine was also formally presented to the department chair "for his commendation," and the editorial committee once even "hunted up the president of the college that he might praise them for their work" ("Creative Composition" 2). Such activities suggest—and perhaps require—a small, close-knit campus.

Increasing Systematization

By the time of Scott's and Vance's experimental courses in the 1930s, the public women's colleges were beginning to experience a greater systemization in curricula, a result of expanding enrollments and increasing integration into their respective state university systems. Within English departments, this systematization resulted in the production of department-wide instruction manuals for composition. Though these manuals suggest evidence of a rule-driven, prescriptive curriculum, they also suggest evidence of instructors seeking to establish composition curricula appropriate to the context of women's collegiate education.

At Mississippi State College for Women, Ardrey Shields McIlwaine, composition director from 1928 to 1931, published an enormously detailed, professionally typeset manual for a two-semester composition sequence encouraging women students to think and write about college life and the meaning of college for women. McIlwaine, an early cultural historian who would go on to write a pioneering literary history of poor southern whites, was keenly interested in the social uses of writing.[16]

During the first semester's "college life" unit, students read books and contemporary magazine articles on campus life and specifically women in college. Its stated aim is to "aid you in making an intelligent adjustment to M.S.C.W.; it will encourage you to think about matters which you might take for granted; it will show you the importance of some things which you would not otherwise recognize until your Junior or Senior year" (*Freshman English Manual* 4). Addressing issues such as attitudes toward women, extracurricular activities, students who must work, and careers for women after graduation, the course is ambitious: one of the themes for library research is "Why is every woman in debt to Mary Wollstonecraft and to Mary Lyon?" (9). The reading list is extensive, and, as keeping with the standard practice of weekly or near-weekly writing, twenty-six themes are required over the course of the year; throughout, the readings and writing assignments are meant to be relevant to students, with many centering on life in the South and small towns. Despite some of the more prescriptivist aspects of the curriculum—one assignment in the "diction" unit directs students, "Be able to recite from memory on: *Collegiate Handbook*, 67–68, 69D" (11)—the course sequence is remarkable in its explicit addressing of students' own contexts and concerns. Unfortunately, this ambitious cultural approach did not last long. Whether it was controversial or whether it lasted only as long as McIlwaine remained at the college is not known.

More long lasting was North Carolina College for Women's composition program. The 1930–31 instruction manual suggests that the social emphasis in composition pedagogy came late to the college, despite a campus environment that generally promoted student interest in public affairs. Notable faculty included outspoken philosophy chair Anna Forbes Liddell, who in her long life fought for both suffrage and the Equal Rights Amendment; history professor and dean of the college Walter Clinton Jackson, who was active in cooperative interracial activities; history professor and later dean of women Harriett Elliot, an outspoken feminist who had encouraged student government and had brought suffragist Anna Howard Shaw to deliver the 1919 commencement address;[17] and English professor Arnold McKay, who by this time was teaching a two-semester course on protest literature, "illustrating the common man's long struggle toward economic justice and social improvement" (*Catalogue 1929–30* 78). During this time, the English chair and dean of liberal arts was William Cunningham Smith (1900–1941); though an able administrator and popular teacher closely involved in the life of the campus, his primary interests were in literature.

As perhaps befits the influence of Smith, who had earned his bachelor's degree in 1896, the 1930–31 instruction manual suggests the persistence of the old clarity-elegance-force model of nineteenth-century current-traditional handbooks, emphasizing the development of expressive faculties and correctness. "The Freshman English course is designed to develop in each student the ability to think with clearness, to read with comprehension and with appreciation of literary values, and to write with ease and effectiveness. It is distinctly a composition course, and themes or other forms of written work will be required throughout the year. It does not aim, however, to make theme writing a laborious and unpleasant task. It seeks to develop the individual's latent powers and to guide each one in forming correct habits of expression" (North Carolina College for Women, *Manual 1930–31* 1). Revision seems to be constructed largely as responding to error, though conferences for the purposes of planning essays are required.

By 1942, perhaps in part as a result of Smith's retirement as chair and the arrival of Winfield H. Rogers (1941–45), the department had begun to acknowledge the wider turn toward the social in composition studies, as well as literature: "The objective of this year's course, and of its continuation in the sophomore year . . . is to give the student the degree of literacy expected of an educated person in a modern democracy. . . . [This] implies the aim of reading complicated writing, the intelligent interpretation of adult exposition, drama, and narrative, and finally, through intelligible and grammatical writing, the relating of these to democracy and the democratic way of life" (North Carolina College for Women, *Manual 1942–43* 2). Toward this end, the course makes use of what one reviewer called "propaganda for democracy" (Arnold), the recently published reader *Explorations in Living: A Record of the Democratic Spirit*, edited by a team led by Rogers.[18]

Following both progressive educational ideals and linguistically informed composition pedagogy, the course also aims to teach grammar in the context of writing: "It will seldom be necessary for the instructor to begin with a formal rule; rather he will show grammar and punctuation functioning, being used for some good purpose and with taste and discrimination." The writer of the manual's introduction, almost certainly Rogers, acknowledges that this approach may be "new and strange to the student" (*Manual 1942–43* 3), and there is some evidence that it may have been to some instructors as well; the instructions for "correcting, revising, and rewriting" remain almost identical to those from a decade before, and the copyediting symbols denoting errors have even increased. While the course is meant to teach grammar in "context" (3), papers can still be failed—and students sent to the writing lab—for comma splices and sentence fragments.

Despite the overall intentions of the course, sample assignments suggest a conceptual struggle to balance correctness of expression with belletristic literary analysis and expository meditations on topics of social import. In one typical four-week block, for example, students begin by studying diction, using their grammar handbook, then read Spinoza's "Freedom of Thought and Speech," Locke's "Toleration," and Milton's "Areopagitica" from *Explorations in Living*, analyzing these texts for "definition, diction, and vocabulary." They then write short, concrete paragraphs of definition "concerned with democratic ideas and problems," then a longer essay (*Manual 1942–43* 4). The second semester shifts to more traditional—and for some instructors, perhaps more comfortable—genre-based literary analysis. Though students read authors chosen presumably for their social themes, such as Henrik Ibsen, Thornton Wilder, John Dos Passos, and Ivan Turgenev, their writing assignments appear to primarily stress analysis of literary techniques.

In its somewhat vague aims and use of professional essays to provide topics for writing, the course represents the maturation of the belletristic composition course. Indeed, it is reminiscent of contemporary readers meant for instructors with little theoretical grounding in composition studies. This course, coming at the end of our period of study, suggests the full ascendency of literary studies as the center of English departments. Yet it also suggests the continual struggle of the public women's colleges since their inception to develop relevant curricula for their women students.

Student Public Writing

In his extended study of rhetorical instruction and student writing at Texas State College for Women in *Rhetoric at the Margins*, David Gold found a campus in which students were actively involved in debating issues of the day. Though students faced many rhetorical constraints outside the institution, within it they were largely provided an encouraging space to test out newly emerging personal, public, and professional identities for women. Despite composition courses that on the surface shared many features of current-traditional rhetoric, students were expected to engage as rhetors. A confluence of forces—some particular to Texas, some to public women's colleges, and some to emerging national trends—contributed to a robust climate of expression: a tradition of activist women's clubs in the state, which publicly supported the college and provided role models for students; a focus on vocational education and teacher training, which kept the question of women's professional opportunities at the forefront of curricular conversations and served as a check on the belletristic impulses of traditional liberal arts study; a high percentage of female faculty, who acted as role models for students; close interpersonal relations between students and faculty, both female and male; an ideologically flexible male administration sympathetic to the concerns of women; an emphasis on oral expression, promoted by speech faculty members who had studied at Emerson College of Oratory; and, perhaps most importantly, a student body of modest means who had come to the college for the sake of economic opportunity and thus had a vested interest in utilitarian ends of education.

A key question that emerges from Gold's work, which largely set Texas State College for Women in conversation with work on private women's colleges, is the extent to which it was exceptional or representative of other public women's colleges. We find it representative, though it, along with North Carolina College for Women and Florida State College for Women,[19] is perhaps at the more progressive end on the continuum of instruction and student public engagement. In particular, Texas benefited from strong activist woman's organizations that closely supported the school and a certain distance from the plantation culture of the Deep South, which meant less investment in a racialized regional identity. At some of the public women's campuses, students received decidedly more mixed messages.

At all these campuses, however, students received ample opportunity to engage in public writing, through campus newspapers, literary journals, and yearbooks. And we here stress the word *public*, as student writing on these campuses was intensely so. Literary journals, newspapers, and yearbooks were treated as a community enterprise, read and contributed to by student and teacher alike. Likewise, classroom assignments frequently ended up in these student publications. In short, there was a robust climate of expression at these campuses concomitant with their mission of training women for careers and public life. Though students struggled to constitute an identity in a changing society in which women's roles were in flux, they did so in supportive campus environments and generally exhibited great optimism about the future. For many of the students at the public women's colleges, the world was not changing fast enough—and they were not shy to say so. In chapter 5, we will treat student writing more in depth through the lens of race.

3

Evolution of Expression: Speech Arts and Public Speaking

HISTORIANS OF RHETORIC have for several decades now worked to recover women's written rhetoric in the late nineteenth and early twentieth
centuries.[1] As this work has evolved beyond what Jacqueline Jones Royster
and Gesa E. Kirsch have called "rescue, recovery, and (re)inscription" (31)
to more robustly examining the full range of women's rhetorical practices
within their contemporary contexts in a wider range of periods, scholars have
begun to take an increasing interest in women's *speaking* practices, from the
parlor (Donawerth; N. Johnson, *Gender and Rhetorical Space*) to the platform
(Buchanan; Logan, *We Are Coming*; Mattingly; Mountford) to the varied
types of particular institutions where women learned elocution and oratorical
skills in preparation for professional and public life (Bordelon, "Composing";
Enoch; Kates). Such work has encouraged scholars to revisit and complicate
earlier claims made about the decline of oratorical culture, the limits of gendered oratorical spaces, and the role of elocutionary training (see Gold and
Hobbs). Within educational institutions, professionally on public platforms
or in Chautauquas, or more privately in homes or women's clubs, women
orators have practiced speaking and leadership in ways we are just beginning
to credit and understand. By examining the speaking curricula at the public
women's colleges, we hope to contribute to this emerging, multidimensional
understanding of the varied ways women learned to speak in this era.

As with many contemporary revisionist histories of women's rhetorical
education, comparisons and contrasts with New England's Seven Sisters

colleges are not a significant part of our framework here, in part because we wish to focus on the specific rhetorical context of the public women's colleges. In general, both sets of colleges have common roots in both northern and southern female academies and seminaries that developed in postrevolutionary and antebellum America and which themselves diverged from the British male academies after which they were modeled. Mary Kelley attributes to these early women's schools "one of the most profound changes in gender relations in the course of the nation's history" because of the movement of women into civil society (1). These early educational institutions for girls and young women of both the "middling classes" as well as the elite (27–28) encouraged students to "envision themselves as historical actors who had claim to rights and obligations of citizenship" (17), teaching history, polite letters, and natural sciences, as well as rhetoric and speaking for evaluation purposes or student displays at commencement.

The Seven Sisters colleges, which began emerging roughly two decades before the southern public women's colleges, evolved from these early academies and seminaries while the nation was in an intensely oratorical period.[2] All began with courses in oral and written rhetoric,[3] and, like their men's college counterparts, then followed the general nineteenth-century trend toward emphasizing writing over speaking over time, especially in newly forming English departments. In its late-nineteenth-century inception, English was a capacious subject that could embrace textual but also oral and aural activities involving literature, drama, philology, and also rhetoric. As Gerald Graff points out, elocution and the reading aloud of great literature was central to early literary education in the United States (43–44). But as early as the third quarter of the nineteenth century, English began to professionalize and narrow, making rhetoric into a written art and usually pushing to the margins what came to be variously called oral or spoken English, interpretive reading, or drama. Faculty who claimed central allegiance to the new field of literary studies in English joined the Modern Language Association, which formed in 1883, but in the wake of the MLA's rejection of pedagogy as a focus early in the twentieth century, writing teachers, along with early teachers of speech, formed the National Council of Teachers of English (NCTE) in 1911. Professionalizing public speaking teachers, feeling sidelined within the NCTE, then pulled out to form their own organization, the National Association of Academic Teachers of Public Speaking, now the National Communication Association (NCA), in 1914 (Berlin, *Rhetoric and Reality* 32–35; Cohen 30–36; Graff 121; Miller, *Evolution* 134–35). This disciplinary dance meant that rhetoric, speech, drama, and their variants were taught under various institutional configurations in American colleges, sometimes as stand-alone departments, sometimes subsumed under English.

As English as a subject increasingly came to mean the belletristic study of literary texts, these early configurations could have great impact on the development of speech and rhetoric at a given campus.

As with private women's colleges elsewhere, the arts of both speech and writing were taught to students at these eight southern public colleges for women, at first in English departments as rhetoric, then as the interpretive reading of great literature. However, another system, often unacknowledged today, may have stamped these schools even more deeply, the feminized arts of elocution, primarily arts of delivery for the public platform. This chapter weaves these disciplinary and cultural trends into the histories of speech curricula and extracurricula at these colleges. These forces shaped each college differently in different decades, yet until World War II, elocution remained a force, shaping the cultures of all these colleges.

Disciplining Speech into Literature

With the rise of the German university model used by Johns Hopkins University, established in 1876, academic fields were beginning to emerge, defined primarily by their attempts at adopting distinct research methods and methodologies. Literature and philology had European models for scientific approaches to research, but as a performance art, speech training, especially elocution, had remained an umbrella field encompassing theater and movement as well as being a general pedagogical and humanistic subject. Declining in status in the new university because it was part of the older generalist program, elocution became embarrassing to both academicians in English, where after some struggle it was vanquished, and the emerging discipline of what would become communication, where those teachers associated under the term "speech arts"—the elocutionists—gave way to their colleagues, professionals who founded a new field they agreed to call "public speaking." Existing disciplinary histories suggest the primacy of this narrative (Cohen; Gehrke; Graff; Keith), but an examination of speech at these eight southern colleges complicates the tale of public speaking's independence from English, its quick development, and its conquest over elocution, primarily by taking gender into account.

Three-quarters of the way through the nineteenth century, British versions of elocution in the academy began to wane, and Harvard's establishment of a composition requirement in 1873 is often taken as a signal shift in the transformation of traditional rhetoric and elocutionary studies into composition (Graff 44). Meanwhile, a French-influenced elocutionary practice was becoming popular with American women. But this elocution or expression became coded as "feminine" along with modern languages and music, in contrast to the masculine virility of more scientific research fields such as philology. Its association with the feminine, the body, and Victorian morality, while weakening its influence in the academy, nonetheless gave elocution resilience and a long life, if not continuing respect, in these eight southern and other women's colleges, where it contributed to a rhetorical ethos for women.

By the 1930s, Anglo- and French-American elocution traditions and a continuing strand of persuasion in classical rhetoric served as a base on which to develop courses in public speaking, argument, debate, and theater, as well as new studies of speech defects, mental hygiene, and personality improvement. In addition to curricula in English and public speaking, a panoply of extracurricular activities such as literary and debate societies, gymnastics and other bodily exercises (sometimes called physical culture and aligned with speaking and performance), acting, and pageantry enriched students' perspectives and abilities in speaking, particularly in these eight women's colleges. Our inquiry into elocution shows us that it would not be possible to understand the peculiar features of these and perhaps many other women's colleges—their styles of oratory and expression, Greek dances, theatrical forms, pageants, Zouave military drill teams, and Swedish gymnastics—without understanding their origins in a feminized elocutionary theory and practice. The early intertwining of elocutionary arts with reading and teacher training programs also gave elocution a long life in these eight institutions.

History of Elocution in Relation to the Colleges

By the time of the chartering of the first southern public women's college, Mississippi State College for Women, in 1884, women's popular elocution had become an established movement, with formal institutional training in numerous schools as well as informal and popular sites (N. Johnson, *Gender and Rhetorical Space*; Renshaw; Ruyter). After pushing back against restrictions on women's public speaking for much of the nineteenth century, women must have relished the opportunity to learn to speak and perform for broader audiences and even train for speaking careers.[4] As Herman Cohen notes in his comprehensive disciplinary history, *The History of Speech Communication*, in a society with little-to-no technological mediation, speech arts were valued, from literary readings to public speaking (9).

Women, of course, had long taken the role of home entertainer, singing and playing music, performing dramas, and reading aloud to family and friends. These activities have long been a contested site of women's oratorical performance. On the one hand, the consolidation of a feminized private sphere in the early nineteenth century limited women's public roles and speaking opportunities (K. Campbell; Norton). Nan Johnson has found that even as popular "parlor rhetorics" began circulating among both sexes after the Civil War, they still tended to reinscribe limits on women's access to public rhetorical space through the end of the century (*Gender and Rhetorical Space* 19–47).

Of course, these were not the only spaces available for women to speak. As Carolyn Eastman and Mary Kelley have recently shown, throughout the nineteenth century, women had increasing access to robust instruction in forms of oratory through the rapid expansion of female academies, seminaries, and, later, colleges.[5] Even if their *political* speech was still limited, by the end of the century, women had also increased their presence on the platform, and some were even making a living speaking on the public stage in lyceums and other series on the model of the Chautauqua. Moreover, inspired by the popular elocution movement, a number of schools of expression and oratory began to open in the last quarter of the nineteenth century, proving enormously attractive to women. Rhetorical studies is only just beginning to piece together the various forms of elocutionary and oratorical training available to women in these diverse locales.

Complicating our understanding of the development of women's oratorical education in this period is that these expanded opportunities for women to engage in oratory came at a time when the hold of classical "oratorical culture" was weakening (Clark and Halloran; Graff). By the end of the century, academic institutions were beginning to specialize into departments, and a reaction against elocution was setting in. The academic skepticism of and distaste for elocution and, as it was later called, expression grew over the first two decades of the twentieth century. Graff describes the residual strain of elocution and interpretive "reading" in early English departments as a minority enterprise that lost out to the hegemonic force of disciplinary pressures, and in some ways the elocutionary arts, having no strict research program or system of research methods, were better suited to the old humanist and generalist college. They thus held on in normal schools and small general colleges, often even after the founding of public speaking as a separate discipline.

By the time the first of the eight public colleges for women was founded in the mid-1880s, elocution and expression study were at their peak, but the fashion would be short-lived. Across the country, however, many women had just discovered the power of speech arts for both teaching and performing publicly. They had discovered the resonance of a morally centered, holistic art that disciplined women's bodies into acceptable vehicles for public speech delivery. Indeed, elocutionary arts and debate appear to have had particular resonance for those formerly denied the public platform, and thus were taught at both black and women's colleges.[6]

Our exploration of the development of speech at these eight public colleges for women shows that elocution and expression played a significant role at all these schools and that these forms and values of speech arts remained in place longer than historians have previously recognized. Though the status of elocution and expression fell in these women's colleges as well by the 1930s, faculty trained in late-nineteenth- and early-twentieth-century popular forms of elocution and expression held onto and continued to teach these arts, sometimes in only slightly modified form, into the 1940s and even 1950s. Our examination of these arts at public women's colleges sets into clear relief the centrality of speaking for women as part of the rhetorical curriculum as well as the gendered nature of late elocution in a way heretofore not addressed by our field's histories.

Elocution's Appeal to Nineteenth-Century Women's Culture

The art of elocution focusing on public presentation was something women had been denied and perhaps felt that they needed. It was a generalist study of self-culture in the vein of Margaret Fuller's "conversations" and early Transcendentalism.[7] "Elocution," wrote Robert I. Fulton and Thomas C. Trueblood in their 1893 textbook *Practical Elements of Elocution*, "is not an exact science but a liberal one through which the highest excellence in the art is attained. . . . It is the purpose of Elocution to develop individuality, to correct bad habits of speech and gesture, and to make the body a fit instrument to serve the mind and soul" (1). As Cohen describes elocutionary study, it is centrally linked to philosophy, ethics, and even mysticism, a holistic view appealing to Victorian women. But to appease the later scientific spirit, it also adopted a veneer of scientific language.

In the eighteenth century, elocution developed as a field from Thomas Sheridan and John Walker in the British tradition, focused on delivery and stressing pronunciation and interpretive reading (see Miller, *Formation* 136–41). Janet Carey Eldred and Peter Mortensen point out that oral reading from collections of British and American literature was a staple of early nineteenth-century girls' education. But the later French tradition of elocutionary training became particularly resonant with and adaptable by the late Victorian women's culture that Carroll Smith-Rosenberg describes in *Disorderly Conduct*. This culture developed from women's communal, domestic lives and contained rituals of childbirth, child rearing, personal care, and deathbeds that were primarily women's responsibilities. As such, it was collaborative, intensely emotional, patterned, and concerned with religion and morality. Elocution as practiced by women adopted and fostered similar values.

Of elocutionary training, speech historian Cohen writes, "Elocution assumed the characteristics of a philosophy and a way of life as well as a science" (2). This approach would seem to appeal to either sex, but here we suggest some tentative reasons why elocution was so appealing to women. First, it was not only associated with women in their role as students, but was developed with women's texts and active pedagogical collaboration, and it was often taught by women in schools exclusively for women or attended in high numbers by women. It solved the problem of the rhetorical canon of delivery being developed for men, particularly the difficult choice of whether to choose a male or female style of delivery (see Buchanan 66–105). It did so by creating its own feminine style of presentation with the values of nineteenth-century women's culture. This style, centered on beauty and self-culture, was specifically designed for enhancing and presenting women's bodies in public, with pathos-filled readings of literature and movement arts such as Greek-clad dance, statue-poses, tableaux, and pageantry. Its spiritual and emotional tone, lofty ideals, and morality suited late-Victorian women's culture, with its still-present elements of True Womanhood affirming the need for women to maintain the mantle of nurturance, purity, and piety. Less loftily, it served as an acceptable model and style for self-promotion for formerly private women who might be marketing themselves publicly as platform performers or owners of schools. Elocution also developed as Victorian women's culture was part of the transformation to the "new woman" of the Progressive era, as women broadened their culture through hybrids such as "civic housekeeping," organized and administered through the growing women's club movement. Moreover, elocution's emphasis on physical exercise and freedom of movement encouraged a regendering of delivery of particular value to women at this time (Banaji; Suter).

Thus allied with rhetoric, and developed through the nineteenth century as various arts of delivery primarily for public speech, acting performance, and interpretive reading of literary works, elocution became important for women at the turn of the twentieth century. Literary reading was an art of display, and women could display themselves well on the platform. As Nan Johnson has shown (*Gender and Rhetorical Space*), it was a popular art available to women through home manuals and readers helping women speak and read in the home parlor and at the women's club. But it was also training that led to paid work—platform careers in major cities, speaking tours, appearances at women's clubs and colleges, and various entertainment circuits. Future teachers, too, needed to be able to effectively read literature aloud. These characteristics may have made elocutionary arts seem appropriate to these colleges, with their hybrid programs of liberal arts, vocational training, and teacher education. It may also have resonated with southern women's history of displaying their intellectual achievements socially.

Delsartean Schools and Participation by Women

Rhetoric scholar Wilbur Samuel Howell terms the elocutionary movement "that strange phenomenon" (3), and the particular "brand" of elocution women were most drawn to might seem peculiar to us today. Originated by François Delsarte (1811–71), a French teacher of acting and voice, the "Delsarte System of Expression" has been called "probably the most popular method of speech training in the United States" at the end of the nineteenth century (Shaver 202). A system of physical culture as well as performance, it was introduced into the U.S. in the 1870s by Steele MacKaye. Dance historian Nancy Lee Chalfa Ruyter argues that "through Delsartean training, a considerable number of late-nine-teenth-century white middle- and upper-class American women and [female] children were able to pay attention to their bodies in a socially acceptable manner, to undergo training in physical and expressive techniques, and even to present themselves to selected audiences in public performances" (xvii).

As Cohen suggests, Delsarte's work, full of scientific-sounding natural laws and "replete with diagrams, charts, and drawings," was so complex "that is it not possible to summarize the totality of his thought" (3), but a general abstract will give some feeling for its otherworldly flavor. Influenced by Emmanuel Swedenborg's theories of the correspondence between the natural and the spiritual world and steeped in nineteenth-century scientific mysticism, Delsarte posited that physical gesture reveals or corresponds to movements of the soul; as such, gesture was central to communication, and he devoted much effort to developing an elaborate taxonomy of gestures and their corresponding emotions.[8] Closely tied to what he termed this "Law of Correspondence" was the "Law of Trinity," which suggested a complex of tripartite relationships among elements in the natural world.[9] Thus the various parts of the body can exist in three states, *eccentric* (rising, expanding), *concentric* (falling, contracting), and *normal*, each corresponding to various states of the body, mind, and soul. For example, a raised, lowered, or normal eyebrow together with a dilated, contracted, or normal pupil combine to produce nine primary expressions of the eye (*Delsarte System of Oratory* 71–77), which can in turn be combined with various combinations of other parts of the body to represent an almost infinite number of emotive states. Though some American followers would reject abstractions of this system— or construct equally complex ones of their own—most followed Delsarte in connecting speech and gesture to emotions and the soul.

Ethereal, scientistic, romantic and freeing in its positive tone, encouraging of individual development, and grounded in aesthetics, this system found fertile ground in the United States, particularly in the Northeast, where the climate for its acceptance may have been prepared by the residual Transcendentalism and self-culture of New England. Combining idealistic Swedenborgianism and Delsartean training, hybrids of this elocutionary system spread across the nation between the 1870s and 1900, with private schools of expression, elocution, and oratory opening in New York, Chicago, Philadelphia, and especially Boston, which by 1880 boasted five thousand students of oratory and elocution (Ruyter 58; Renshaw 302).

Though sometimes linked with the decline of oratorical culture because of their emphasis on elocution and Delsartean methods, these schools of expression found new energy as centers of progressive education in the late nineteenth and early twentieth centuries, in particular two influential schools in Boston, the Emerson College of Oratory (1880, now Emerson College), founded by Charles Wesley Emerson, and the School of Expression, sometimes called the Curry School (1879, now Curry College), founded by Anna Baright and eventually run with her later husband, Samuel Silas Curry. Graduates from both these schools would play important roles in the public women's colleges, where they sometimes comprised the bulk of the speech faculty. Other schools of this pattern include Philadelphia's National School of Elocution and Oratory (1875), operated by J. W. Shoemaker and his wife, Rachel; Chicago's Columbia School of Oratory (1890), headed by Mary Blood and Ida Riley; and the Leland Powers School of the Spoken Word (1904), founded by Leland Todd Powers with his wife, Carol Hoyt Powers.

As suggested by the founding faculty of these schools, women were prominent in the elocution movement and likely attracted many women students and influenced others through their textbooks. At Emerson, Susie J. Rogers, whom Emerson married in 1888, directed the department of physical culture and gave popular dramatic readings, and Jessie Eldridge Southwick, an Emerson graduate and later instructor of dramatic expression and voice culture, wrote several texts based on the Emerson system (*Emerson Philosophy of Expression, Expressive Voice Culture*). Particularly influential was Genevieve Stebbins, who developed American Delsartism and publicized it through her *Delsarte System of Expression* (1885), republished in several editions, the sixth in 1902. In her New York School of Expression, Stebbins, who focused on Delsarte's practical exercises, finding them much more valuable than his somewhat esoteric philosophy (Stebbins 385–86), taught many future leaders in the elocutionary movement, including the Currys and Mary Adams Currier, who became a professor of elocution at Wellesley (Ruyter 55–56).

As Ruyter documents it, American Delsartism was largely a female-driven movement; of the more than four hundred instructors and performers active during this period who either identified as Delsarteans or acknowledged the influence of the method, about 85 percent were women (57–58). At least twenty founded or headed schools, while most earned their living by teaching, either privately or in established institutions. They were also performers of "nonverbal genres: statue poses, *tableaux movants*, pantomime, and dances." In contrast, male Delsarteans, traditional speakers, were much less likely to participate in these aesthetic activities or in the various gymnastics or "drills" (58–59; see also N. Johnson, *Gender and Rhetorical Space*).

These women elocutionists were middle class and well educated, especially in literary matters. Many wrote books or wrote for elocutionist magazines such as *Werner's* (Ruyter 58). They were active in the National Association of Elocutionists (1892), although not all elocutionists were Delsarteans. Just after the turn of the twentieth century, this elocutionist organization was renamed the National Speech Arts Association, though it still retained the echo of its elocutionist origins. (In contrast, the organization, formed when speech teachers walked out of the NCTE in 1914, called itself the National Association of Academic Teachers of Public Speaking explicitly to differentiate itself from elocutionists, who soon infiltrated the group anyway.)

In addition to showing the centrality of women to its history, Ruyter defends Delsartean practice as not "merely a silly surface activity; it engaged mind, body, and feelings." She writes that having tried and taught some exercises, "I do not consider the Delsartean exercises as banal and unimportant. Rather, they represented . . . stages—in the understanding of how the body works and the relation of that to health; in the analysis of bodily design in space and time; in the development of movement as an expressive medium; and in finding effective physical training methods for the general public as well as for performing artists" (131; see also Banaji). These key educational theories of body and mind as well as major figures in elocution, their schools, and their textbooks become directly important to the earliest decades of rhetoric and composition at the eight publicly supported colleges for women in the South.

Elocution in the Public Women's Colleges

In the first decade of the twentieth century, most of these public women's colleges had someone teaching oratory or elocution, often mixed with physical culture. At Alabama College for Women, besides early English literature faculty such as Anne Kennedy, hired in 1886, Anna McCoy Francis taught oratory and physical culture with a mixture of the "Swedish and Delsarte systems" of club swinging and freehand exercises, "which helps toward muscular control, correct breathing, walking, and standing. There cannot be grace and freedom without strength; so the first work is for strength through the proper use of the lungs. The breathing exercise will greatly help all who expect to use the voice in any way" (*Catalogue 1907* 32).

Also at Alabama, Nannie B. Granberry taught elocution, apparently as a lower-level preparatory study, and Maude Hayes, in fine arts, taught elocution in the first decade of the twentieth century, having earned a music degree from the Nashville College for Young Ladies; she used the textbook *The Evolution of Expression* by Emerson. In one of many examples of such networking between the colleges, Hayes later spent a year at Winthrop. At Alabama, Lucyle Hook, trained in expression at Texas State College for Women and at Columbia, adopted and continued to use Emerson through the 1920s in expression (although the summer classes most likely populated by teachers seeking continuing education used a Curry textbook).

Emerson's *Evolution of Expression* was an important textbook for these southern women, used also at Texas State College for Women and for several decades at Oklahoma by Frances Dinsmore Davis. Davis relied even longer on a companion reader by Emerson, *The Sixteen Perfective Laws of Art Applied to Oratory*, used through the 1930s. One OCW alumna said in an interview that she studied speech with Davis in 1937; when she grew rattled when reciting a piece from memory in private lessons, her professor made her lie down on the floor and practice relaxation exercises until she could continue, a practice of "decomposing" right out of American Delsartean elocution (Student at Oklahoma; Ruyter 84).

Texas State College for Women, which renamed its elocution department the Department of Reading in 1918, was strongly influenced by Emerson and his texts. The department's first two directors, Jessie McClymonds (1903–5) and S. Justina Smith (1905–24) were Emerson graduates, as would be five out of six department members by 1920. McClymonds, who based her program on Emerson's *Evolution of Expression*, saw expression as a teachable art, not a natural talent, and sought through her teaching "to secure the harmonious development of the powers of expression in the individual." Coursework emphasized both "literary interpretation" and "technique, including exercises for securing correct pronunciation, distinct enunciation and perfect articulation . . . [and] drill in the easy and natural use of the physical agents of expression in obedience to the mind" (*Catalogue 1903* 25). She also taught physical culture "according to the Emerson system, which seeks for the highest condition of health and beauty" (*Catalogue 1904* 34).

As Edyth Renshaw explains, a key to Emerson's theory was the belief that "expression is necessary for impression just as impression is necessary for expression. He believed that in the act of expression the student gained insight as well as technique, and through insight was self-propelled to the next stage of evolution." This is all based on a philosophy that "a person becomes what he thinks." Renshaw emphasizes that "Emerson wanted to elevate elocution from the level of a parlor trick to a social art" (313).[10]

In a similar vein to that of Emerson's, Samuel Silas Curry's approach to expression combined elements of faculty psychology, transcendental philosophy, and Pestalozzian regard for the needs of the individual student to produce an almost mystic vision of the power of oratory to transform not merely the listener but the speaker. Curry was dismayed by what he saw as the reduction of elocution to mere mechanical tricks or formulaic modulations of the voice or gestures. True expression, he insisted, came not from external manipulation, but from within; the more truly understood and deeply felt a passage to be spoken, the truer the expression. "Expression is the result not of physical but of psychic action at the moment of utterance" (*Province of Expression* xi).

Like Emerson's somewhat Romantic approach, Curry's goal was to provide students with confidence as speakers by unlocking the power inherent within themselves. He also tied oratory to civic discourse, believing that a "free people must be a race of speakers" (*Foundations* 3) and arguing that "however beautiful a method for the development of expression may seem, if it fails to develop public speakers, it must be fundamentally wrong" (*Province of Expression* 427). Though Curry's texts would be used in several of the public women's colleges, his greatest impact was felt at Florida State College for Women, where, through 1945, nearly every speech instructor at the school was a Curry graduate, thus shaping the curriculum for decades.

These lofty ideals and the encouragement of self-culture fostered by the elocution movement drew many women faculty to devote themselves to this philosophy of oratory. But later, when some administrators and other faculty disrespected their ambitious, philosophically grounded programs, idealistic expression faculty seem to have been dismayed. In all eight colleges, however, local conditions including power and personality intersected with national forces to shape disciplinary formations. The early histories of speech and elocution pedagogy at these colleges show how the interrelationship of local and national can play out.

Early Days in the Western Colleges

Western influences on women's education may have led rhetorical education at Oklahoma and Texas to form a different pattern from those schools in the Deep South. Culture in the West was closer to the frontier, more open in general, and more open to women's speaking; active speaking and performance programs may have given women more latitude there. For example, at its inception, the Texas State College for Women formed a Department of Elocution (later Expression), Physical Culture, and Vocal Music, and two years of study were required of all students. The second director, Justina Smith, an Emerson graduate with extensive training in music and an interest in drama, further refined the elocution program, creating a three-year sequence in expression, consisting of reading, based on *Evolution of Expression*, dramatic interpretation, and elocution. Like her predecessor McClymonds, Smith strove for an unornamented, "natural" expression, noting that the aim of the reading course was "not for elocutionary effect, but for simple, intelligent reading. . . . Imagination, concentration and continuity of thought are developed by quickening the appreciation, and teaching that reading in its highest sense is interpretation" (*Catalogue 1913–14* 62).

The department, by 1920 larger than the University of Texas's Department of Public Speaking, integrated reading, writing, and speaking instruction through an interdisciplinary degree in literary interpretation.[11] At a time when women were prohibited from participating in debate at the state's coeducational flagship, TSCW students were encouraged to study public speaking and performance; reading majors took a structured sequence of courses in English, drama, debate, public speaking, literary interpretation, and physical training, with *Evolution of Expression* remaining the "basis for the work of [the] department" (*Catalogue 1920–21* 132).[12]

Emerson's influence was evident at TSCW: in freshman expression, the aim was "not for elocutionary effect, but for simple, intelligent reading of the lines—a development of the student's capacity to respond to the spiritual life of a poem or any form of literature." Expression courses were popular enough that nearly all were offered each quarter; the department also offered numerous sections each quarter of a four-year sequence in individual instruction in reading for students outside the department (*Catalogue 1920–21* 130–36).

As with Texas, spoken English and expression were also emphasized at the westernmost of the public women's colleges, Oklahoma College for Women in Chickasha. The first president, Hosea Baker Abernethy, was a rhetoric scholar from Columbus, Mississippi (the home of Mississippi State College for Women); he appointed a professor of German and oratory named Olive Leaman McClintic, a speaker, performer, and educator, who began a degree program in expression. She must have been popular, for the young women soon named their literary society after her. Soon the young women were out in the community giving both speeches and interpretive readings publicly at events such as Confederate memorials.

McClintic held a bachelor of oratory from Texas Christian University (1901) and had also served on the faculty there. Well-qualified, she had earlier attended Emerson College of Oratory in Boston and had earned a certificate from Northwestern University's School of Oratory. As first director of the new Department of Reading and Expression, she explains her position in the 1910 catalogue, revealing much about public attitudes to elocution: "In no other branch of our educational system has so great a change been made in the last 10 years as in the teaching of Elocution. Many sins have been committed in the name of Elocution and in consequence it had fallen into disfavor so much that its exponents were obligated to search out a new name by which to designate the noblest of all arts, the art of public address; thus we have the name expression" (*Catalogue 1910* 17). McClintic required every student working for graduation to take oral reading courses, "not necessarily to make entertainers, but to read and speak better" (17). This comment shows that elocution/expression training was a serious educational enterprise, still associated with women's platform and club presentations. With the reading requirement, expression soon became the largest area in the new school. But McClintic soon married, became Olive McClintic Johnson, and returned to Texas, where she became a prolific writer.[13]

A new Oklahoma College for Women president, George Washington Austin, came in 1915–16 with his own expression professor, Frances Dinsmore Davis, whose mother had been a teacher of voice at OCW in 1910 just after the school opened. Davis would rise to be dean of fine arts, a position she held until 1959. She came with a bachelor of oratory in expression from a nominal college, Texas Fairmont Seminary, in Weatherford, Texas, and later took summers and leaves to earn a bachelor's degree in speech and theater at the Carnegie Institute of Technology (one of the predecessors to Carnegie Mellon University) in 1924 and a master's degree at the University of Michigan in 1937.[14] One of the earliest and longest serving faculty, she remained a strong presence at OCW for decades, dying in 1973.

The 1916 bulletin lists the degree Davis supervises as "Bachelor of Arts in Expression," and her department is called "Expression and Dramatic Arts." That year she first used the Emerson textbooks she would rely on for many decades, especially the four-volume *Sixteen Perfective Laws of Art* and *Evolution of Expression*. While the readings in these volumes do contain some public argument, they are primarily literary prose, poetry, and classical epideictic readings. The catalogue course description for beginning expression for 1916 reads true to the high register of elocutionary theory: "Study of the principles of public discourse; development of the power of self-command and directness. Aim: Development of the Intellect. 2 hours" (*Catalogue 1916* 106).

In 1917, Davis took the first of many leaves, and her student assistant Mary Thompson, who would become the internationally famous Indian performer Te Ata under Davis's tutelage, helped fill in. During this time in speech, storytelling courses became popular, training students in the arts of selecting, shaping, and performing myths, stories, and lore (and not just in Oklahoma).[15]

In 1919, Davis returned with further credentials from the Dramatic School of Chicago Musical College and Washington Square School of Theater in

New York; she immediately changed the program title "Expression" to "Public Speaking," along with adding further dramatic arts and contemporary drama to the program, marking the influence of the "modern" speech field.

By 1920, public speaking was located in the Department of Fine Arts, with Davis as head. The formal debate club formed, and debate was a one-hour class, sponsored by younger speech faculty. Theater and speech activities continued to expand under Davis's direction. She was assisted by Claribel Baird, née Buford, an OCW alumna who later earned an M.A. at Michigan, and Ruth Ball, with a degree from Emerson College of Oratory and further study at Wisconsin and Boston. Baird and Ball also taught freshman composition, so there was some crossover between the disciplines.

In 1919–20, the Department of Fine Arts offered a public speaking diploma requiring three years of study and a public recital. Two semesters of "technique" were required, with private lessons possible. Technique was described as "Study of the principles underlying oral reading, training in committing and repeating lines from the best writers, drill in pronunciation and enunciation, drills to overcome slovenly habits of speech. . . . Aim: to cultivate the imagination, to encourage original thinking, to instill the habit of consulting the dictionary and all reference books; to arouse a wholesome respect for words; to create a love for good literature. Text: *Evolution of Expression*, Vols. I and II." Volumes three and four of the series were used in the next course, Oral Interpretation, with the "Aim: To Deepen the Sympathies, to Widen the Vision, to acquire poise, both mental and physical" (*Catalogue 1919–20* 98). Here we can see that despite the terminology of "Public Speaking" Davis, primarily interested in acting and theater, continued to teach the old elocutionary courses in the same way, as she did for decades. In fact, the courses themselves continued to be called "Speech Arts."

By 1922, fine arts at Oklahoma College for Women had become a school, and Davis was now a dean, making her one of the highest-paid faculty members, at $3,000 per year, though she had by then only a questionable oratory degree. She also reported working long hours, no doubt because of the expanding scope of the new field of public speaking. New elements began to be added to the program, at the same time as traditional elocutionary movement arts such as Greek dances were at their peak; a Greek theater was built along a creek on campus for dancers' performances as well as those of the new Greek drama class. These extraordinary performances as well as ambitious regular theater were whole-campus events, enlisting students in home economics to construct the elaborate costumes.

Development and Expansion of Public Speaking

Because of the long life of these elocutionary pedagogies and activities at these southern colleges, it is not easy to demarcate when "modern" public speaking education began. The emphasis on elocution and performance led easily into modern studies of theater and speech therapy. One sign that the new field of public speaking had become influential can be seen in faculty membership in its regional and national associations and the expansion of speech education into various components under the umbrella of modern speech. These components include debate, argumentation, and public speaking by the early 1920s, as well as a continued emphasis on expression, theater arts, and movement studies; an emerging line of pedagogy on correct speech and speech defects; then a broadening into "euthenics" (or "better living") and "personality" training. As Cohen writes, "orphans" from other activities without academic homes joined with public speaking, including faculty interested in voice and diction, anatomy, physiology, phonetics, dialects, and speech defects. The field later added radio broadcasting. As public speaking developed, some of these groups moved out to form their own disciplines and associations, including the American Speech and Hearing Association and the American Theatre Association (x).

Along with the residual elocution strand, which probably also existed in some measure in the new field as a whole, many of these eight colleges moved in the direction of professionalizing their speech programs in the years before World War II. Most had elements showing that the early period of the speech profession had shaped their studies, especially components that might be of particular interest to women, such as studies of self-presentation. This new field of public speaking began to make its mark on the westernmost colleges of Oklahoma and Texas especially early. It is not clear whether this is because of the relative freedom and egalitarianism of the western frontier or if powerful individuals influenced programs, or perhaps both. At Oklahoma College for Women, Frances Davis was active in public speaking professional associations. In 1928, she attended the nineteenth meeting of the Eastern Public Speaking Conference in New Haven, Connecticut. She delivered a lecture there, "The Place of Speech Training in the General Education Process," in which she describes the scope of the field as including interpretive reading, speech problems, and, of course, dramatics (Oklahoma College for Women, *Trend* 27 Apr. 1928 1). Though she incorporated the new approaches to speech she learned at the Carnegie Institute and the University of Michigan in her later studies, she never gave up her Emerson texts or her elocutionary approach.

As with most of the other southern public women's colleges in the 1920s and 1930s, Oklahoma College for Women had a debate team and a debate club, supervised by one of Davis's assistants. At OCW competitions, the auditorium would fill with young women and townsfolk cheering and clapping for their team, especially when the opponent was the major state university up the road, the University of Oklahoma (OU), headed by Josh Lee, later U.S. senator from that state. The year 1924 was a big one for debate because OCW beat OU 3–0, in addition to beating Texas A&M, Oklahoma Baptist University, and other regional colleges. The 1924 *Argus* yearbook wrote, "The Debate Club claims the distinction of doing more for O.C.W. in an intercollegiate way than any other organization on campus" (n. pag.).

Under Davis's leadership, by the early 1930s, like the field itself, speech at Oklahoma College for Women also expanded into "euthenics" and "better living" courses. New courses in speech problems became the basis for a future program in speech therapy. Davis, a powerful personality, kept up with the times as well as keeping a tight rein on standards: students early on needed her permission to enroll in fine arts and did not major in speech unless "Miss Davis" asked them to. In 1927, she personally began the Green Masquers Honor Society for Drama, comprised of students she herself chose (D. Hobbs 105). She directed plays, began radio training, performed frequently herself, organized curricular and extracurricular activities, and began the Personality Clinic. This clinic, also called the Culture Clinic, helped give young women from rural Oklahoma polished "movie star" bearings, grooming them in not only how to speak but how to sit, stand, walk, dress, and behave (*Catalogue 1942–43* 33).

Davis was a remarkably powerful woman who often went up against presidents under whom she served—on such minor points as moving a piano or larger ones like building a new theater—and won. The college theater building today bears her name, and her influence is still felt in the present college's emphasis on theater arts.

Just across the Red River from Oklahoma, in Texas, in the 1920s, in keeping with the school's mission of training young women for domestic as well as professional and public life, the Texas State College for Women's reading department advertised its work as "vocational as well as cultural," fitting students for "the work of the home, the church, and the community . . . the many responsibilities of social life and for teaching the subject of Reading." A year-long sequence in debate, designed to help students "acquire ease and fluency while speaking from the platform," was open to all students, no matter what their major, "interested in becoming successful demonstrators, public speakers, club leaders, teachers, or church, settlement or extension workers." Public Speaking was designed to aid students in "meeting the demands of social and public life" through practice in extemporaneous occasions such as "the response to toasts, the introduction of speakers, discussions and elementary debate." In Platform Art, students were required to write and present original works to the class, as well as cast and direct either a dramatization of a work of fiction or an original one-act play (*Catalogue 1920* 130–36).

Other colleges also became part of the "modern" field of public speaking, but these professional activities might still be housed in English. Sometimes this could limit speech activities, but in at least one case, that of Florida State College for Women, English sponsored and promoted the new field.

Another Evolutionary Path: Speech and "Speech Arts" in English Departments

For most of a century, rhetoric was the property of English departments. However, as Cohen documents, disciplinary struggles occurred as English focused on literary texts and professionalized, until 1914, when speech teachers in the NCTE formed their own public speaking organization and field. "The new profession," he notes, "by the testimony of its founders, came into being, primarily, to escape the domination of English departments, where the teachers of Oral English occupied a place below the teachers of Literature and English Composition" (ix–x). From 1915 to 1945, a sorting out, sometimes involving conflict, occurred between teachers of English and public speaking and within each field as both fields developed and solidified. Whether speech was allowed to develop as a separate discipline from English in these eight schools depended on many factors, from the previous training, vision, and orientation of college leaders, to powerful personalities in English, and even to funding constraints on forming new units for speech and drama studies.

In some of the more traditional colleges, public speaking, debate, and closely related training in elocution or theater were never allowed to usurp the central mission of a textually based literary education. If a talented or ambitious expression or speech teacher proposed a wider program, it was quickly reined in. In fact, this textual reading and writing model dominated over others at many of these eight colleges. In these colleges, "oral English" or "spoken English" and other speech and theater training remained within or controlled by the English department. Yet we believe that women most often received adequate training across the curriculum and extracurriculum to meet their personal commitment to leadership and their career needs.

Although all these eight colleges provided students with education in both oral and written arts of composition somewhere in the curriculum or in student clubs outside class, Mississippi, the first of the colleges to be founded, in 1884, set the pattern of having strong written composition, language, and literary study in English. As time went on, literature took center stage in the English department, although first-year composition, journalism (until 1939), and some advanced writing courses were offered. Mississippi represented one of the most traditional colleges—for example, it did not drop the requirement that students wear uniforms until 1945, many years after most of the other schools.

The classical philological-literary bent of its first "Mistress of English," Pauline V. Orr, born in 1861, set the standard for classics and English for years to come. In the first college bulletin, Orr was called "Mistress of English and Elocution," but she had dropped the "elocution" by 1893, a fact that may signal the profession's declining respect for elocution at this historical moment. As Mississippi had few graded public high schools at the time of MSCW's founding, the college was originally largely preparatory in nature, then early on provided two-year normal degrees, which did encompass training in literature, grammar, and elocution.

All this the classically trained Orr could easily provide or supervise in her assistants. Her father had been a wealthy plantation owner and judge who provided her with the finest education of the day, equal to men's higher education. She attended Brooklyn's Packer Institute, completing a four-year classical and literary program in two years, and then went to New York for more study in Latin and also oratory. Following that, she studied philology, German, Old Gothic, and Anglo Saxon at universities in Switzerland and Germany. Thus Orr had no lack of resources for carrying out what she envisioned as a full collegiate language program—equal to a men's program—at Mississippi.

The School of English at the turn of the century had three foci: language study, rhetoric and literature, and composition.[16] Texts used in composition before and just after the turn to the twentieth century included David Jayne Hill's *Science of Rhetoric,* James McCosh's *The Laws of Discursive Thought,* and John Franklin Genung's *Outlines of Rhetoric.* Orr herself used Gertrude Buck and Elisabeth Woodbridge's 1899 *A Course in Expository Writing* in English 3 (sophomore composition) after the turn to the new century. Buck and Woodbridge's was a progressive text from the Vassar curriculum that eschewed rule-driven instruction in favor of "a nondogmatic inquiry into the context and situations of writing" (Carr, Carr, and Schultz 72). Orr was primarily oriented to written literature, teaching at first in classical languages, and evidently her composition classes were highly based in textual literary studies rather than elocutionary in emphasis. Her eye was on the highest standard, and elocution by then had come to be associated with preparatory and normal school education.

Because of Orr's high standards, her early true college graduates, six of whom stayed to teach at Mississippi, were leaders in women's college English departments. These included Miriam Paslay, mistress of Latin at Mississippi State College for Women for thirty years and Orr's lifelong friend. Other early graduates included Blanche Colton Williams (1898), who became head of English at Hunter College and a biographer of George Eliot. Rose Peebles (1891) went on to earn a Ph.D. from Bryn Mawr and became the head of English at Vassar. Emma Laney (1906) worked for decades in English at Agnes Scott; and Minor White Latham (1910) became head of English at Barnard. Frances Jones Gaither (1909), class poet and author of the college's original alma mater, became a best-selling novelist.

In 1893, Orr was thirty-two and at the height of her career, but her strong character stirred up controversy and threatened men in power because she wanted women on the board of trustees. Male board members, fearing that she wanted to be president—and was popular enough to achieve it—passed a ruling that the college presidency would be open to men only. In 1913, Orr resigned in protest (along with other strong early women faculty) when the college decided to drop Latin and modern language study from its new B.S. in home economics. She feared it was the first step in relaxing standards so that the women's college would not be equal to four-year men's programs.[17]

The tendency to classical and literary study at Mississippi set by Pauline Orr did not mean there was no speaking or elocution training. Emma Ody Pohl, trained in Delsartean methods, came in 1907 to teach physical education and also taught some performance arts and dance, leading later to large-scale pageants. The pattern of combining physical education with performance reveals the influence of the New England elocution schools.

But in English, the elocutionary thread would continue. Orr's replacement as head of English was Lawrence Painter, who held a master's degree from Harvard (1909). He came in 1913, married his student Mary, and was the captivating oral reader of literature as described by Eudora Welty in her memoir *One Writer's Beginnings*, which outlines her experiences as a student at MSCW from 1925 to 1927.[18] She described Painter, her sophomore English literature teacher, as "a handsome, learned, sandy-haired man—wildly popular" with students. "He got instant silence when he would throw open the book and begin to read aloud to us" (87). This art of "rendering" or orally interpreting written literature traveled usefully into the literature classroom from the public speaking and reading platform and was part of the quiver of both the generalist in literature and the elocutionist for many decades.[19]

Other English faculty at Mississippi at the time of Welty included Mary Margaret Whipple, who had studied at the Leland Powers School in Boston, and who taught expression under the title "Spoken English" in the English department through the 1920s. Nonetheless, "Oratorical and Oral Expression" as a Mississippi catalogue heading was gone by 1918. Not until 1938 was the speech department separated physically and relocated in the Old Chapel, although from 1935, a student could major or minor in speech. The establishment of speech as a separate department coincided with a highly successful fiftieth anniversary pageant telling the college's history that was performed that year. From this time on, plays were produced from the speech department, but all drama study was still located in English.

Winthrop College represents another case where the English department maintained power over speech. Winthrop's James Pickney Kinard, a Johns Hopkins Ph.D. who came to Winthrop in 1896 having completed a philological dissertation on the style and sources of Archbishop's Wulfstan's homilies, was head of English.[20] Although literature became the heart of English at Winthrop under his influence, English early maintained a fusion curriculum including language study, composition, grammar, rhetoric, spoken English, and later creative writing and journalism in one strong department. This was in part because of the normal school program at Winthrop.

Kinard, born in 1864, a native South Carolinian and a graduate of the Citadel, was a Southern Colonel/Victorian Knight figure. His father had died in Virginia in the Civil War. A gentleman, medieval scholar, Anglo-Saxonist, and defender of the English language and southern womanhood, he rose fast in the Winthrop hierarchy. He married one of his students, Miss Lee Wicker, educated at Peabody Normal (later the influential George Peabody College for Teachers, now part of Vanderbilt University), and who subsequently taught elocution and reading at Winthrop. The yearbook *The Tatler* was frequently dedicated to him, from the first one in 1898. Kinard rose to be dean and then president. He published composition and grammar textbooks and wrote at least one novel. Obviously, the English department under his sway felt his particular philological and literary stamp. Standard textbooks used in composition during this period included Genung's *Outlines of Rhetoric*, Sara E. Husted Lockwood's *Lessons in English*, Fred Newton Scott and Joseph Villiers Denney's *Composition-Rhetoric*, and Adams Sherman Hill's *Principles of Rhetoric*.[21]

But while Kinard was on leave from 1913 to 1915, a new, evidently brilliant personality showed up, Miss Lillian A. Crane, of the Laughton School of Expression in Boston, whose courses were listed under reading and expression. Suddenly extensive new Department of Expression descriptions and courses were listed at the bottom of the English listings in the college catalogue. This apparently was an ambitious attempt to form a separate unit from English for the speech arts. Kinard returned to Winthrop in 1916 with expanded duties in psychology and education and soon became dean of the college. The timing of his return and the subsequent fate of the elocution program suggests he quashed its expansion into a full program.

The catalogue shows that soon the expression department also ambitiously expanded to offer more courses than English despite having only two (or maybe three) faculty. Miss Sybil Snell of the (Curry) School of Expression in Boston and Chalif's School of Dancing in New York came to boost the department offerings to twenty-four courses, including storytelling, debate, pantomime, philosophy of expression, and educational dramatics. By 1923–24, Crane and Snell together had formed an ambitious Department of Public Speaking, the "modern" term for the field. But almost immediately after this complete reorganization of expression into public speaking, the next catalogue revealed that suddenly, there was no Miss Crane, and no Miss Snell!

There should be a story here that tells as much about historical disciplinary formation as about personalities, but archival materials can provide only the barest outline of the drama. Miss Crane, from Philadelphia, who had lived in New York and Boston, had previously taught in Columbia, South Carolina. At Winthrop, she taught elocution and gymnastics or physical culture, as noted, a common configuration in women's colleges under Delsarte-influenced expression pedagogies. Miss Crane proved herself capable—she once organized a popular pageant on a massive scale involving the entire school and thousands of attendees, "The History of South Carolina," which she may have written with Kinard.

But in 1924, she resigned, explaining in a letter, first, because of the "uncertain position and fluctuating policy in regard to the Department of Public Speaking." (The new department was evidently a shimmering mirage rather than the solid body portrayed in catalogue listings.) Second, she complained "of the superintending of my extra-curricular activities by a Board of Censorship, which naturally strangles initiative and deadens most effectively all creative impulse" (Crane).[22] Returning to New York, Crane tried to get into graduate school at Syracuse but was denied entry. This was apparently because her expression degree from the Laughton School of Oratory was not seen as an academically valid B.A. In fact, at this time, the private schools of oratory were increasing requirements in response to increasing B.A. standards, and the prestige of elocution was falling. Crane went on to live in poverty in New York City, even desperately—but unsuccessfully—requesting summer teaching at Winthrop in later years.

At Winthrop, requirements for spoken English and oral interpretation continued, taught by Miss Florence Adams Mims, who came in 1925 but was firmly anchored in the English department. Mims was no slouch, an assistant professor who attended the Central School of Speech and Drama and graduated from Leland Powers School of the Spoken Word, and also attended Henry Jewett's School of Acting, Boston University, and Philadelphia's Rice School of the Spoken Word. From her "spoken English" post, she performed and directed student drama and debate for two decades. At Winthrop in 1945, journalism finally earned its own major. But in 1945, speech arts were still listed under the English department, although speech had become a distinct professional discipline at least three decades earlier.

A notable exception to patterns in which English kept control over speech and thereby subordinated speech to literature was Florida State College for Women. At Florida, speech instruction had a central place in the curriculum from the start. At the school's inception, elocution was a required freshman class, while in the sophomore through senior classes, students were required to deliver original orations each year. Several factors combined to promote further development. Influential English chair and dean of the college William Dodd, who served from 1910 to 1944, saw "oral composition" as an important part of study in the discipline, believing that learning to tell a story, debate, and think on one's feet promoted students' resourcefulness and confidence (*Some Objects* 10–11). He therefore encouraged the development of a speech program and departmental major.[23] The college's tacit mission in training teachers, meanwhile, ensured the popularity of such courses. Most early graduates became teachers, and as late as 1930, 57 percent of first-year students listed teaching as their first career choice (Andrews 8). Teachers not only had to be well read, but able to lead reading, speak in public, and organize public events.

As was common at the other public women's colleges, oratory at the school followed a progression from an initial elocution model emphasizing expression and physical culture to training in literary interpretation and dramatic production for teachers to a comprehensive speech and communication program. By the 1920s, in addition to traditional offerings in diction and literary interpretation, the school offered a three-year sequence in public speaking, with an emphasis on argumentation and debate. Students studied "arguments, fallacies, sources, and drawing of briefs," "psychology of audience behavior," "applications of principles of persuasion and suggestion," and "criticism of great orators" and participated in formal team debate (*Catalogue 1928–29* 117–18). By 1935, speech was established as a major department, offering a comprehensive sequence of courses in speech "fundamentals," public speaking, debate, literary interpretation, and speech writing for students who, it was expected, would be speaking in public in a wide range of professional and public roles: "those planning for work on the public platform as readers or lecturers; those preparing to teach speech (reading, public speaking, debate and dramatics) in high school or college; those expecting to be teachers of literature who wish to develop their interpretive powers; those preparing for business life who find themselves handicapped by inability to express themselves clearly and convincingly; and those pursuing the work for purely cultural ends" (*Catalogue 1934–35* 204–5).

Curry's influence is in explicit evidence in Florida State College for Women's curriculum and catalogue copy; through 1945, nearly every speech instructor at the school was a Curry graduate. These included its first expression director, Edith W. Moses, who saw the field as breaking away from being taught as a mere "imitative art" (*Catalogue 1905–6* 101); Mary Hollingsworth Buford, who headed the department from 1921 to 1948 and oversaw significant expansion of the curriculum; and Buford's student and self-described "Curryite" Elizabeth Thomson, who taught from 1929 to 1971 and introduced the school's first radio broadcast course.[24] DuBois Elder, director of expression from 1912 to 1920, was also influenced by Curry, using his textbooks in her courses and promoting expression as a way for students to study "their own processes of mind" (*Catalogue 1913–14* 115). By 1935, the department had four members, by 1945 five, all of whom were Curry graduates, and all of whom were women. The department's stability was enhanced by the fact that four of them, Buford, Thomson, Margaret Wyly, and Kemper Martin Moore, worked together as its core for nearly twenty years.

Coeducation would largely erase this influence; upon Buford's retirement in 1948, a male chair, Clarence W. Edney, was hired, and "his first move was to get rid of all the women from the speech faculty," except for Thomson, who had tenure. After that, she "was the only female teacher for years" (Thomson 9). In ridding FSCW of its women speech faculty, was Edney attempting at long last to rid the institution of the strong hand of a feminized elocution to institute a modern professional public speaking program? If so, he had banished one of the longest-lasting and perhaps broadest in scope of the shaping influences of these colleges, elocution-trained women faculty.

Extracurricular Opportunities to Speak and Perform

Women at the eight southern public colleges for women learned to speak and write as much, if not more so, outside their formal classes through extracurricular activities such as special events, drama, debate, literary study clubs, and other club or YWCA programs. As we have seen thus far, their education, despite emphasizing "industrial" or "teacher" training, was generally humanistic and liberal arts. As such, it was holistic, and the intensive nature of students' lives on campus meant that learning took place in a wide spectrum of activities planned to keep the young women busy and out of trouble as well as to entertain and educate them. Most young women received some training in public speaking in their classes, and the more active had regular opportunities to speak, read papers or poems, or act in drama productions in all eight schools.

For example, at Alabama College for Women, in 1924 on the occasion of the Armistice Celebration, classes were dismissed, and students attended a program in which Lucyle Hook, head of expression, read a war poem; many students also spoke or read poems. (Hook was a popular figure who also directed the Alabama Players and organized May Day there.) Young women at Alabama could practice parliamentary skills and speaking in student senate after 1925. The Drama Club began in 1921, and the Forensic Club in 1925, although debates were popular from the mid-1920s through the 1940s, with student newspapers giving extensive debate coverage during those decades. Throughout the 1930s and 1940s, Pi Kappa Delta, the national honor fraternity in public speaking, was active. Alabama also had three chapters of the Story Tellers League in the early twentieth century: one for classic and literary stories, one for folk tales, and one for the best of contemporary stories. Storytelling was a popular speech activity in other colleges as well.

As with the other colleges, Oklahoma College for Women also had its literary societies such as Literatae, begun in 1917, the Leaman Literary Society, 1911, and others including the Othana and Utopian clubs. The Ruth Bryan Owens Club was often in charge of daily assemblies. Speaking also took place in oratorical contests sponsored by different groups, as well as at programs like the 1921 Old South commemoration. Most special programs featured young women reading poetry or literature or less frequently giving speeches. Forensics were strong at Oklahoma until into the forties. The college, along with others, also participated in Pi Kappa Delta.

Winthrop in South Carolina also had its debaters before the turn of the twentieth century, with the Debates League created early on. Drama activities and the drama club Masquers were active by the early 1930s. Even when the college was still called the Winthrop Training School, the literary society met every two weeks. By 1895, Winthrop had two literary societies, Winthrop and Curry, each with a printed bulletin. By the 1930s, there were three literary societies, the Curry, Wade Hampton, and Winthrop. Young women spoke at YWCA events, class and sorority meetings, and local clubs. The college had a chapter of the United Daughters of the Confederacy, which each year entertained the state legislature on its annual visit to the college on Robert E. Lee's birthday. Student government at Winthrop started in 1911, giving the young women organizational and leadership training.

Public speaking opportunities at Mississippi seemed less frequent than at the other colleges, and student groups were social in nature into the early twentieth century. In contrast to the other schools in our study, where participation in a literary club early was common or even de facto required, at MSCW the earliest literary clubs became exclusive membership clubs, and they later disbanded when the president asked them to after rivalry led to conflicts (Pieschel and Pieschel 51).[25] However, it seems likely that all the colleges' literary society programs featured young women discussing, speaking, or reading papers, as that was the usual pattern for student clubs and for the General Federation of Women's Clubs literature study groups.

Drama and Pageants

At Mississippi, drama and play production remained the responsibility of the English department. But like at the other colleges, drama and other dramatic entertainments such as pageants were major events offered for citizens from miles around. Many pageants were held, including one celebrating Joan of Arc (Pieschel 3). MSCW graduate and best-selling novelist Frances Jones Gaither's contributions included the ambitious 1915 "The Book of Words: The Pageant of Columbus," about the early history of the state and the school, and later "The Clock and the Fountain," written for the college's fiftieth anniversary, celebrated in 1935.[26] The latter pageant was a drama about the history of the college for unaware students. It featured music as well as dance. Also at the fiftieth anniversary celebration, Emma Ody Pohl (who came from Greenville in 1907 to teach physical education and drama and founded the college's May Day celebrations in 1909) created and led "Les Sylphides," after a ballet she had seen in New York City. Pohl also led the Zouave drill team, mentioned in Eudora Welty's *Losing Battles* (247). She also early on established the annual Junior-Freshman Wedding pageant (Pieschel and Pieschel 61). Such physical and acting training, even when not directly leading to speaking parts, helped train young women in public presentation.

At Alabama, one popular pageant was "The Great White Rabbit." As at Mississippi, many of the pageants at Alabama had Native American themes, including "The Passing of the Red Man, a pantomime in one act, the Advance of the White Man" and "The Way of Life, a Dramatic Pageant," supposedly depicting a "fairly authentic" portrayal of Indian religion.

At Winthrop, medieval scholar Kinard wrote, directed, and acted in the "Old English Pageant," sometimes called the "Medieval Pageant," reenacting the visit of Queen Elizabeth and her court to Kenilworth Castle in 1575. Later, J. E. Walmsley, the chair of history, wrote and directed "The Making of South Carolina," a popular spectacle with a cast of more than fourteen hundred, along with sixteen hundred costumes, and a reported seven thousand spectators.

At Oklahoma during the 1920s, traditional elocutionary movement arts such as Greek dances were at their peak, and a Greek theater was built along a creek on campus for their performances as well as those of the new Greek drama class, with events attended by townsfolk for miles around. Pageants sponsored by the speech and drama program were also at their height by this time. The May Day Fete was another campus tradition that Oklahoma adopted from the other colleges during the 1920s. Full of pageantry, music, drama, and athletic competitions, the May Day affair grew to involve hundreds of students and thousands of spectators. The most spectacular event of all took place on May 4, 1926, when the local press reported that "500 OCW girls performed before a crowd of 3,000 spectators." The theme of the fete was "Alice in Looking Glass Land."

> All of the characters were in costumes as depicted by the original "Alice" illustrator John Tenniel. Alice arrived first, attended by living, costumed flowers, butterflies, dragonflies, rabbits, flamingos, dormice, chessmen, the Mad Hatter, the White Queen, Father William, and other Lewis Carroll characters and creations. There were myriad dances, drills, songs, and capers. The *Chickasha Daily Express* pronounced it a "big success." The day was marred only by the collapse of a section of bleachers on the north end of the oval, injuring a half-dozen people and shattering one or two leg-bones. Dr. Rebecca Mason, resident physician at OCW, assisted the wounded and set one of the broken bones. (D. Hobbs 95)

Although the young women were taught to write and give speeches, and although many of these performance events did not involve traditional rhetoric, they were valuable experiences for students. They allowed young women, often rural and family-oriented, to learn to present themselves publicly in a variety of rhetorical situations. The experiences, including the ubiquitous rituals of graduation, and others such as Winthrop's daisy chain and Mississippi's magnolia chain, must have given them an ease with appearing on the public stage and interacting with community leaders and important visitors to campus, government officials, legislators, and at least one U.S. president, Taft, who loved to visit the women's colleges.[27]

Public speaking was at first part of a general oratorical culture, but it developed into a skill for teachers on the one hand, or for platform or dramatic performance arts on the other, although no distinction was made. What we today think of as training in speaking for civic or citizenship purposes was inchoate in the curricula in most colleges, marginalized in favor of dramatic readings of literature, storytelling, or theatrical acting. Yet in their extracurricular experiences, these young women learned how to do what they needed to do in their lives—lead a meeting, speak before an audience, administer a large organization, teach, entertain, or devote themselves to performance in an artistic career. The graduates of the eight southern public women's colleges did all these activities over their lives, and more. While their disciplinary training in formal speech may have at times been less than it could have been, the accomplishments of alumnae show that their education in public speaking was more than enough to empower them to develop their abilities and to succeed in their chosen lifework.

4

Useful Careers: Professional Training for Women of the New South

"THE GROWTH OF INDUSTRIALISM has favored women workers": this finding came from a 1936 study sponsored by National Federation of Business and Professional Women's Clubs in conjunction with the Alabama state chapter and Alabama College for Women (National Federation 15).[1] How the study's authors could arrive at these conclusions and how the southern public women's colleges prepared women to succeed in available occupations in the region is this chapter's theme.

The eight colleges all offered vocational training in various business and industrial areas as well as teacher preparation in addition to general college work. Home economics, given federal funding in the second decade of the twentieth century, remained at the heart of the curriculum until after coeducation. The importance of such "practical" curricula at the public women's colleges cannot be overstated. Though students at both public and private women's colleges sought expanded educational and economic opportunity, significant demographic differences persisted between these types of institutions well into the twentieth century. In 1933, Doak Sheridan Campbell of George Peabody College for Teachers published a survey of approximately fifteen hundred women graduates of southern colleges from 1920 and 1925, including over five hundred from seven of the eight public colleges for women.[2] He found that, compared to graduates of private women's colleges, the graduates of the southern public women's colleges were more likely to have worked after graduation, continued working after marriage, chosen a vocation before entering college, and chosen coursework for practical home-making or vocational value (see table 4.1).

Table 4.1
Comparison of 1920 and 1925 graduates of southern
public and private women's colleges

Percentage who	Worked		Chose vocation before entering	Chose courses for*		
	Postcollege	Postmarriage		Homemaking	Vocation	General culture
Public	92.0	59.4	60.0	12.3	31.4	13.5
Private	81.3	52.1	46.6	1.6	27.1	18.6

Source: D. Campbell, *Problems in the Education of College Women* (25, 30, 67, 77).
* Open-ended question; figures represent answer as percentage of total responses.

This is not to say that students at the public women's colleges did not value the liberal arts, or that private women's college graduates disparaged home-making. Indeed, they shared many cultural traits; both had similar literary tastes and were about equally as likely to marry, be politically engaged (about two-thirds were frequent voters), and take responsibility for housework. Campbell also asked graduates which courses they had not taken in college that they "have since felt the need of" (52); though he did not break down this question by institutional type, the answers suggest a wide-felt need among women for both practical and cultural education, with the most popular responses being courses in home economics, followed by English (60–61).[3] Though it is not our primary focus here, this chapter also considers how women made use of their education in rhetoric and writing at the public women's colleges and the relationship of writing and speaking to many of their career choices. We begin with historical background about how these colleges contributed to Progressive-era industrial education, before addressing three major areas of professional education—industrial and commercial, teaching, and home economics.

Industrial Education for White Women

If industrialism was good for women, it came slowly to the South and was just gaining ground by the late nineteenth century, when the earliest public women's colleges opened. Although wood and textile industries and tobacco processing existed in the South before the Civil War and cotton mills were strong by the 1880s, industrial development itself was often viewed as an idea linked with northern values. The agrarian movement was suspicious of business and banking, yet some southerners felt industry could free their region from northern dependence (Fisher 144–45).

The argument between W. E. B. DuBois and Booker T. Washington over whether higher education should emphasize the training of a "talented tenth" or the broader population, leaders or workers, was not a controversy limited to African American education. Industrial education for ordinary workers was then a burgeoning movement in the North, seen by many as a democratic form of education as opposed to the old elitist classical education. Progressive domestic feminists often supported manual and household education as addressing the whole person. By the time southern Reconstruction ended in 1877, a new middle class, comprised of small farmers, businessmen, and professionals, was emerging in the South, and increasingly looking to industrialization as a means of increasing its and the region's prosperity.

Southerners were not alone in their efforts to rebuild. New England minister and philanthropist Amory Dwight Mayo, associate editor of the *Journal of Education* in the 1880s, campaigned throughout the South, calling for southerners to support public education, still slow to catch on in the region. In South Carolina, he early on supported the Winthrop Training School for Teachers (1866), a precursor to what would become Winthrop College, itself established in 1891. Mayo was a particular proponent of industrial education for both black southerners and what he termed the "third estate" of the South, descendants of nonslaveholding whites now coming into their own, especially women.[4] "Industrial education," he declared, "in its broadest and most practical form, with good schooling in the elements of English, must become a great factor in the uplift of the new South" (281). He thus supported the early Mississippi State College for Women's plan of industrial education and advocated it as a model for other schools. Thus the history of these eight colleges is an important part of the history of industrial and vocational education for women in America.

Industrial education developed in America on the heels of industrialism and industrial work. After the Civil War, studies in science and technology grew along with enthusiasm over the possibilities for using them to improve the human condition. European-style trade schools with hands-on practice influenced the New York Trade School (1881, now the New York City College of Technology), the Pratt Institute (1887), and other early schools such as Rennselaer Polytechnic Institute (1824) and the Massachusetts Institute of Technology (MIT, 1861). With the Morrill Acts of 1861 and 1890, the public land-grant colleges were born, greatly expanding opportunities for industrial education to a wide range of students through a blend of liberal arts and vocational subjects.[5]

Still, opportunities for women lagged somewhat behind.[6] With the notable exception of the coeducational Pratt Institute, many early industrial schools were exclusively or primarily for men. In the West and Midwest, land-grant agricultural and mechanical (A&M) colleges were typically coed, as were those established for black students nationwide. In the South, however, a pattern developed of state-funded A&M schools for white men only; with the exception of Florida, each of the states in our study had such a school. Indeed, part of the impetus for the founding of the public women's colleges was the desire among many citizens to extend such education to their states' white daughters. In South Carolina, for example, Clemson University was founded in 1889 as an agricultural school for the sons of farmers. In 1891, when the state created Winthrop, its women's normal and industrial college, the two institutions were seen as "paired" male-female colleges by the governor. The founding of black coeducational land-grant institutions in these southern states also created pressure to provide similar institutions for white women; as we describe in chapters 1 and 5, key to the founding of the public women's colleges were calls for the state to provide the same opportunity to white women as it did to black women, lest the former be left behind. The paradox of this rhetoric, at once progressive regarding gender and reactionary regarding race, would remain a conflicted part of the histories of these colleges through their integration in the 1950s and 1960s. Though the white public colleges for women did not model themselves after black land-grant institutions, they shared in the contemporary milieu of offering a hybridized liberal arts–industrial higher education.

Other hybrid models of industrial education were also developing at this time. Ezra Cornell's university in New York, established as the state's land-grant university in 1865, aimed to produce leaders of the old liberal arts model and at the same time practical men of modern science; this dual goal influenced the direction of the land-grant colleges. In Chicago, Clara Mitchell worked with John Dewey in the School of Education at the University of Chicago, where the arts and crafts movement was linked with industrial arts. At Chicago's Hull House, Jane Addams sponsored vocational classes and created a labor museum in tribute to women's historical production. Early models from Europe may also have inspired the idea to combine normal and industrial education for women.[7]

Thus various models of industrial education were available—or developing—when the first southern public colleges for women were founded. Nonetheless, these colleges helped pioneer this synthesis of industrial and general education in the United States. All these schools were chartered and operational by the first decade of the twentieth century, when the nation was arguing over whether to follow the German model and have separate tracks for industrial/vocational education in high schools or combine them with general education. The colleges, which already featured "domestic" arts and sciences, were the beneficiaries of federal funding for vocational education for home economics from the earliest disbursal of these funds under the Smith-Lever Act of 1914. These funds led to an emphasis in the schools on home economics over industrial education. Along with the existing commercial courses (not included under federal vocational education until 1963), federally funded home economics and its teaching became the premier vocational education offered to students of the public colleges for women.

This chapter first discusses the industrial courses of study offered to women in the early days of these colleges, then turns to their teacher-training education, and finally to home economics, which, combined with home economics teacher training, became stronger in the second decade of the twentieth century and remained a staple of the curriculum as long as the colleges were for women only.

Education for Industrial and Commercial Careers

Early in the twentieth century, long after the earliest of the public women's colleges were founded, women themselves were campaigning for girls to receive industrial education as part of a proposed National Act for Vocational Education. Women on a committee to help frame the bill included Florence Marshall, director of the Manhattan Trade School for Girls, and Agnes Nestor, president of the International Glove Workers' Union. But the General Federation of Women's Clubs lobbied for home economics training, which was favored over industrial education when the bill that ultimately became the Smith-Hughes Act was signed in 1917 (Kliebard 135).[8] Whenever there was a conflict between traditional values and practices for women and industrial education, the former typically won the public's hearts and minds. That is why the kind of industrial education offered initially by the southern public women's colleges was such a radical idea.

The earliest of the public women's colleges were founded at the dawn of the "new South" era, when the region's boosters began calling for industrial development to supplant the previous plantation model of the southern aristocracy, which, though thought to be culturally superior to the northern industrial model—indeed, the source of the South's putative cultural superiority—was increasingly acknowledged to have been economically unsustainable. In new South "spokesman" Henry W. Grady's oft-quoted words, "The old South rested everything on slavery and agriculture, unconscious that these could neither give nor maintain healthy growth. The new South presents a perfect democracy . . . a hundred farms for every plantation, fifty homes for every palace; and a diversified industry that meets the complex needs of this complex age" (19).

Despite pronouncements such as these, the people of the South still had to be persuaded of the benefit of industry, particularly in regard to women, and a rhetoric was put in place to do just this. It is clear from the colleges' earliest bulletins that industrial education for women was a new phenomenon whose rationale had to be articulated and argued for. For example, the first Alabama College for Women catalogue in 1896–97 begins with a plea for "more light," based on the death cry of "the great Goethe. In an extended agrarian metaphor, women are likened to plants, albeit distorted ones, because they have been used to light coming only from one side. While they may appear to be flourishing, "if we look at the other side we shall find them neglected, deficient, and deformed. What they want is more light—light on the other side. . . . So in education we must open new windows . . . and let every luminous characteristic of modern life shine in upon our school rooms. We must pay less heed to what the world was two or three hundred years ago, and regard with greater respect what the world is today" (*Catalogue 1896–97* 2). The author knew that the school catalogue served as marketing and would be closely read by anxious parents who were perhaps hoping for a more traditional liberal arts education for their daughters. At the same time, progressive agrarians had fought for their daughters as well as their sons to benefit from the taxes they already paid for education. In the 1870s and 1880s, they knew it was possible their daughters might never marry and would need to be able to support themselves. Nevertheless, embracing the industrial education model was a stretch for many, and a rhetoric setting forth and making sense of the conflicting values helped persuade them to support it.

This kind of rhetorical repositioning of southern ideals for women, with all its inherent contradictions, occurs in speeches at the laying of the cornerstone at South Carolina's Winthrop in 1894, particularly that of Governor Benjamin Ryan Tillman.[9] Tillman first acknowledges the need to move beyond antebellum ways, particularly the old seminary-type schools for women. "The effects of slavery upon our habits and customs are . . . still plainly visible. We are disinclined as a people to have our women leave home to seek their fortunes or enter industrial life. The consequence is that . . . our women have been altogether helpless and our system of education has been a fatal blunder." In this radically new school, however, the industrial arts "will lead to independence." Music is to be taught, but only as an art to "insure livelihood," and not for display or "ornament" (qtd. in Chepesiuk and Chepesiuk 30). At the same time, traditional values will be promoted through domestic subjects: "Chemistry and practice of cookery will be taught, and. . . . those thousand and one things which a woman has to do to make a pleasant home, will be taught" (32). Tillman thus helps reframe his listeners' ideas of the industrial arts while assuring them that the new institution will not be *too* radical.

Indeed, Tillman takes great pains to assure his listeners that the new institution will not do anything to "rub the bloom off the peach":

God forbid that this school shall ever send forth a woman who has been unsexed. We would have the clinging, helpless creature able to stand erect and walk; we would have the trembling bird given wings to fly from home—seek avenues of independence—until she can find a mate and build a nest for herself; but never, never have any of the daughters in South Carolina, who shall be trained in those walls . . . become other than helpful wives and happy self-respecting mothers. Women's special province in life is that of the home-maker. (33)

Here Tillman soars to rhetorical heights, asserting that the college will produce *not* "a strong minded, bold, brazen, pert, self-asserting female, prating of 'woman's rights,' 'man's selfishness and tyranny,' the 'degradation of nursing children'" (33–34) but a "woman trained in all the domestic arts and economics, and some bread winning occupation; self-reliant and strong, yet withal modest, self-respecting and lady-like" (33). Women were to be educated for competence, which bred confidence, but this would not result in changing ideals for womanhood. Obviously, the necessary rhetorical repositioning required the advancing and intertwining of competing tropes to form the necessary appeals.

With this kind of rhetorical repositioning taking place by leaders early on, this notion of industrial education soon became the model, even in the most traditional areas of the South.[10] But lofty arguments aside, what did industrial education mean, nationally, or in the region at that time? In *The "Girl" Question in Education*, Jane Bernard Powers argues that industrial or trade education was always undermined by traditional feminine ideals and overlapped with home economics—needlework, millinery, cooking, and sewing being staples of all of the above (16, 102). What compromises took place between what was possible and what was available and acceptable work for women? For example, we know women at first were trained in printing. But at one school at least, Mississippi, the training program in printing was dropped because male printers were reluctant to hire the graduates (Pieschel and Pieschel 32). Programs of study from individual colleges, along with evidence of work women could (and, in certain cases, could not) do help define the meaning and scope of industrial education in the Progressive era.

In Mississippi, the original charter and later legislative acts indicated that the school was expected to be vocationally oriented and not a liberal arts institution. Yet there was an ongoing struggle between industrial and traditional education, and a compromise was not reached for many decades. Early industrial education at the college included telegraphy, phonography (an early form of stenography) and typewriting, bookkeeping, drawing, design, modeling, wood carving, needlework, repoussé, leather working, photography, pharmacy, dressmaking, millinery, cooking, and printing. Many of these industrial courses were actually commercial courses: Bookkeeping included two hours of penmanship a week. Telegraphy "comprise[d] a thorough knowledge of commercial and railroad telegraphy." Phonography used "Pittman's system" of dictation and shorthand for "speech and sermon reporting," including writing of dictated letters. Typewriting included a "thorough knowledge of the machine" (*Catalogue 1885–86* 25).

Appeals set forth for Mississippi State College for Women's benchmark program of industrial and decorative art, as prefaced in an early bulletin, made the case that U.S. companies need not go to Europe for good design: "Hitherto American people have, in a great measure, been dependent upon foreign inventors and designers, but with drawing taught in our schools, as it should be taught, our manufacturing companies need not go abroad for designs" (*Catalogue 1885–86* 23). The catalogue notes that the course is also training for art education in the schools. "By diligent study, a pupil may complete the Preparatory Course and perfect herself in one branch of designing in two years." Design applications were, for example, for wallpapers, oil cloths or prints, or carpet designing. An award of a "fine American" sewing machine was given to the pupil who makes the "most progress in cutting, fitting and making garments and in nice sewing" (*Catalogue 1885–86* 35).

Mississippi's president Henry Lewis Whitfield (1907–20) expanded and transformed the nature of industrial education into home economics. Under the previous president, plans were made to strengthen the industrial department, and an industrial hall (1902) and science hall (1906) had been added (Pieschel and Pieschel 43, 46). But Whitfield continued to strengthen industrial studies and turned the Department of Industrial Science, founded in 1910, into the first home economics department in the state in 1915. He also argued that *his* college women should study agriculture, along with their studies in horticulture and floriculture, though this goal was apparently not shared by the board of trustees. In 1920, having been "repeatedly . . . denied funding" to start a practice farm on campus, he secured a donation from a Mississippi philanthropist of 343 acres with buildings, equipment, and livestock. Home economics professors were to be in charge of supervising students at the farm. But the trustees refused the donation, and Whitfield was fired soon thereafter (Pieschel and Pieschel 67–68). The tensions between the southern ideals for women and the new realities were palpable. Yet most of the colleges, like their male A&M counterparts, owned farms with full approval of their publics. The flap over the Mississippi farm exposes the conflict over ideals for womanhood in Mississippi. Past ideals, whether the agrarian yeoman ideal of a small family farm or the competing aristocratic Cavalier ideal of a large estate, worked to conceal women's active participation in farm work.

White women did farm work, and even fieldwork in the South, but because it violated "ideals" for womanhood as well as myths about racial destinies, they—and their men—usually weren't proud of it. In Georgia, for example, the campaign for a women's college was begun by the wife of a state legislator, Susan Milton Atkinson, inspired by seeing rural white girls working in the fields hide their faces in shame as she passed by in her car (Curl 4).

This emphasis on industrial education would eventually diminish as the colleges matured, supplanted by home economics and teacher education. In 1916, Oklahoma's Industrial Institute and College for Girls became the first to drop any reference to industrial or technical education from its name, becoming Oklahoma College for Women. Nationally, trade education for women was diminishing, and the appellation "industrial" had garnered unpleasant associations by that time, suggesting to some members of the public prisons or reform schools, to the chagrin of administrators. That shift in meaning for industrial colleges, soon after home economics had won the battle for federal vocational educational funding, signaled the end of the original "industrial education" model.[11] By 1923, all of the colleges had dropped the term "industrial" from their names, save Florida, which having been established as a liberal arts college had never used it, and Texas, which officially retained it until 1934, though it had long followed the hybrid model of the other public women's colleges and had included the designation "the State College for Women" in its catalogues since at least 1921 (for a list of all college name changes, see the appendix).

Whatever designs the state legislatures or more practical women supporters of industrial education had for these colleges, southern women knew that the prestigious Seven Sisters of the North and other revered women's colleges were primarily liberal arts in orientation. As Amy Thompson McCandless notes, while the South's industrial and normal colleges were "designed primarily for the middle and lower classes . . . liberal arts colleges were viewed as the preserve of the region's elite" (*Past in the Present* 11). That fact and the long history of traditional southern educational values favoring liberal arts studies ultimately held sway. Many faculty and students at these colleges wanted a general education including literature, fine arts, and music—although the model many aspired to was now a traditional, even outdated one sometimes resembling that of the old seminaries—and over time, their strong desires transformed each college. These tensions would long resonate in the public women's colleges and their descendants. Three colleges today, Georgia College and State University, the University of Science and Arts of Oklahoma, and Alabama's Montevallo University, after initially struggling in the era of coeducation, were reborn as public liberal arts colleges, while the rest have held onto professional training programs of various types along with their fine arts and liberal studies as comprehensive public universities.[12]

Commercial Education

Over time, industrial efforts at the public women's colleges were supplanted by commercial education courses. Such programs were a success because many young women wanted to work in business; likewise, the colleges' presidents tended to brag about their successful business alumnae, whom they saw as having an advantage over graduates of private business schools. Clerical jobs were usually plentiful, so women enrolled in the popular commercial courses and programs. Another factor making commercial studies attractive was that clerical work was considered a middle-class vocation like teaching (Powers 39). Commercial education was for students who could go to high school and beyond, who could consider a middle-class career. It often required advanced literacy skills, which, as we have seen, English classes could help provide. Parents had little reason to be concerned about the office, which was now considered a respectable place to work, especially in comparison to the factory, where the work was considered rough and lower in status.

Commercial studies were not a new thing, coming into being in the late nineteenth century. The introduction of the commercial typewriter in the 1870s and subsequent standardization led to the feminization of secretarial work; this opened many jobs, as did the bureaucratization of business and government in the industrial era. The number of women office workers rose from fewer than one thousand in 1870 to one hundred thousand by 1910 and to one million by 1920 (Powers 40). The labor market needed inexpensive and docile workers, and willing and educated public college women were thought to fit the bill. Women who did not want to teach but who wanted to meet a man and marry could do so in an office setting. Commercial work also included the possibility of advancement, from pool stenographer to private secretary or administrator. It thus held promise as either a short- or long-term career.

Winthrop College, founded as the South Carolina Industrial and Winthrop Normal College in 1891, initially offered three areas of study—normal, industrial, and domestic science. Like at Mississippi, the industrial course early on included many commercial subjects such as stenography, typewriting, and bookkeeping, but also freehand and industrial drawing, professional sewing, dressmaking, and millinery; the domestic science area taught cooking, personal sewing, and housekeeping. Reading and elocution were taught to all. Trustee Dr. E. S. Joynes was sent to France and Germany in 1895 to visit industrial schools for women in Paris, Hamburg, Berlin, Dresden, Munich, and Karlsruhe (Webb 21). His enthusiastic report resulted in changes in curricula at Winthrop in academic, business, industrial, and domestic science areas of study (Webb 29).

At Alabama, the first catalogue (1896–97) calls the institution the "Girls' Industrial School of Alabama, A Polytechnic Institute," listing faculty in the areas of mathematics, English and history, pedagogy, stenography and typewriting, telegraphy, art, dressmaking and needlework, scientific cooking, and music and voice. The bulletin notes in its section on English and history that the "department of Stenography and Typewriting has been of special value to the department of English, because of its practical application of the principles taught in the English department." The experience of the first year, it continues, "proves that our school, of many Industrial departments, can develop a strong, clear mastery of English, beyond that possible in ordinary institutions" (*Catalogue 1896–97* 25).

The conflict between the old elite literary education and the new industrial one at Mississippi was also evident at Alabama. However, early proponents of industrial education were ambitious. Alabama's first catalogue described the school as "grand and noble work," its purpose "to train young women for certain lines of work, thus preparing them to cope with the world should they ever be thrown upon their own resources." As the field of women's usefulness is broadening, the school prepares the girls to enter a new world. Yet, "a great building cannot be erected upon an imperfect foundation"; therefore, "the literary department is especially thorough, and no pupil is permitted to enter advanced classes when she is deficient in the elementary branches" (*Catalogue 1896–97* 14).

At this earliest incarnation of Alabama College for Women, the chartering legislative act included mention of indoor carpentry, plumbing, and electrical construction, along with business courses and others preparing girls for "the practical industries of the age."[13] Courses actually taught were somewhat narrower, omitting construction trades, but, like the other early schools, encompassing telegraphy, typewriting, stenography, dressmaking, needlework, scientific cooking, art, and instrumental and vocal music under its industrial branch.[14] These were dispersed among three lines of study, business, normal, and collegiate, although students took industrial courses and cooking no matter which course of study they chose. Hat making later was offered and, in a time when many women wore hats, was so successful that the study of millinery was adopted back at the first industrial college, Mississippi.

Unlike the earliest public women's college, the last chartered, Oklahoma College for Women, founded in 1908 and opened in 1909 as the Oklahoma Industrial Institute and College for Girls, early on had a full business or "commercial department." Business courses could be taken alongside the literary sequence and included bookkeeping, typing, stenography, domestic science, cooking, chemistry, bacteriology, sewing, tailoring, embroidery, and fine arts. Although later the studies were separated into different departments, business studies were always popular at the college.

Through much of the public women's colleges' histories, students took a variety of practical courses, even when they majored in teaching or a liberal arts program. Such courses as upholstering, dressmaking, and millinery were popular with young women who knew they needed to be able to do a variety of practical tasks, or perhaps these just appealed to their creativity. One Oklahoma alumna, Connie Vann Jackson, now a retired teacher, took many such courses in the 1950s because they were practical or pleasurable, or she liked the instructor. Credits earned, of course, counted toward graduation, and she was eager to graduate and get married after World War II (Jackson).

Teaching as a Profession

Because the South was just establishing its system of public schools after the Civil War and even into the twentieth century, school teachers were sorely needed; thus, as with the Seven Sisters and other private women's colleges in this era, teaching remained a significant career area for graduates of the public women's colleges.[15] The expectation that a primary career path of public women's college graduates would be teaching is reflected in the founding appellations of three of the colleges, North Carolina, Georgia, and Winthrop, classified as "normal and industrial" colleges. Mississippi, as usual a model, began the pattern at the public women's colleges of having academic, industrial, and normal areas combined, but this was a pattern that was already well established by coeducational public African American colleges. While not all the eight colleges stressed teaching as a career area, all provided pedagogy and education strands in their curricula. In part because of domestic ideology, teaching was long one of the most popular careers for women in both the North and South. As one historian notes, "At no time between 1870 and 1970 did teaching fall below fifth among the ten leading occupations of *all* women workers" (Clifford 256).

A significant difference between North and South, however, and one critical to our study, is the different rate at which teaching became a career option for women in the South. By 1880, teaching was a feminized profession in the Northeast, where 71.2 percent of public school teachers were women; in the South Atlantic and South Central regions (encompassing the former slave states from Maryland to Texas, including Oklahoma), women were only 37.5 percent and 32.8 percent of total teachers respectively. In the years to follow, which would see the founding of the public colleges for women, teaching would increasingly become a career path for southern women; by 1906 67.8 percent of South Atlantic and 60.7 percent of South Central teachers were women (see table 4.2). The eight public colleges trained many of the women who would build the white public school systems in their states.

Table 4.2
Percentage of female public school teachers by
region, 1879–80 through 1905–6

	1879–80	1889–90	1899–1900	1905–6
North Atlantic	71.2	80.0	81.6	85.8
South Atlantic	37.5	50.9	59.3	67.8
South Central	32.8	42.5	52.6	60.7
U.S. average	57.2	65.5	70.1	76.4

Source: U.S. Bureau of Education, Report of the Commissioner, 1906 (304).

In the years before the Civil War, the South began to identify itself as a distinctive region with chivalrous, Cavalier values and aristocratic mythology. Private and denominational schools were the tradition, and after the war, segregation and its financial and social costs slowed the development of public education. Interest in public education for whites rose suddenly after literacy tests for voting aimed at disenfranchising black citizens were instituted in the 1890s. Though illiterate whites were typically exempted through "grandfather," "good character," or other clauses, most states had time limits on these; thus, "if the white masses were to retain suffrage, they had to be educated" (McCandless, Past in the Present 22). Even progressive advocates for public education tended to view it through a racialized lens. North Carolina's Charles Duncan McIver, for example, as president of the North Carolina Teachers' Assembly, would be instrumental in the founding of North Carolina College for Women and later serve as its first president. Though he saw education as universally important—"For the white race and the black race; the rich and the poor . . . the paramount question of the southern states is, how shall the great mass of our people be educated?"—he also believed that "the most important factor . . . affecting the civilization of the south is the white girl of the country" (354–55).[16] McIver's genuine interest in advocating for economically and educationally disenfranchised white women and progressive educational ideals, coupled with traditional southern notions of white womanhood and civilization, was common among administrators at these institutions.

New Englanders in collaboration with southerners were often prime movers for public education in the South. New York industrialist Robert C. Ogden would tap McIver in 1901 to serve as secretary of the newly founded Southern Education Board, established to persuade local communities to tax themselves for free public schools (McCandless, Past in the Present 23). International banker George Peabody, born in Massachusetts, created the Peabody Education Fund in 1867; though he died soon after in 1869, the fund, under the leadership of chair Robert Charles Winthrop and general agents Barnas Sears (1867–80) and J. L. M. (Jabez Lamar Monroe) Curry (1881–1903), greatly influenced the direction of public education in the South.[17] In 1875, it helped establish the State Normal College in Nashville (later George Peabody College for Teachers and now part of Vanderbilt University), and in 1886, the Winthrop Training School for Teachers, the precursor to the public women's college Winthrop. The training school was established by David Bancroft Johnson, a dynamic progressive educator who, while serving as superintendent of schools in Columbia, South Carolina, secured Peabody funds to create a normal school for the city, which lacked teachers. When the new public women's college was established (and moved to Rock Hill), Johnson continued on as president, serving until his death in 1928.

In the more western states, attitudes toward women were more egalitarian than in the Deep South, and this helped open up teaching as a career. Women followed the frontier and helped build it and thus had influence as pioneers, when dedicated teachers were needed. In some states, such as Kentucky (1838), women were granted limited rights to vote in elections concerning education. In 1893, North Dakota became the first state to elect a female superintendent of schools; by 1922, nine western states had placed women in superintendent roles (Vaughn-Roberson 17).

In Oklahoma in 1907, women gained the vote in school-related elections, but four years later the state board of education ruled they could not serve as state superintendents (Vaughn-Roberson 17). But Alice Robertson, a nineteenth-century teacher and founder of Indian schools, began the Indian Territory Teachers Association in 1884, and sixteen years later became superintendent of education for the Creek Nation. She became NEA vice president in 1905 and, in 1920, became a U.S. representative, the second woman ever to serve in Congress. (Conservative and driven by domestic ideology, she had fought against suffrage for women.)

In Texas, where women had won the right to vote in primary elections in 1918, they were crucial to the election of Annie Webb Blanton as state superintendent of public instruction that same year. Blanton was then chair of the English Department at North Texas State Normal College (now the University of North Texas) and president of the Texas State Teachers Association. In 1929, Blanton helped found the Kappa Gamma Delta Society (now the Delta Kappa Gamma Society International) for white female educators with high credentials. Oklahoma and Colorado and other states followed. Domestic ideology was strongly at work in this early professional group. The organization later fully integrated and became active in progressive campaigns such as the ERA (Vaughn-Roberson 24). Meanwhile in the Northeast, more labor-oriented teachers were founding teachers' unions.

By 1946, in Oklahoma, 29.3 percent of teachers had not acquired a bachelor's degree, and by 1948 in Texas, 18.6 percent lacked that credential (Vaughn-Roberson 20). Yet many women from professional pride earned a bachelor's degree long before their states required it and even earned graduate degrees. Women at the public colleges for women were leaders in professionalizing teaching across the South.

Finally, preparation to teach home economics became a dominant teaching area in these colleges after the 1914 Smith-Lever Act and especially the 1917 Smith-Hughes Act funding vocational home economics education. This shifted the emphasis in the field of education by establishing a related service-and-outreach bureaucracy, creating a field with various potential jobs and steady funding, something few of these colleges had ever experienced.

Home Economics and the Professionalization of Women

"Home economics has not fared well at the hands of historians." Thus begins Sarah Stage in the introduction to her and Virginia B. Vincenti's 1997 edited collection, *Rethinking Home Economics* (Stage 1). For second-wave feminists, many of whom associated the term with "visions of girls learning to . . . prepare potato salad" (Apple 79), the field appeared "little more than a conspiracy to keep women in the kitchen" (Stage 1). In correcting these and similar misreadings of the field's history, the contributors to this volume argue that the central concerns of home economics as a field were careers for women and the professionalization of women's work.

Spurred on by early advocates for domestic education for women such as Catharine Beecher, by the burgeoning industrial and vocational education movement, by late-nineteenth-century concerns with the place of both science and women in society, and by Progressive-era interest in the democratization of education, home economics emerged as a field of study in the U.S. in the last quarter of the nineteenth century.[18] The first courses in "domestic economy" at the college level were offered by midwestern land-grant colleges beginning in the early 1870s, with Iowa State reportedly the first in 1872. Influenced as they were by Beecher and Mount Holyoke's Mary Lyon, several of the Seven Sisters colleges early on included domestic duties for students and gave "a slight nod to the particularities of feminine education" in courses such as physiology, but courses in domestic economy as such were not a part of their curricula (Turpin 155). In describing Bryn Mawr president M. Carey Thomas's repudiation of such coursework in 1893, Stage notes that as an academic subject, home economics "suffered from being confused in the public mind with household skills . . . and from its association with the agricultural colleges in the Midwest" (7).

Such tensions permeated home economics from the profession's start. In 1899, at the first of a series of conferences in Lake Placid, New York, that would lead to the establishment of the American Home Economics Association in 1909, a conflict broke out over what to call the field. "Household arts" suggested domestic skills, with links to industrial education in the schools; "domestic economy" suggested middle-class housewives and the "servant problem"; and "domestic science" the rigors of the laboratory applied to the home. "Home economics," the term that eventually won out, seemed to best encompass the field's interest in linking private and public spheres, particularly the areas of health reform and "municipal housekeeping" (Stage 5).

Chemist Ellen H. Richards, foremother of what would have been a different kind of home economics, preferred a more scientific and research-oriented approach that included research studies in domestic science, chemistry, nutrition, and sanitation.[19] Seeking scholarly recognition for her field and professional opportunities for its educated women, she proposed the term "oekology" (later "ecology"), reflecting a holistic view of the home and surrounding environment.[20] Though never happy with the term "home economics"—she had little interest in the domestic "arts" or the problems of "middle-class clubwomen" (Stage 6), she did concede to its adoption.[21] As defined by the 1902 Lake Placid Conference, home economics was to be, in its "most comprehensive sense . . . the study of the laws, conditions, principles and ideals which are concerned on the one hand with man's immediate physical environment and on the other hand with his nature as a social being, and is the study specially of the relation between these two factors," and in a "narrow sense . . . the study of the empirical sciences with special reference to the practical problems of housework" (Lake Placid Conference, 70–71).

Despite the centrality of women's professionalization to home economics and its contributions to expanding domestic activities into the public sphere—early advocates advanced social reforms such as food and sanitation laws—the field would come to reflect more traditional gender values, in part because of its success in the establishment of governmental funding for home economics training. As both a study and a government-sponsored bureaucracy, home economics would create new gender differentiations through school curricula, curricula created and administered by women, including the graduates of these eight colleges, where home economics would be an important part of their programs. Like many issues in southern history, the dominance of home economics in women's education and lives is two-faced, a Janus, with revolutionary and conservative forces bound tightly together.

By the second decade of the twentieth century, power had shifted to the land-grant colleges and Department of Agriculture, which provided money and jobs. Stage argues that this had the effect of tying home economics to more traditional notions of domesticity and lessened its early radical nature (9). In 1914, the Smith-Lever Act created the Agricultural Extension Service, which was to provide farm women with home economics education and men with education in agriculture.[22] Many educated women served as cooperative extension agents, which helped link the field to rural life and paid women a living wage, and sometimes more; in 1939, Texas State College for Women graduates working as home demonstration agents made, on average, twice the salary of those working as teachers, and those working in the field of home economics overall made approximately 50 percent more (Bentinck 94).[23] The Smith-Hughes Act of 1917 was even more important for the southern public women's colleges, as it funded training for vocational education and home economics in primary and secondary schools. This moved home economics further away from research and linked it with the unfortunately less academically respected teacher training programs. Yet both extension agents and teachers of home economics had paid, professional careers, careers that further expanded career choices for other women.

The Smith-Hughes Act had a significant impact on high school curricula. A 1932 Office of Education study showed that the number of high schools offering home economics rose from 53 percent in the period 1915–17, to 95 percent in 1930–31. Herbert M. Kliebard argues that this shift accelerated the gender based curriculum differentiation in U.S. high schools (135–36) Kliebard also argues that home economics accelerated racial, ethnic, class, and gender differentiations, with many school programs designed to lead black or immigrant students into domestic service (137). Stage concurs that an emphasis on professionalization "took on distinct class and racial biases," with white extension agents enforcing white cultural assumptions about the "good life" (11).

As time went on, home economists began to work in business, "negotiating between the consumer and the company" (Stage 12). But the role of consumer advocate that became central to the field conflicted with business roles in product design, marketing, and sales. In 1926, the American Home Economics Association opened its convention floor to commercial displays, and food corporations began employing home economists, leading to the question of whether the field was going to protect consumers or target them for sales.

Nutrition and food continued in importance, especially during food crises during World Wars I and II. Four-year degree programs became mandatory for nutritionists, and many women home economists took part in wartime efforts such as the 1941 National Nutrition Conference for Defense. Reflecting this trend, in 1943, the USDA Bureau of Home Economics became the Bureau of Human Nutrition and Home Economics.

The federal Smith-Hughes funding impacted the public women's colleges and significantly reshaped their curricula after 1917. This provided many women with broadened career opportunities in teaching, nutrition, business, and agricultural extension services, while also allowing a space for women to maintain their traditional roles and seek higher education. Home economics departments, strengthened by federal funds, often had significant power in determining their curricula and degree program requirements. In many cases, this strength helped move the public women's colleges to a more modern scientific curriculum. Home economics faculty over time became more and more powerful and confident in these institutions. They were strong and frequent speakers and writers themselves, although they most often relied on the English and speech faculty to teach their students what they would need to know to communicate in their own professional field.

Winthrop College's Domestic Science Department from its earliest days included a cooking school modeled on that of the cooking department at Philadelphia's Drexel Institute, termed in an early catalogue "one of the best institutions of its kind anywhere." Besides lessons in various types of meals, on "small stoves" provided for each pupil, the courses included lessons on "invalid cookery" as well as nutritional lessons and the study of food safety (*Catalogue 1895–96* 26). The Winthrop farm was 259 1/2 acres, and the school offered floriculture, horticulture, and dairying from its earliest days. A B.S. degree was begun in 1909–10 for these students.

Winthrop began offering extension work in home economics as early as 1910. Carrie Hyde, matron of the Practice House, along with two graduate assistants, took a demonstration train, the "Farmer's Institute Train," sponsored by Clemson, to every county in the state to help improve agriculture and rural life.[24] Two fully equipped coaches were assigned to Winthrop, and stoves and other kitchen equipment were used to give lectures and demonstrations in cooking, sanitation, and other homemaking skills. The 1911 *Report of the Board of Trustees* said the train traveled more than 2,063 miles and visited forty-seven different locations, with eleven thousand women attending and viewing the exhibits (Webb 49).

In 1914, with the Smith-Lever Act, Clemson and Winthrop split the funds for state agricultural colleges, with Clemson, the official A&M school, getting agriculture and Winthrop getting home economics demonstration programs (for white women only) (Webb 158).[25] Clemson administered the funds and supervised agents at Winthrop. A quarter of all funds received by Clemson would be devoted to home economics work at Winthrop. Home economics agents were nominated by Winthrop but were administered by Clemson, which proved a complicated and conflicted arrangement.[26]

At Winthrop, by 1915–16 the white county home demonstration agents were listed in the college catalogue along with the faculty. These agents performed public service in home economics, agriculture, dairying, poultry, and marketing and did mill village work with the United States Department of

Agriculture and Clemson College. Among them were Dora D. Walker, one of the first home demonstration agents in South Carolina, and Mary E. Frayser, noted for her work in South Carolina education, in home economics, as a club woman, and for the tax support she helped raise for public libraries.[27] As "State Agent for Rural and Mill Village Community Improvement," she persuaded twenty-five mill presidents to hire community agents to do social work in their mill villages. Her work in nutrition and hygiene helped defeat pellagra and hookworm in rural areas.

Frayser advised South Carolinians to throw "out the frying pan" and eat fresh vegetables (qtd. in Webb 34). In 1914, she organized the first Home Economics Institute for South Carolina women at Winthrop. That year, the Smith-Lever Act was passed, and the home demonstration work that Winthrop had already begun was more securely funded. Active with the South Carolina Federation of Women's Clubs, she helped establish the Women's Council for the Public Good and the state Department of Labor in 1936. A feminist, she helped promote women into public offices (36).[28]

Home economics was a later innovation at the earliest public women's college. Early at Mississippi, programs included only arts and sciences education, vocational studies, and teacher training. A two-year industrial course was offered, and President Robert Frazer (1881–98) recommended adding courses in domestic economy, home decoration, and landscape gardening, which was done (Pieschel and Pieschel 37). The next president, Andrew Armstrong Kincannon (1898–1907), increased the industrial department and built a new Industrial Hall in 1902. He introduced millinery, photography, pharmacy, and domestic science and began a proper Department of Domestic Science. He hired Mabel Ward, the first teacher of home economics in Mississippi, who had been trained at the Oread Institute of Domestic Science in Worcester, Massachusetts, through a scholarship granted by the Mississippi Federation of Women's Clubs (Pieschel and Pieschel 49).

"Mississippi needs better schools, better teachers, longer school terms, better health, better babies, and better biscuits," the next president, Henry Lewis Whitfield (1907–20), declared (qtd. in Pieschel and Pieschel 55). Whitfield upgraded domestic science, and the Department of Industrial Science became the first real home economics department in the state. By 1911, home economics was required of every student. Whitfield also encouraged Tomato Clubs and home extension work, with extension workers traveling in Model T Fords to rural areas: "They became soldiers in the fight against botulism, hook-worm, pellagra, and nutritional deficiency" (Pieschel and Pieschel 65).

Whitfield's emphasis on and support for the new home economics B.S. program was primarily responsible for ending the dominant reign of the traditional classical curriculum at Mississippi State College for Women.

Head of English and member of the original faculty Pauline Orr, and Miriam Paslay, Mistress of Latin and member of the first graduating class, resigned over the decision to drop Latin and modern language from the B.S. in home economics. Thus ended nearly three decades of these women's strong intellectual leadership in the college (Pieschel and Pieschel 65–66). It also signaled the beginning of the dominance of home economics and scientific studies. This shift resulted in successful alumnae such as Marietta Eichelberger (1912), who became director of nutrition for the trade association the Evaporated Milk Association, and her sister Dr. Lillian Eichelberger (1914), the first woman to become a member of the University of Chicago School of Medicine.

This influence of the dominant home economics program was felt throughout the curriculum at Mississippi. In 1915, English offered a course entitled "Literature of the Home," at first as part of the industrial track, then later in the English department. The title was later changed to "Literature of Home and Nation." The school was into its thirtieth catalogue, and the first-year writing course was now officially called "Composition." As always, it was required of home economics students as well as all other majors.

At Alabama College for Women, though household work and other courses had been taught, it was not until Smith-Hughes work was required in standard high schools that President Thomas Waverly Palmer (1907–26) realized his school was the only institute in the state prepared to train home economics teachers for such work. Beginning in 1913, Palmer had begun to strengthen home economics and other departments. The establishment and professionalization of home economics raised standards across the college (Griffith 87). The first graduate of the school's four-year program was Miss John Williams Pridgen of Enterprise, who received her B.S. degree in home economics in 1922. By 1944, home economics was the largest department on campus.

Like the other institutions, Oklahoma College for Women early on had a commercial department, whose courses could be taken alongside the literary sequence, and included bookkeeping, typing, stenography, domestic science, cooking, chemistry, bacteriology, sewing, tailoring, embroidery, and fine arts. What soon became home economics was at first divided into domestic arts and domestic sciences, each with its own faculty and occupying its own floor in the same building.[29] In 1929, a contract was signed to build a new $10,000 Home Management House, to be located east of the president's home. A separate practice home allowed the young women to realistically hone their skills. For example, a real baby was brought in from social services to allow students to learn to care for infants. Every six weeks a new baby came to the college, and the OCW yearbooks include pictures of these infants with their adoring practice "mothers."

At Oklahoma, home economics was also actively involved with fine arts. This interlacing of the arts and sciences was part of the founding philosophy of home economics as a field. In domestic arts, students studied design, china painting, home decoration, flower arranging, and the like. These skills were frequently put to use when the fine arts department put on theatrical productions. The design and sewing of costumes by home economics students became an integral part of many college performances. Those same skills produced dozens of dresses for style shows produced annually by the home economics department.

Relationship of Speaking and Writing to Home Economics

College extension agents and home economics teachers both had teaching roles. But extension agents probably did more public speaking and writing, preparing written materials such as pamphlets and contributing articles to farm magazines. Because graduates were expected to be educators in both schools and communities, home economics had a strong communication and teaching emphasis; although it is clear that these women's college graduates had many options, many of them chose to teach home economics primarily in high schools and other colleges.

In a study, "Objectives for a Home Economics Education Program at Alabama College," Allene Bell (in her M.S. thesis at Iowa State University, 1929) surveyed home economics teachers and teacher trainers about their teaching practices. She found numerous activities and objectives such as making bulletin boards, leading discussions, writing tests, keeping records, and developing habits of good thinking in students (54), but reports no explicit objectives among instructors to help students write or communicate better. Nor does Bell's own list of major objectives for home economics education relate specifically to developing writing or speaking abilities. It seems that as a field, home economics at most schools relied heavily on general English and speech curricula to prepare its students for their professional careers. Writing in English classes and for student publications and practicing speaking in English or speech classes were skills increasingly important as home economics developed as a professional area based on the communication of expert information to various publics.

Career Choices for Graduates

The earliest pattern of expanding industrial and commercial studies in the colleges forecasts the expanded careers of later women graduates. For example, at Mississippi State College for Women, Katy Boyd George, a graduate of 1904, was invited to speak at the 1918 Alumni Day celebration. George had taught at the college and undertook further studies at the University of Chicago and in Paris. She had served as Boston's Young Women's Christian Association (YWCA) secretary and had traveled to France to organize Red Cross nurses at a hospital at the World War I front. Thought worthy of reprinting in the school's bulletin, the introduction to George's speech, by Mississippi's dean and vice president Miss Nellie Keirn, rehearsed the careers of many other Mississippi graduates:

> One of our number is a foreign missionary in China; another an ex-missionary to the same country; one, a physician in a children's hospital in London; one, a professor at Vassar; one a professor of English in New York City, and a writer; one, a teacher at Barnard; one, a teacher in Wisconsin College; one, in a public library in New York City; one, an osteopath in Louisiana; one, at the head of government work for women in Arkansas; one a physician in Mississippi.... In our own State our alumnae are scattered in every nook and corner, doing effective work in almost every line. They constitute a large per cent of the home economic agents that thread Mississippi throughout its boundaries.
>
> They furnish the teachers for Mississippi in such large numbers that were they withdrawn many schools would have to close their doors. They are expert stenographers and clerical workers, a host of them working at present in Washington; they are finished musicians; they are bacteriologists, doing health work in this and other states. (*Alumnae Yearbook* 10–12)

During World War I, women from the college were actively pursuing a variety of professional careers and making contributions to not only the state but the nation.

By the 1930s, women who had attended or graduated from the public women's colleges were teaching in public schools and in higher education as well as holding secretarial posts and doing various other types of work. Their business careers follow the history of the typewriter, telegraph, and telephone. They were involved in women's organizational work and government work, including home economics.

The 1936 National Federation of Business and Professional Women's Clubs (BPWC) study of women's employment in Alabama supports these depictions of expanding career options for women. Surveying 318 "business and professional women" (all Alabama BPWC members or eligible for membership), of whom 317 reported employment, the report gives a rare picture of women's work in the area in the early 1930s.[30] It found the largest group, 45 percent, engaged in clerical work (serving as stenographers, secretaries, bookkeepers, clerical assistants, and vault custodians), followed by education, 18 percent, and production and exchange, 11 percent (see table 4.3).

The survey found little difference in distribution of careers by age group except in clerical work, where 62 percent were forty years old or younger, suggesting the more recent opening up of this field, in part a result of increasing educational opportunities for women (National Federation 41).[31]

Table 4.3

Occupational distribution of 318 Alabama business and professional women, 1936

Field	Percentage
Clerical	45
Education	18
Production and exchange	11
Miscellaneous	8
Health	7
Food, housing, personal service	6
Social service	4
Professional	1

Source: National Federation of Business and Professional Women's Clubs (41).

The report showed that by 1936, education was providing enhanced professional opportunities for women, suggesting the role of the public women's colleges in educating and training women for jobs that were available to them in the South. It revealed that racial discrimination in the South may have raised the level of work available to white women; as the report noted, African Americans generally did the physical labor in the region. It also showed that the colleges were collaborating with women's organizations to investigate careers and working conditions for women as well as other issues pertinent to women. The same Alabama College for Women faculty member who did the data analysis for the 1936 report, Minnie Steckel, authored another report in 1937 on the development of women's suffrage in the state, *The Alabama Business Woman as Citizen*. Steckel found that even among employed white women, voting eligibility was sometimes limited by a poll tax originally intended to discourage African Americans from voting. If white women could benefit from the oppression of blacks, they could also at times suffer some of the same consequences.

Women who were educated and trained for careers at the eight public colleges worked at careers both inside and outside of the field of education. They were also businesswomen, nurses, industrial workers, home economists, social workers, and leaders in a wide variety of fields. Many were also mothers, wives, and clubwomen and active citizens, making significant contributions to their towns and states, and not infrequently to national and international arenas. If their education guided them into the traditional, if expanded, lifework it had also helped to create, it also prepared them for labor in fields unforeseen by their own teachers or themselves. Education in the public women's colleges gave many graduates the confidence to take the path less chosen and to undertake the unknown as they launched into a changing social and economic climate.

5

The Absent Presence of Race

THE SOUTHERN PUBLIC COLLEGES FOR WOMEN were founded in an era when, in both popular and scholarly parlance, to be "southern" meant to be white. Prior to the Civil War, southern identity coalesced around the race question as the region sought to defend—and began to define itself through—its peculiar institution. In the 1880s, new South leaders, while beginning to acknowledge the wrongs of slavery, also sought to rehabilitate antebellum southern society and tacitly justify white supremacy. During what has been termed the nadir of race relations in America, from roughly the end of Reconstruction through the end of World War I, this white supremacy was codified and enforced in the South through both Jim Crow laws and organized violence against African Americans. By 1928, historian Ulrich B. Phillips could declare that the central theme in southern history and "cardinal test" of a southerner was "a common resolve indomitably maintained—that [the South] shall be and remain a white man's country" (31). Even scholars more pessimistic about antebellum life and less sanguine about the effects of slavery, white supremacy, and segregation took this as a given; for W. J. Cash, the southern "mind" was essentially white.[1] This distinction held for many through the Civil Rights era, as white segregationists reappropriated Civil War symbols in a bitter battle to cling to a racialized regional identity that excluded black participation, and scholars continue to debate the extent to which this racialized discourse remains resonant today.[2]

Though white women were not visibly at the forefront of organized op-position to African American civil rights, they did play an important role in crafting the racialized southern identity and symbols that lay behind it. Following the Civil War, southern white women found themselves in a society in which traditional privileges of race, class, and even gender no longer applied. In negotiating their way through this changing social order, many sought to "fashion the new out of as much of the old as could survive" (Faust, *Mothers of Invention* 8), taking leading roles in Confederate memorial associations, preservation societies, and campaigns to erect public monuments to the war, as well as writing, sponsoring, and providing an audience for histories sympathetic to the southern cause. These historically minded activities—concomitant with a larger, national movement of expanding women's civic participation in the Progressive era—provided women with new forms of cultural power even as they legitimated traditional gender roles as well as race and class privileges. In memorializing and celebrating the Lost Cause, women did not simply reaffirm their role as caretakers of culture but helped shape what it meant to be southern in the new South. Indeed, scholars have long debated the extent to which southern white women after the Civil War were complicit in helping create a racialist and racist regional identity and denying or delaying civil rights for African Americans. These studies have largely focused on the activities of elite white women property owners, club members, and writers (Bishir; Brundage; Censer; Faust, *Mothers of Invention*; J. Johnson, *Southern Ladies*; Whites). Yet few scholars have examined college women's activities in this regard, particularly those of the southern public college for women, designed for young women of more modest circumstances.

As public education in the South was nearly universally segregated by race, these colleges were set up with a shared, explicitly race-conscious ideology, promising to nurture young white women and prepare them for public life even as they sheltered them from "outside" influences, including interaction with black men and women, particularly men. At the same time, as we have seen, these schools quickly proved themselves to be poor agents of legislative and even community will, expanding women's rights and roles and even serving as vehicles of progressive social change. Though emerging out of a new South economic order, the southern public women's colleges had their antecedents in antebellum southern ideals, which, though honoring higher education for white women, valued it less for its practical effects than as a status marker, signaling a lady "worthy of protection, admiration, and chiv-alrous attention" (Farnham 3). This legacy could be a double-edged sword, as Amy Thompson McCandless finds in her own broad survey of women's education in the twentieth-century South:

For some women, the culture of deference and dependence that pervaded Southern institutions did, unfortunately, stifle aspirations and
reinforce the status quo. For others, however, higher education provided the wherewithal for them to expand their intellectual and social
horizons, to understand their regional heritage, to ameliorate its worse
aspects, and to build on its best elements. (*Past in the Present* 14)

As segregated and separatist institutions, the public women's colleges owed
their existence to deeply ingrained and intertwined attitudes about both race
and gender. Their separatism served to raise students' consciousness of their
identities as women, even as it reinforced certain gendered notions of identity
and public space. Their segregation, meanwhile, helped reinforce both a protectionist ideology concerned with black male threat and a southern identity
resistant to questioning racial inequality. Scholars who have examined the
history of women's rights activism have found white women in the South to be
extremely conflicted over the extension of civil rights for African Americans.
Many white women suffragists were silent on the issue of black suffrage, while
many otherwise civically active white women opposed suffrage in part because
they were troubled by the extension of the vote to black women and the legal
protection of the vote for black men (Green; Newman). Indeed, a number of
scholars have found postwar southern white women to be more concerned
with reestablishing race and class privileges than advocating for women's rights
(Brundage; Faust, *Mothers of Invention*; Fox-Genovese; Whites).

An examination of rhetorical education at the southern public women's
colleges would not be complete without addressing this historical context;
while we have treated it in chapter 1 and elsewhere through the text, here we
would like to take it up in detail. To what extent were students at southern
public women's colleges complicit in contributing to what Joan Marie Johnson
has called the "culture of segregation" promulgated by racialized constructions of southern, American, and female identity? ("Drill" 527). What role, if
any, did these colleges play in breaking down racial divisions and promoting
interracial understanding? And how did students' racial attitudes change over
time? To address these questions, in this chapter we explore student attitudes
on race through the lens of their public writing. Although students express
a continuum of attitudes, both within and across institutions, we find that
student treatment of African Americans in their writing often offers a more
sympathetic range than that of contemporary elite white clubwomen and professional women writers. Though students adopted many tropes of Lost Cause
rhetoric, in particular the romance of a glorious antebellum past and umbrage
at northern interference in southern affairs, they also were more willing than
their elders to critique the economy and society of both the pre- and postwar

South, align themselves with progressive and populist ideals, and espouse the cause of postwar national unity. While rarely overtly hostile to African Americans, their portrayals of them, following contemporary stereotypes, remain relatively stock through the 1910s. It is not until the 1920s—when students had begun reading black authors in English classes, taking courses treating race relations in the emergent field of sociology, and participating in the interracial cooperation activities of the Young Women's Christian Association (YWCA)—that they began to engage African Americans as individuals, at least through their writing. Though still betraying a paternalism typical of middle-class reform efforts in their treatments of blacks—a treatment also extended to poor whites—and an essentialism typical of writers of the period, some of these college women appear ahead of community norms in advocating for more equitable treatment of African Americans. To this extent, they were led by the examples of progressive teachers, themselves subject to institutional and cultural constraints. Likewise, in those schools in which African American civil rights did not register on the consciousness of college leaders, students were likely to follow this lead.

School and State Differences

Since W. J. Cash's declaration in his 1941 *The Mind of the South* that "if it can be said there are many Souths, the fact remains that there is also one South" (viii), scholars have debated the extent to which the region can be said to have a shared identity. Certainly the eight public colleges for white women in the South are linked by common regional features; they had similar missions, student bodies, and curricula. Systemically, they were linked by legislated segregation and separatism. Most importantly, perhaps, students in each of these schools—from the border states of Texas and Oklahoma to the Deep South of Alabama and Mississippi—saw themselves as *southern*, and increasingly so through the early years of the twentieth century as state identification gave way to a regional consciousness, aided by Lost Cause romanticism, new South boosterism, and struggles against what was perceived as northern hegemony regarding federalist policies from the New Deal to civil rights legislation.

The southern public colleges for women were thus established against the shared backdrop of a white, southern, segregationist discourse that exploited both racial fear and a long-persistent ideology of protectionism toward women. With the exception of Oklahoma, each state had a large black population, and fear of this presence, either as imagined physical threat or actual economic competition, played a role in the establishment of these colleges (table 5.1 shows the percentage of African Americans in the county and state in which each college was located). In Mississippi, where the first of the schools, Mississippi State College for Women, was established by the legislature in 1884, old South ideologies venerating white women were prevalent, but harsh economic realities awakened many to the need for poor white women's vocational education. Though in founding the school legislators were responding to populist pressure—the school was backed by the Grange, the Women's Christian Temperance Union, and the Mississippi Teachers' Association—they were also motivated by the availability of public-supported higher education for black women at the coeducational Tougaloo University (1869) and Mississippi State Normal School at Holly Springs (1870).[3] Mississippi would become a model for other white public women's colleges in both its curriculum and explicit mission of educating its state's white daughters. In Georgia, Susan Milton Atkinson, who initiated the campaign to establish a women's college, was inspired to action by seeing rural white girls shamed by "having to work in the fields" (qtd. in Curl 4). During the campaign for the college, one prominent woman petitioned the legislature by decrying the unfair advantage had by black citizens, who she argued enjoyed not only parity in state educational funding, but millions of dollars in private funding that put "colored girls upon a higher educational plane above our white girls. . . . Northern philanthropy proposes to prepare negro girls for earning first class wages in the marts of the world, while the . . . Georgia legislature says to our white girls 'We found you in ignorance, and we leave you there. Ta, ta.' . . . If the supremacy of the white race is to continue, now is the time to set the ball of female education . . . in motion" ("Vital Question" 15). Oklahoma, though having a small back population and the last of the states to establish a public women's college, was also influenced by protectionist ideology; though the state's flagship, the University of Oklahoma, was coeducational from its founding in 1890, as was the state's black public college (Oklahoma Colored Agricultural and Normal, 1897, now Langston University), the state saw fit to establish a white women's college in 1908, one year after passing a comprehensive set of Jim Crow laws. The school, opened in 1909 for "white female citizens . . . known to possess a good moral character" (Oklahoma, Session Laws 616–17), was founded by transplanted Mississippians and modeled itself on the Mississippi school.

Table 5.1

Percentage of black citizens by college's state and county, 1900

	MS	SC	GA	AL	FL	NC	TX	OK (1910)*
State	58.5	58.4	46.7	45.2	43.7	33.0	20.4	8.3
County	75.5	52.4	63.3	24.4	80.4	28.4	7.3	5.7

* Oklahoma achieved statehood in 1907.
Source: U.S. Bureau of the Census, *Thirteenth Census of the United States.*

At Florida State College for Women, racial fear played an active role in early campus affairs. In 1900, Leon County, of which Tallahassee was the county seat, had the highest percentage of black citizens of any county in Florida, 80.4 compared to a statewide average of 43.7. Fear of racial intermixing was high on the minds of campus administrators, who sought to protect not merely students, but themselves. In 1909, University of Florida (UF) president Andrew Sledd was forced to resign, in part because of the resurfacing of a 1902 antilynching article he had written for the *Atlantic Monthly* "which offended the public" (Dodd, "Florida State" 25; see also Sledd).[4] Just two years later, UF history professor Enoch Banks, by no means a progressive on race—indeed, he opposed black suffrage—was publicly excoriated and forced to resign after publishing an article in which he suggested that "the North was relatively in the right, while the South was relatively in the wrong" on the issues of slavery and secession (Bailey; Banks 303). In light of such events and under the watchful eye of the legislature and the state press, Florida State College for Women officials were particularly careful to err on the side of caution. For many years, classes were held on Saturday, the local market day, in order to discourage students from going into town and potentially mixing with black citizens. Remembered dean of the college William Dodd, "In keeping with the wishes of their parents, the Administration exercised with the students a sort of benevolent paternalism. . . . They were chaperoned to church in groups on Sunday and to town on week-days. But they never went to town on Saturday: there were too many negroes on the streets that day" ("Florida State" 61–62). In 1911, President Edward Conradi (1909–41), in his report to the board of control noted with pride the installment of a steam laundry on campus. Previously, laundry had been sent out: "This was a constant source of danger, in so far as it exposed the students to various contagious diseases always more or less prevalent among the colored people" (Florida, *Report of the Board of Control* 96). The legacy of racism at Florida State College for Women was longstanding. The school did not integrate until 1962, fifteen years after it went coeducational, and black students were not even permitted on campus for public events.

Despite commonalities, each state had a markedly distinct history that affected the schools within them. North Carolina and Texas had perhaps the least conflicted response to the race question, North Carolina because it aligned itself with progressivism and the new South, and Texas because it had comparatively weak links to the plantation economies that sustained slavery. At the other end, states such as South Carolina, the first to secede from the union, and Mississippi subscribed to a more rigorous form of southern nationalism. Complicating this continuum further were variations among the schools in attitudes of key faculty and administrative personnel. At small, close-knit schools such as these, one faculty member could make a difference in campus culture, and given the hierarchal nature of campus administration, a president or dean could make—or remake—a campus in his image.

At Texas State College for Women, administration officials displayed either indifference to or ignorance of black sociopolitical struggles. President Louis Hubbard (1926–50) freely told ethnic jokes in the classroom, which he recounted in his 1964 autobiography (81–86). Dean Edmund White's 1948 memoir, *Lengthening Shadows*, is replete with dialect jokes and "mammy" stories; indeed, he thought himself something of a connoisseur of African American culture, publishing at least two books of dialect stories (*Senegambian Sizzles*; *Chocolate Drops from the South*) that circulated fairly well in the state, receiving favorable reviews in the Texas State Teachers Association publication the *Texas Outlook* and even from Eleanor Roosevelt.[5] At Alabama College for Women, the wife of President Thomas Palmer (1907–26) served as state president of the United Daughters of the Confederacy (UDC) and was eighteen years president of the local chapter. It is perhaps not surprising then, that scholarships from the UDC were listed prominently in the school's bulletins. As the UDC was a standard bearer for Lost Cause ideology, the campus was less than friendly to black civil rights.

At North Carolina College for Women, in contrast, Lula McIver, the wife of founding president Charles Duncan McIver, was courted by and became friends with Charlotte Hawkins Brown, who headed the Palmer Memorial Institute, a black preparatory school in nearby Sedalia, and was instrumental in getting her husband to support Brown's fundraising efforts. An outspoken feminist at the time of her marriage, she became an advocate for black women's education and suffrage. Although Charles McIver died in 1906, Lula lived in the president's residence until her own death in 1944. For years after her husband's death, "and to the eternal perplexity of Greensboro whites," Lula invited a male student from the city's black A&T to board with her on campus: "There, surrounded by young white women students, Lula McIver offered an object lesson in race relations" (Gilmore 188). Of the eight schools, North Carolina College for Women was perhaps the most forward thinking in terms of race. Its faculty maintained the closest ties with nearby black educational institutions, it was the earliest to integrate its undergraduate program, in 1956, and in 1960 some students from the college joined the Woolworth's lunch counter sit-ins led by black students from North Carolina A&T. The atmosphere at North Carolina was further aided by having an at-times progressive YWCA chapter, led by Lois McDonald in the early 1920s and later by Wilmina Rowland in the late 1930s and early 1940s, that encouraged students to take part in interracial activities. Greensboro likely also benefited from being something of an educational center; at the time of the founding of the public women's college, the town boasted the Quaker Guilford College (1837), the Methodist Greensboro Female College (1838, now Greensboro College), and the black Methodist Bennett Seminary (1873, now Bennett College); the black Agricultural and Mechanical College for the Colored Race (now North Carolina A&T) was chartered in 1891 and also established in Greensboro.

North Carolina College for Women's history suggests the importance of individual faculty members and administrators in setting the tone of campus culture at these small institutions. It also suggests that even progressive faculty could push only so much against the dominant culture. In *The Emergence of the American University*, Laurence R. Veysey notes the pressure on college administrators to act in ways "congenial to the reputable elements of the American population" (381). In the South, such "reputable elements" could exert much pressure, especially at the nexus of race and gender. As William Dodd noted in his history of Florida State College for Women, "the public was extremely tenacious of its inherited ideas and customs, especially those which related to women." The college's administrators, "as leaders in educational affairs . . . had to keep some what in advance of their patrons. But not too far in advance" ("Florida State" 2). Neither of North Carolina's first two presidents, Charles Duncan McIver (1896–1906) and Julius Isaac Foust (1906–34) had supremacist agendas. McIver in particular was a pioneering progressive educator and advocate of school reform, and Foust presided over a period of enormous growth for the college. However, neither were they particularly warm to black civil rights. Greensboro, despite a notable black middle class and white Quaker population, remained fiercely segregated, and both men, acutely aware of the tenuousness of public support for the public education of white women, were reluctant to court controversy for their institutions by taking stands at odds with public opinion. In 1905, when Sue Hollowell, an officer of the Women's Association for the Betterment of Public School Houses, tried to organize an integrated chapter, she was censured by President McIver and the state superintendent of public instruction: "That reprimand stood as clear warning that the participation of white women in public school reform was contingent upon their willingness to subordinate humanitarian concerns to prior racial and class loyalties" (Leloudis, "School Reform" 906)

Foust in particular appeared sensitive to potential controversy. In 1922, he pressured sociology professor Eduard Lindeman into leaving after he upset the Ku Klux Klan for, among other things, allowing his black maid to invite friends over for a birthday party, sparking rumors he was entertaining blacks as guests in his home (Trelease 96).[6] Almost without exception, he refused to allow local black residents to attend campus events or local black schools to use campus buildings for their own events. Though he did allow students to attend interracial meetings through the YWCA off campus, "he put his foot down when they asked to hold one on campus." In 1929, when sociologist and history professor Walter Clinton Jackson asked that students from the nearby black North Carolina A&T be allowed to borrow books from the library, he agreed but asked the campus physician, Dr. Anna Gove, to report on possible communicable diseases (Trelease 127).

Jackson, who served at NCCW nearly forty years, was an important tempering influence on race relations at the school.[7] As an administrator, he pushed for the inclusion of the newly emergent fields of sociology and political science in the school's curriculum. Jackson had a scholarly interest in black culture and was publicly active in the Commission on Interracial Cooperation, serving terms as both president of the organization and chair of the North Carolina state chapter. A popular teacher and administrator, he coedited an anthology of black poetry (White and Jackson) and wrote a children's biography of Booker T. Washington (*A Boys' Life*); taught the school's first sociology course in interracial relations; and served as chair of the board of trustees of Bennett College from 1938 to 1953. He encouraged students and faculty from Bennett to use the library; invited Charlotte Hawkins Brown to campus as a speaker; and sponsored interracial events, inviting singer Marian Anderson to campus in 1935, four years before her Lincoln Memorial concert. Yet Jackson, like William Dodd at Florida, "could not appear too far in advance of public opinion" (Trelease 196). After receiving criticism for allowing blacks to attend a concert at the campus auditorium in 1937, Jackson thereafter limited such events, and after being chastised by the trustees for allowing an interracial meeting to take place on campus in 1947, he forbade another group permission two years later (Trelease 196–97).

But the groundwork had been laid. In 1952, the student newspaper took—and thereafter maintained—a desegregationist stance (Trelease 279). Through the early 1950s, there were increasing calls by faculty to integrate the campus, and restrictions on interracial activities slowly lifted. The campus quietly integrated in 1956, but not before one final act of paternalistic protectionism. Male students, mostly working teachers, had been allowed to take summer and graduate courses at the school, and the board of trustees, fearing the presence of black men on campus in the wake of desegregation, voted to ban all new male enrollments, white and black, an order that remained in place at the graduate level until 1962 and the undergraduate level until 1964, when the campus went fully coeducational.

Race and Campus Culture

Such events undoubtedly resonated with students. How did they respond? To what extent did they adopt racial norms as played out on campus and in the wider culture? Though these are difficult questions to answer, examining students' public writing may provide one entry point. Jane Turner Censer, in her examination of white southern women writers after the Civil War, finds a surprising willingness to critique southern institutions and a concomitant interest in the North through the 1870s and 1880s. Not until the 1890s do women more commonly echo the tropes usually associated with southern writing of the period, at which point they begin adopting Lost Cause ideology in earnest. However, Censer finds that white southern women writers, "despite their racist writings," did not pioneer and were less likely than male writers to depict "the plantation myth or the image of blacks as beast-rapists" (274).

Despite the availability to students of the trope of black violence and the explicit protectionist ideology of public women's colleges vis-à-vis men, black men do not appear as threatening in early student writing. Censer argues that white southern women writers were in general not interested in "black pathologies" (272); her conclusions seem to hold for the student writers at the public women's colleges as well. In general, portrayals of African Americans, though often stereotypical or superficial, are not antagonistic. Frequently black characters appear in a stock loyal servant role. Occasionally they are the superstitious subject of comic folk tales, but these seem less an explicit attempt to explore black character and culture than to render a local scene. As Censer reminds us, "local color" stories were popular at the time, revealing perhaps as much a middle-class fascination with class as with color (262, 270). Moreover, a common exercise in composition classes of the early twentieth century was the daily theme, in which students were frequently expected to write descriptive episodes and sketches of settings and scenes. Poor rural whites, also speaking in dialect and similarly depicted, also appear in student writing at this time.

Students' racial attitudes may have been affected by their close proximity to black workers on campus in staff positions. Many of the schools began with girls doing all their own housework, but the schools soon hired help, usually African American, for cooking, cleaning, and maintenance work. Students write of these men and women warmly, if infrequently, and they occasionally appear in yearbook photos. At North Carolina College for Women, for example, the college's physical plant staff were almost all local African Americans, around forty in 1894–95 for a campus of approximately four hundred students (Trelease 35). Though treated paternalistically—through the 1940s they were called by their first names—they were considered to some degree part of the life of the college. A special 1902 *Decennial* yearbook features a full-page photo of head cook Henderson Faribault and a full-page testimonial to head of maintenance Ezekiel Robinson, praising him for his calm handling of flustered freshmen: "If a Freshman, upon arriving at the College for the first time, hands to him the check which her father has given her for tuition, in a response to a call for 'checks for trunks,' Zeke knows exactly how to act, what to say, and how to maintain his equilibrium, so that the Freshman shall suffer no embarrassment" (149).

Of course, proximity alone is not enough, and since students largely encountered African Americans in service roles, their paternalism toward them may have been reinforced. Within the social sciences, contact theory suggests that interpersonal interactions between racial groups can reduce prejudice, but for lasting, systemic behavioral changes to take place, there must be shared goals, equal status, intergroup cooperation, and wider social or legal sanction (Emerson, Kimbro, and Yancey; Pettigrew). These were clearly lacking at the public women's colleges. Moreover, the struggles of black women against prejudice, even in interracially cooperative organizations such as the YWCA, and of black educators for control of their institutions against white benefactors and educational authorities suggest the limits of contact in eliminating prejudice, particularly where power imbalances exist. Interpreting southern race relations for a national audience, North Carolina native and College of the City of New York professor Holland Thompson observed in 1919, "So long as the negro is plainly dependent and recognizes that dependency . . . there is much kindly intimacy between individuals. . . . If a suggestion of race equality creeps in, antagonism is at once aroused" (142).

Perhaps not surprisingly, the absence of African Americans at other campuses may have led to increased and more overt forms of racism. At Texas State College for Women in Denton County (only 7.3 percent black at the time of founding), Edmund White's racially tinged humor during his long tenure as dean of the college (1915–48) may have been more easily taken for granted. At Oklahoma College for Women in Grady County (5.7 percent black at the time of founding), the campus newspaper in 1922 celebrated an "awe-inspiring" visit by the Klan that had full approval of the administration:

These people in their mysterious uniforms paraded around this campus, visited Nellie Sparks Hall . . . the Fine Arts building, the Library and Willard Hall. Their very unusual "calling cards" remind us that our college is essentially a center of interest, as is indicated in the inscription, "1,600 eyes are upon you." The following morning in chapel [college president] Mr. Austin read the letter left by them which contained a message of approval of the work of O.C.W. in the past and a sincere hope for its successful continuation in the future. We feel confident that our college life will always be such that it will receive the hearty indorsement [sic] of all societies and all people. (Trend 24 Oct. 1922 1)

While North Carolina College for Women students could display gross insensitivity toward African Americans, more obvious provocations such as these would have likely not occurred at their campus, where Lula McIver and Walter Jackson publicly supported interracial cooperation and black speakers and occasionally black students visited the campus.

As college students, some of these young women were also learning to view race as a subject of legitimate scholarly inquiry. African Americans as subjects appear regularly in the college's yearly lists of "representative essays" of its graduating classes included in early commencement programs. During the period 1905–11, these included "The Religion of the Negro," "The Negro of Yesterday and Today," "The Influence of Superstition on the Negro," "Education of the Southern Negro," and "Uncle Remus." The issue of race relations as a subject is also evident in such titles as "How the Other Half Lives," "The Conditions of Domestic Service," "Social Life in the Old South," "Our Heritage from the Old South," "The Rebuilding of the South," "The Work of the United Daughters of the Confederacy in North Carolina," and "Women of the Confederacy: Their Contribution to the Lost Cause" (North Carolina College for Women, *Representative Essays*).[8] In 1916, the Cornelian literary society debated the subject of black education: "Resolved, That the negro should have a liberal rather than an industrial training." Perhaps not surprisingly, the negative won (*State Normal Magazine* Feb./Mar. 1916 241). But at a time when few southern whites were willing to publicly support liberal arts education for African Americans—most arguments in favor were articulated by black writers such as DuBois—it is significant that the topic was being debated.

Another influence on student attitudes was the impact of environmental theories of learning and social development. Students at these southern public schools for women largely bought into and celebrated the progressive ideal of the democratizing effects of education. At North Carolina, President McIver, a leading proponent of the "new" education, hoped to modernize the state by sending out a cadre of teachers. Moral uplift in this context applied equally to whites and blacks. Thus in 1900, the *State Normal Magazine* argues against a Virginia proposal to fund public schools in proportion to the taxes each race pays.

> Should the races receive for their schools only the amount they pay in taxes, the Negroes would be deprived of all education. . . . The grossest crimes, as a rule, are committed by the illiterate man. For the sake of our safety, if for no higher reason, it is the duty of the white man and woman to elevate rather than lower the standard among the colored people. The negro is a part of the South. (Oct. 1900 30)

Perhaps not surprisingly then, the earliest awareness of and sympathy for black civil rights at these schools comes through the lens of the transformative power of education, a trope that these young women adopted in regard to themselves. In 1901, the North Carolina campus held a debate, "Resolved, That Hereditary Nature has more influence than Education in the formation of character." In taking the negative, Daisy B. Allen argues,

> If heredity is more powerful than education, how have we emerged from savagery? Why, the one hope for the negro now is in education, because that alone can cure his tainted morals. And he has been made just what he is by his lack of education, or education in the wrong direction, and the force of his environment which is a part of education. If heredity is so powerful, why do we find so many new schools springing into existence? Why not leave the child to his hereditary nature? . . . Heredity ends and education begins with the cradle. (*State Normal Magazine* Apr. 1901 212–14)

Despite her paternalism and tacit acceptance of black social pathology, she advocates for an environmentalist view of human nature not widely shared by the white community in 1901, even among the educated elite.

Of course, these explorations must be weighed against a wider campus and regional culture that did not take black civil rights or culture seriously. Indeed, the blitheness with which students reference African Americans throughout the period of this study is frequently disturbing. The 1907 Alabama College for Women yearbook alludes to the Ku Klux Klan in a light vein with its featuring of a "Kandy Kooking Klub," its colors "Chockolate and Kream," while the 1908 yearbook for South Carolina's Winthrop College lists a "Ku-Klux Klub." In Florida State College for Women's 1922 yearbook, student Margaret Boyle, voted "cutest," is dressed in blackface in a "pickaninny" costume, waving from atop a bale of cotton. Student minstrel shows appear to have been common through the 1920s at the campuses. At Mississippi State College for Women, even faculty participated in minstrel events, and the student newspaper at Oklahoma College for Women reports several minstrel shows put on by visiting Rotarian and American Legion troupes. The Florida student newspaper reports on several student minstrel shows, including one by visiting men from the University of Florida: "They completely forgot the fact that they were members of the dignified Sophomore class of the College . . . and, in the forgetting, delighted their audience with a real negro minstrel—not to be improved upon by the most popular colored jiggers and singers ever produced" (*Florida Flambeau* 8 Feb. 1918 1). If such events were not officially condoned by campus authorities, neither were they censured. That the campus literary journals would publish dialect stories or the newspaper or yearbook publicize minstrel and blackface events suggests a tacit acknowledgement of the range of views the campus community—and a wider public—found acceptable. And no doubt many students never interrogated their views; speaking of her time as a student at Oklahoma College for Women in the 1930s, one alumna commented that "no one ever even thought about race" (Student at Oklahoma).

Though it may be impossible to directly gauge African American response to instruction at the public women's colleges, numerous southern black writers have criticized the culture of white womanhood in general for allowing race privilege to trump sisterhood. Anna Julia Cooper indicts the white "Southern woman—I beg her pardon—the Southern *lady* . . . never renowned for her reasoning powers" (108) for perpetuating an irrational prejudice that harmed her own cause as well as that of black women by denying their common humanity. Temperance leader and suffragist Frances Willard infamously drew Ida B. Wells's ire for her silence on lynching and acceptance of the southern ideology of black male threat, and Wells's frustration with the racism of some suffrage leaders—in 1903, the National American Woman Suffrage Association adopted a states' rights policy that tacitly accepted white supremacism in its southern chapters—eventually led her to form the first known black women's suffrage group, the Alpha Suffrage Club, in 1913 (Wells 138–48; D. White 103–4). North Carolina educator Charlotte Hawkins Brown, whose success often required public deference to her school's white southern benefactors, male and female, privately bristled at their prejudice. Of her efforts to gain a "good strong southern backing," she wrote, "I've had to close my eyes sometimes to many things that hurt my heart to make this friendship. . . . [T]he question in my heart and mind, and God only knows how it hurts, is just what are they going to ask me to submit to as a negro woman to get their interest, for there are some men who occupy high places who feel that no negro woman whether she be cook, criminal or principal of a school should ever be addressed as Mrs." (Brown, Letter to Galen Stone).

Certainly, many graduates of the southern public colleges for women opposed black suffrage and assumed an unreconstructed and supremacist identity. Even in the relatively progressive environs of Greensboro, Brown endured snubs by white women and North Carolina College for Women campus authorities. Scholars have also noted that both Cooper and Brown tacitly accepted certain norms of southern white femininity even as they challenged them; that nationally known, accomplished black women as these felt such pressures suggests the extent to which a racialized construction of female identity prevailed in the American South. Altogether, we still know too little about these interpersonal, interracial relationships; as Deborah Gray White notes, black women in the struggle for civil rights often "had to make 'the cause' and their lives indistinguishable," leaving behind too few records "that revealed their private selves" (88). Much further work will be required to uncover the voices of black women and men who interacted with students and faculty at these colleges as well as those of students, faculty, and administrators at black schools and colleges in the region.

Racial Ideology and Early Student Writing

Despite the erasure of black voices from public discourse and dearth of inter-racial dialogue in the South, southern whites retained an intense fascination with race, in part because their regional identity and cultural myths were so dependent on racial demarcation. In particular, the antebellum ideal of the southern lady, as Christie Anne Farnham argues, represented "a romantici-zation of white domination in a slave society. By merging the lady of separate spheres ideology . . . with notions drawn from chivalry and a glorification of myths of Anglo-Saxon culture, the hierarchal similarities between lady and serf and lady and slave were reinforced and extended" (2). Though the image of the southern lady was always more idealized than real, among elite white women the social upheavals following the Civil War helped engender romanticism for the lost glory of the imagined antebellum past. Joan Marie Johnson, examining white clubwomen in South Carolina, finds that they "embraced a past in which the Confederate cause was just, slavery benign, and slaves racially inferior" (*Southern Ladies* 3). Typical was one 1921 rem-iniscence: "The *Old South* is gone forever but memory serves to dwell on the happy, prosperous, wonderful conditions which characterized our dear Southland" (qtd. in J. Johnson, *Southern Ladies* 32).

Though students at the public women's colleges often romanticized the old South, they did not buy wholesale into Lost Cause rhetoric or atten-dant idealized notions of the southern belle. This difference may be par-tially generational. In *The Reconstruction of White Southern Womanhood, 1865–1895*, Jane Turner Censer attempts to close the gap between differing historical interpretations of women's activities—particularly those of Anne Firor Scott and her critics—by looking at elite women writers by generation. She finds that those women born between 1850 and 1869, with little or no adult memory of antebellum life, had the most expansive views of women's public roles. At the same time, they were more likely than their parents to be polarized in regard to the "Confederate legacy" and women's rights, be-coming actively engaged on both sides of these issues (Censer 275–76). This polarization would continue into the twentieth century, with southern white women playing prominent roles both in supremacist organizations such as the UDC and in interracial cooperation movements such as that sponsored by the YWCA. Though this polarization can be seen in the authorization of persistent stereotyping of African Americans by student writers at the public women's colleges, outright hostile treatments are rare.

During this time, social roles for women were also changing. A number of scholars have argued that the Lost Cause rhetoric adopted by white women to reconstruct southern identity reaffirmed patriarchal values, "celebrat[ing] manly men and womanly women" (J. Johnson, *Southern Ladies* 5). The first generation of public women's college students, born into the emergent new South, were happy to fulfill their role as protectors of southern traditions but were less inclined to wish to be protected. Students also seem unconcerned with charges that education might somehow unsex them; schools emerged largely through increasing public acceptance that new and practical education was needed for women, and educators at these colleges were particularly eager to distinguish their institutions from the "ornamental" finishing school of the antebellum South. Class difference may have also played a role in tempering student nostalgia. The middle- and upper-class white clubwomen who supported Lost Cause ideology largely had men who could protect them economically; the students who attended public women's colleges in the early years of the twentieth century frequently did not, tending to come from rural families of modest economic means. Indeed, they went to school largely because they needed to work, and many were their family's best hope for economic mobility.[9]

In writing about race, these students did not remain static in their attitudes. Early student writing, from approximately 1890 to 1910, reflects the emergent old South romanticism that flourished toward the end of Reconstruction and into the new century. Students during this time frequently write what can best be described as plantation pastorals, romanticizing an antebellum past, in particular, attendant privileges that few of them or their families would have shared. The narrator of North Carolina student Lina O. Wiggins's 1898 "Way Down South in Dixie" spends an afternoon on her lawn daydreaming of the old South, inspired by her "mammy" singing longingly of "de ole plantation." She envisions gallant young men, charming young maidens, and slaves who "lived lives of contentment, being well cared for always and especially in times of sickness." Although she happily enjoys the advantages of the new South that has risen out of the ashes of war, particularly the welcome new feature of "liberal education of [its] children," she retains an uncomplicated and unselfconscious nostalgia for the old (*State Normal Magazine* June 1898 282–86). Likewise, Annie L. Harrison's 1902 "A Southerner's Debt to Thomas Nelson Page and Joel Chandler Harris" lauds these authors for countering northern misrepresentations of the antebellum South such as that of *Uncle Tom's Cabin*, "which [no] Southerner would willingly have stand as a portrait of Southern life. . . . The majority of slave-owners were kind and considerate, and, as a rule, the most affectionate relation existed between master and slave" (*State Normal Magazine* Apr. 1902 316). When African Americans appear in these early stories and essays, they do so largely as stock characters in dialect stories and character sketches, rarely as individuals; the 1909 "Aunt Sally's First Ride," by an anonymous Alabama College for Women student, portrays a domestic servant on her first train ride as an ignorant and wide-eyed rustic (*Technala 1909* 80). Student writing at this time also exhibits a large degree of state identity, suggesting how thoroughly states' rights ideology had established itself as a trope in southern discourse. This identification seems particularly acute in those states where southern nationalism and Lost Cause ideology were strongest and Progressive-era reform viewed with the most suspicion. Students long not simply for an old South, but an old Florida, South Carolina, or Alabama.

Yet their romanticization of the old South is not uncomplicated. These students, after all, are pioneers in the new South, which offered expanded economic, social, and political opportunities for women. Unlike their elders in the UDC, they are willing to critique, if somewhat hesitantly, the old social order. They wish to be recognized for the uniqueness of their regional culture but also partake in the new national one. Florida State College for Women student Estelle Koege's 1910 essay "Tallahassee—A Sketch for the Benefit of New Students" embodies these tensions. She writes glowingly of Tallahassee's "palmy days" before the war, with its "fortunate people" and "beautiful homes." Yet she acknowledges the "somewhat superficial culture" of Tallahassee's old white elite and its "unstable basis of a social system long before abolished elsewhere," as forceful a critique of slavery as a student at the college could probably safely write. Yet these criticisms are at last trumped by her indignation at the effrontery of the North in imposing its will on the South. "But Tallahassee enjoys the distinction of being the only capital of the Confederacy which was not entered at some time by the Union solders. Also Florida, with South Carolina and Mississippi, was the first state to withdraw from the Union when she felt that her rights were being infringed upon" (*Talisman* Nov. 1910 6–7).

At North Carolina, Mary Milam's 1901 "Ring Out False Pride in Place and Blood" acknowledges the glory of the lost past but also takes to task those who sit "in idleness" on their formerly grand plantations bemoaning their fate, "living in the past, too proud to work . . . unwilling to mingle with the common people." This false pride, she maintains, is dying: "In our female schools, the cook-stove is taking its place by the side of the piano. . . . Young men and women are learning the dignity of manual labor, and are being trained for useful careers." For Milam, the future economic progress of the new South is dependent on breaking the hold of the romance of the old South and accepting the new language of industry and economic reform. Yet in true southern fashion, Milam will not break completely from the past but rather aims for reconciliation with it (*State Normal Magazine* Feb. 1901 117–18).

Despite this nostalgia, students also recognized that the new social order must mean reconciliation with the North. Florida student Frances Long's 1914 "The South of Yesterday and Today" is, at first glance, textbook Lost Cause propaganda.[10] Of Reconstruction, she writes, "No other civilized people has ever been subjected to such treatment at the hands of the conqueror as the South received from her Northern brothers." Despite her marked regional chauvinism, she closes with an appeal for union. Referencing Father Abram Ryan's "Reunited"—in which the poet-priest of the Confederacy called for reconciliation in the wake of northern assistance to the South during the 1878 yellow fever epidemic—she envisions a future in which North and South, "hands clasped 'across the tears' . . . shall consolidate in a mightier union" (*Talisman* Jan. 1914 7–10; Ryan 211–13).

Other students, even in this early era, did begin to acknowledge flaws in the antebellum South, particularly the wrong of slavery, even if they did not go so far as to acknowledge black civil rights. In 1906, Florida student Gertrude Westgaard wrote approvingly of Lincoln, finding him a healing and unifying figure for showing restraint toward the South, obliquely acknowledging the flaws of the southern cause even as she demands respect for its defenders. "Never did he speak harshly . . . of what many termed 'rebels.' . . . [W]henever he had cause to speak of them he termed them our 'erring countrymen.' . . . He hated slavery because he knew the buying and selling of human souls to be wrong. . . . but so long as the Constitution permitted it, he recognized the legal, if not the moral, right of the slave trader" (*Talisman* May 1906 27–28). By 1927, Lincoln's Gettysburg Address had become such a commonplace of southern education that Texas State College for Women student Marion McElroy could write a satirical piece complaining of being continually forced to read it in everything from classes in typing to American literature (*Daedalian* Winter 1927 21–22).

Even at Oklahoma College for Women, a school in a state that at times embraced southern nationalism even more ferociously than did some Deep South states, Lincoln's birthday was celebrated. The program for the 1913 celebration, produced by the school's Leaman Literary Society, is almost a stand-in in miniature of competing and conjoined motifs in southern women's college culture:

1. Piano solo
2. Lecture, "Life of Lincoln," Mamie Neal
3. Quartet, "My Old Kentucky Home"
4. Reading, "Marse Linkum's Mistek," Louise Crocket

    5. Debate, Resolved, That Lincoln was a greater statesman than
       Washington. Lucy Frey affirmative, Caroline Dawson negative
    6. Piano solo ("Program")

First, traditional finishing school culture: a light piano solo. Then an affir-
mation of the new unified nation: a lecture on Lincoln's life. Then a nostalgic
antebellum ballad, Stephen Foster's "My Old Kentucky Home," followed by a
dialect poem, Mary Fairfax Childs's "Marse Linkum's Mistek." While Foster's
song is relatively mild—defenders of the original lyrics often cite Frederick
Douglass's sympathetic reading—Childs's poem is pure apologia for slavery:
"At Mastah's home 't wuz sho 'nough free—de clo'es, de light, de wood, /
De corn-pone, an' de possum-fat—Lawd, Judy! wa'n't it good?" (Childs 26).[11]
Following this nod to the past, a debate representing the new progressive
education and women's public participation in society, on whether Lincoln
or Washington was the greater statesman. Finally, the dissipation of tension
with another piano solo. Each of the events is given equal weight in the program; that neither students nor faculty seemed to find their juxtaposition
odd suggests perhaps the extent to which contradictory impulses can exist
at once in the same cultural milieu and reminds us that the postbellum
South was, as Censer has said of the antebellum South, "a place of nuances
and complexity" (2).

Student Writing after World War I

Over time, students left antebellum romanticism behind as the new South
became more integrated into the new nation. These changes were precipitated
in part by World War I, which attracted great interest on college campuses
nationwide. For the first time in many schools, world affairs intruded into
campus activities. Women's colleges often became local centers of domestic
war efforts, as students engaged in sock-knitting, bandage-making, and let-
ter-writing campaigns. The war also helped forge and strengthen a burgeoning and unified national identity; this was a cause that both southerners and
northerners could share. The "new" college woman that emerged during this
time was bolder and more worldly than her elder sister, and perhaps more
primed to accept new ideas.

    Following World War I and especially into the 1920s and 1930s, student
writing at some campuses began to exhibit both greater sympathy for African Americans as well as a greater intellectual understanding of the cause
of black civil rights. The earliest part of this period, which witnessed the
release of *Birth of a Nation* in 1915, the rise of Klan membership through
the 1920s, and an explosion of race riots between 1917 and 1921, was arguably
the nadir of race relations in post–Civil War America.[12] At the same time,

race and the "negro problem" were increasingly subjects of public discourse, thanks in part to increasing black activism in this period. On college campuses, three sources likely also contributed to this discourse: the reading of the emergent black writers of the Harlem Renaissance (in 1934, Countee Cullen was among the poets most in demand in the Florida State College for Women library[13]); new race-sensitive sociology and anthropology courses; and the YWCA's efforts on behalf of interracial cooperation. In contrast to the South Carolina clubwomen of 1928 Joan Marie Johnson finds complaining of the "arrogance" of educated young African Americans compared to their ostensibly more compliant forebears ("Drill" 543), at the public women's colleges, students were by this time studying black writers and defending both their humanity and literary ability, even as they accepted essentialized notions of inherent racial characteristics.

During this time period, plantation romances and dialect stories became more sporadic and student treatment of African American subjects became generally more sophisticated, though variations do occur both within and across campuses. Pieces such as the 1931 "Pickaninny Song," written by a 1919 North Carolina graduate (*Coraddi* Feb. 1931 14); Florida student M. Wordworth's atavistic 1930 dialect story "The Speerit O' Mista' Sany Clau'" (*Distaff* 20 Dec. 1930 6–7); and Oklahoma student Rosemary Eells's prize-winning 1943 character sketch of her family's yardman, "Portrait in Black,"[14] which depicts a "happily content, easygoing 'nigger' with a carefree, happy philosophy of life" (*Trend* Christmas Literary Edition 1943 3), suggest a persistent acceptance of racial stereotyping by sponsoring faculty and students. At the same time, however, are essays reflecting a burgeoning if limited consciousness of racial issues. In 1935, Florida State College for Women student Edna Hoffman won first prize in *Harper's* 1935 college student essay contest for "And They Call It Relief," written for a journalism class with Earl Vance (*Florida Flambeau* 10 May 1935), in which she depicts her experiences as a case worker for the Federal Emergency Relief Administration. Though she treats her black clients with a breezy flippancy—"I resolved to tackle the colored ones first—I could practice on them and it wouldn't matter so much" (*Distaff* Nov. 1934 4)—and regards them as largely ignorant and superstitious, she also recognizes the impossibility of her task. She is especially incensed at a benefits cut that reduced weekly payments to white household heads from $1.80 to 90 cents and black household heads from $1.20 to 60 cents and dependent benefits for both white and black families from 60 cents to 30 cents per household member; meanwhile, there were "no drastic cuts on the administrative side. . . . The government was paying me $15.20 a week to tell people I expected them to live on 60c. . . . I couldn't keep my self respect and tell Willie Brown that he was supposed to support his wife and five children on $2.40 a week" (8–9).

Florida student Lylah Scarborough's "Out of Harlem," examining poet Countee Cullen, essentializes his work—"Cullen's love songs are filled with the sensuous warmth that is the heritage of his race, in which pagan fervor has not yet ceased to battle with Christian piety"—but she is also sincerely moved by it, finding him "one of our most noteworthy of contemporary lyric poets," who, if he lives up to his promise, will rank "as one of the great American poets" (*Distaff* 15 May 1929 3–6). Texas State College for Women student Gertrude Thornhill's "The Negro Becomes a Literary Contributor," treating DuBois's *Darkwater*; Georgia Douglas Johnson's *Heart of a Woman*; and poetry by Cullen, Paul Laurence Dunbar, Langston Hughes, and others, also accepts racial stereotypes, finding in African American writing an exotic romanticism: "It is the wild throb of the African heart voicing through rhythmical lines its longings, its sufferings, its passionate yearning that makes one read again and again the work of these black folk." Yet she also acknowledges the effects of prejudice: "Who can say that the Negro could not produce even better work of more universal appeal if his soul were free to be used in the artistry of his calling rather than spent in futile, life-long struggle against closed doors?" (*Daedalian* Winter 1927 16–18).

In *The Ideologies of African American Literature*, Robert E. Washington points out that the Harlem Renaissance movement was concomitant with a "primitivist vogue" in European and white American literary and artistic circles (32). He argues that the movement failed in part to "enlighten white American racial attitudes" (25) because what black writers "promoted and defended as ethnic realism . . . turned out to be a vehicle for a romantic primitivist ideology" (28). The acceptance of this ideology can certainly be seen in student readings of African American literature. At the same time, students also show evidence of being changed—and to some degree enlightened—by the works they are studying.

North Carolina College for Women student Mary Eliason's 1925 "The Negro as Seen through His Poetry" presents a wide-ranging treatment, including Phillis Wheatley, Claude McKay, and James Weldon Johnson, as well as lesser-known writers such as Charles R. Dinkins and George Moses Horton, suggesting that she closely studied *An Anthology of Verse by American Negroes* (1924), coedited by Newman Ivey White and her college's own Walter Clinton Jackson. In her essay, she acknowledges white misperceptions of black culture:

When we look at the Negroes about us we feel that we are looking at a closed book or at the pages of a book made blank because an unsympathetic Anglo-Saxon is trying to read it. It is when we read the poetry and other writings of the Negro that we get the spirit within the mind and the soul of this human being. . . . [It is only] through all of his writings that we are able to truly see the "souls of black folk." (16)

She further acknowledges that she herself once wondered "how much sorrow a Negro can feel." Though her acknowledgment of black literary achievement is often patronizing and she, too, exoticizes black experience, preferring poetry that expresses "racial characteristics," she also finds in Paul Laurence Dunbar a universal "cry of humanity" and Joseph Seaman Cotter an encapsulation of "not how a Negro loves . . . [but] how all people love" (*Coraddi* Apr. 1925 16–17). Eliason somewhat follows White and Jackson's line of reasoning, treating the texts as both sociology and literature, but her approach is more personal; there is more at stake in her reading than simply a class assignment.

In a similar vein, in "Clashing Colors," Florida student Bertha Bloodworth acknowledges her own racial prejudices.[15] "And down to the Southern marrow of my bones, I feel the horror of rubbing shoulders with blacks or accepting them on terms of social equality. I want to sink back on the comfortable platitudes that tell me Negroes are happy as they are and their status is . . . foreordained" (*Distaff* May 1940 21–22). Yet she recognizes that those platitudes are just that, pointing out a litany of examples of the white South's "mob cruelty" and "blind prejudice" (22), from economic exploitation to organized violence to apathy: "All of us can discuss the 'unfortunate conditions' of our servants, but all of us go on paying them as little as they will accept and smiling at their ignorance and superstition and being proud of the 'picturesque' atmosphere they create for us. . . . For our own good if not for his own," she concludes, "we must set the Negro free. . . . And then perhaps we can discover if our race is *really* superior" (21–22).

Conclusions

"The problem of the twentieth century," W. E. B. DuBois famously wrote, "is the problem of the color-line" (17). DuBois was not alone in his assessment. The same year as the publication of *The Souls of Black Folk*, 1903, a white citizen in North Carolina wrote the *Charlotte Observer*, "Look where you may, you cannot avoid . . . the race question. The negro as an unsolved problem faces us daily" (qtd. in Leloudis, *Schooling* 177). Unfortunately, many white southerners did try to avoid the race question. Southern identity in the so-called new South was constructed as *white* identity, requiring the erasure of competing historical narratives. As Glenda Elizabeth Gilmore eloquently confesses, "In the segregated South, whites invented a past for posterity by making up on a daily basis a multitude of justifications and rationalizations for racial oppression. Growing up there as a white girl in the 1950s, I lived that fiction" (xvi). This erasure relied on myths of a glorious past, a Lost Cause, and northern betrayal. It also required a rewriting of black experience and white responsibility for slavery, racism, and racial oppression. Yet race, even in its absence from explicit narratives, was always present. Unease over the race question influenced white women's reluctance to support suffrage and white labor's reluctance to work with black labor for a common cause. Shira Birnbaum has argued that even the rise of domestic science, which expanded women's professional opportunities in the new century, was predicated on redefining white women's work as professional while keeping black women's work unpaid: "Lines had to be drawn very clearly between professional meal preparation (white women's work) and ordinary cooking (black servants' work), between stain removal chemistry and plain laundry" (230).

White public women's colleges were immersed in these tensions and at times complicit in their perpetuation. At the same time, they offered their students real opportunities for addressing these tensions through writing. In 1925, summing up recent volumes on black culture written by white authors—including White and Jackson's *Anthology* and Jackson's own biography of Booker T. Washington (*A Boys' Life of Booker T. Washington*)—the *Journal of Negro History* noted, "Reading these volumes, we are glad to learn that, while the authors are far from a clear understanding of the philosophy underlying the life of the Negro, they are nevertheless exhibiting a change in the attitude toward the study of this neglected aspect of history" (Rev. of *The Negro and His Songs* 775). While student understanding remained far from clear as well, their attitudes did change. Though we may wish to dismiss the worst of their writings through the lens of contemporary understanding, we need to examine them in their full historical context. Notes Gilmore, "As feminist historians rewrite the past to reveal women's agency, we should retain a cautionary approach that takes into account the limits of the possible. Most white women simply could not overcome the racial contexts in which they lived, even if they had thought to try" (xix–xx). Though the students at southern public women's colleges were not at the vanguard of racial reform in their communities, their sometimes surprising willingness to engage race in their writings—and the opportunities they received to do so—suggests a more complicated picture of white women's educational history than has previously been acknowledged.

Conclusion: A Continuing Legacy

IN HER 1930 NOVEL of the Gastonia, North Carolina, millworkers' labor uprising, *Strike!*, writer and activist Mary Heaton Vorse declared, "The South's hard to understand. No one understands it, not even the Southerners" (8). Numerous historians have pointed out the complexity of writing histories of the South, because of what Sheldon Hackney calls the region's "dual identity," born out of its "double history" (41) as a region both part of and apart from the rest of the nation and further marked internally by polar demarcations of race and gender, affecting residents both black and white, male and female. "A knowledge of the twoness of southern culture," writes Amy Thompson McCandless, "is essential to our understanding of southern women's educational experience in the twentieth century" (*Past in the Present* 17). McCandless's assertion remains particularly true for these eight public colleges for women, which steadfastly maintained a Janus-faced doubleness, facing both the past and future while addressing real needs of the present. Educating women meant particularly educating them to speak and to write: this was what "true" higher education still meant in the still-oratorical culture of the nineteenth century, when the first of these colleges was founded. So it is not surprising that these schools gave explicit attention to rhetorical purposes. At the same time, the conservatism of the campuses and surrounding communities and the conflicted rhetoric over the changing meanings of womanhood suggest some ambivalence among civic leaders as to the ends of such education.

The gaps that emerged between the rhetoric and intention of providing vocational higher education for women and the ideologies and realities of the South after the Civil War and into the twentieth century reveal some of the paradoxes of southern history that affect our study along with others. Despite their ambivalence toward the North, many southern men as well as women envied the elite liberal arts colleges of the Northeast and wished to emulate them. Nonetheless, in their earliest founding, these public women's colleges were all charged with providing the poorer and middle classes of young women in their states with "industrial training" and vocational education, which included teaching and domestic science. The rhetoric at these colleges' foundings showed the stresses of this purpose. Repeatedly, their founders stress the promise of higher education to make women *ladies*—a term with particular resonance in the South—as well as good mothers and housewives. Through the 1920s, campus literature suggests that graduates were expected to fill traditional domestic roles, despite acquiring a higher education that might enable them to do otherwise. At the same time, women graduates of these institutions entered the workforce in far greater numbers than women in the general population. In the United States in 1940, 27.4 percent of women aged sixteen and over were working, and among married women, this figure was 16.7 percent (U.S. Bureau of the Census, *Historical Statistics* 133). In contrast, a 1941 survey of 2,775 Texas State College for Women alumnae who graduated between 1915 and 1939 found that, of the 2,652 who reported their employment status, 63 percent were currently employed (97 percent of these full time) and 98 percent had worked at some point following their graduation. Of single women, who made up 45 percent of the graduates, 94 percent were working. Even among those graduates who did marry, 38 percent still worked. As the study's author suggested, the chances of a graduate becoming "a wage-earner and a participator in the economic life of her community [were] exceedingly good" (Bentinck 38–40). Moreover, the majority of these women, whether they worked or not, were active in community life. Another survey that same year of 288 graduates found that they collectively held 548 memberships in various study groups, women's clubs, civic organizations, and professional associations, with 67 percent currently holding a local office (Cornell 26–32). Doubleness and paradox abound in this history: southern women were to uphold tradition and southern ideals in addition to embracing a radical modern form of industrial education.

The experiences of Eudora Welty at Mississippi State College for Women from 1925 to 1927, when she was sixteen to eighteen years old, may best serve as a touchstone for the doubled opportunities and challenges of these campuses' scene of speaking and writing during a peak period in their history. Welty came to the college at sixteen—attending to please her parents—from

Jackson, 150 miles away by steam locomotive. MSCW "in the 'Roaring Twenties' was a crowded and happy world which witnessed and applauded Miss Welty's efforts as an actress, a cartoonist, and a writer," notes Stephen Pieschel in his study of literary connections at the university (iv).[1] Welty began in 1925 by contributing a humorous poem, a prose satire, and a cartoon sequence to the campus newspaper, the *Spectator*, and was one of three freshmen appointed to the staff in the second semester. She contributed cartoons that semester but went on to publish some fine poetry her sophomore year. She wrote a skit, *The Gnat*, a play on a Broadway hit *The Bat*, making fun of college faculty (Marrs 17). She also took part in an abundance of traditional campus dramatic activities the second year, including pageants, follies, burlesques, and at least two minstrel shows (Pieschel v). She was a student representative in government as well as being a fire drill captain in 1926. Though Welty would prove an exceptional talent, her level of participation was not atypical at these close-knit campuses, where women were expected to create their own school traditions and could flourish in leadership roles unavailable to them in coeducational colleges. Several students Welty worked with on these publications and shows went on to become successful writers and teachers of English (Pieschel vi).

Welty, an only child who came from a comfortable home, describes life as it might have been on the Mississippi State College for Women campus as overwhelmingly noisy and overcrowded in her 1970 novel *Losing Battles*: "Not enough of anything to go round, not enough money, not enough beds, not enough electric light bulbs, not enough books" (245). The campus truly was overcrowded because of the popularity of the school and the constant underfunding by the state. One *Spectator* cartoon by Welty shows Old Mother Hubbard going to the bare cupboard labeled "Legislature," her dog dreaming of a bone named "new buildings"; the cutline reads, "and will the poor dog have none?" (20. Feb. 1926 1).[2] Yet despite her focus on the uncomfortable side of campus life, the campus she inhabited in the mid-1920s was culturally lively.

From today's vantage point, despite the hardships, these women students and faculty seem to have inhabited an idyllic aesthetic and social setting, particularly at the most rural of the campuses, which were sited away from the dangers of big cities but easily accessible by train. These are in ambitious yet undeveloped sites: in Alabama's "little valley of the mountains," Montevallo, well outside Birmingham, backed up to a deep forest; in woodsy South Carolina's Rock Hill, in the foothills of the Blue Ridge Mountains; and on the grassy prairie on former Indian land in Oklahoma donated by a deceased Chickasaw girl's family. At Mississippi, with its original thirty acres, girls took their exercise walking for hours on the forested grounds. In

South Carolina, three miles of violet borders were planted on the forty-acre campus so that students could gather all they wished on certain days called Violet Days.[3] In Oklahoma, students rode horses or spent the night in the college cabin near the campus, or wandered in Grimsley's Garden, planted by a faithful landscape staffer who believed, as many southerners seemed to, that young women needed to be surrounded by beauty to better unfurl their own. Even at those campuses located in growing towns such as Tallahassee, Florida, and Greensboro, North Carolina, students took frequent excursions into nearby natural areas.

These campuses were all socially and culturally active in their heydays, often serving as cultural centers in their communities, and, especially in their early years, providing a touch of the pastoral to passersby. Outdoors, students stepped lightly in their Greek dances, wearing diaphanous gowns, lounging in refreshing green bowers—or in Oklahoma, in a fine, pillared Greek theater. Young women wrote and read poetry, acted in skits and plays, and, of course, they sang and played music, so much so that some educators feared the colleges were in danger of becoming conservatories. The sounds of piano practice could be heard throughout the campuses, if not the strains of violin, flute, or zither. Theater performances were frequent, and visiting artists, writers, and dignitaries on lyceum tours were commonplace, with the likes of Robert Frost, Carl Sandburg, Thomas Mann, Vachel Lindsay, Edna St. Vincent Millay, Amelia Earhart, Bertrand Russell, and Eleanor Roosevelt on the women's college circuit, among many others who visited several or more of these campuses. President Taft was a common visitor to these young campuses and told the young women their schools rivaled those of the Northeast and West (Mississippi State College for Women, *Meh Lady* 1935 202). Young women who were encouraged, trained, and even required to be poised, confident, and well spoken seemed to form natural tableaux in the college landscape. No wonder so many local citizens seemed saddened by the shifts to coeducation—as well as other cultural transformations after World War II—that threatened the persistence of this culture.

Despite this cultural backdrop, there remained tensions regarding these colleges' academic programs. Though national educational leaders often saw a need for industrial and normal education, they often still regarded "true" education as liberal arts. Thus, in 1912, Henry Smith Pritchett, president of the Carnegie Foundation for the Advancement of Teaching, could grudgingly acknowledge normal schools served an important function while suggesting that they were inherently inferior to liberal arts colleges (Carnegie Foundation 149–52). In 1916, Elizabeth Avery Colton, president of the Southern Association of College Women—and herself a harsh critic of what she perceived as widespread slack standards in southern women's colleges—

defended the vocationally oriented programs at Florida, Mississippi, North Carolina, Winthrop, and other normal and industrial colleges: "Those who wish a liberal college education should go to a college of that type; but those who wish to major in domestic science, domestic art, and in manual training, and who wish special training in methods of teaching, will find the normal and industrial colleges . . . better equipped for this type of work than colleges of liberal arts" (10).

The early presidents and deans at the public women's colleges were often liberal arts college graduates themselves and, despite their vocational mission and pride in their students, eager to transform their institutions into "true" colleges. All the southern public women's colleges were accredited by their major regional bodies between 1915 and 1925 and long prior had good reputations in their states for producing employable graduates, particularly in the growing field of education (Orr, *State-Supported*). Yet lingering ambivalence in academic circles about the value of industrial and normal education caused some to question the value of their degrees. Eudora Welty, having been accepted at both Randolph-Macon Woman's College in Lynchburg, Virginia, and the University of Wisconsin, first attempted to enroll at the former school but found that it would not accept all her transfer credits, so she got on the train to Wisconsin, where she flourished in her English classes, receiving her B.A. in 1929, but never felt entirely at home (Marrs 20–23). Even at Oklahoma College for Women, accredited in 1920 by the North Central Association of Colleges and Secondary Schools as a standard college, alongside institutions such as the University of Oklahoma and various flagship midwestern state universities, students could find it difficult to pursue their aims after graduation without further study (Student at Oklahoma).

Race and class tensions also lay under the surface at these segregated public colleges. Teachers' colleges in general attracted poorer classes of students; one Mississippi aristocrat, U.S. senator LeRoy Percy, believed it was that population that sparked race violence and so kept a normal college from being situated in his community of Greenville (Barry 154). Institutions that were a bastion of young white women in the Deep South were also seen as needing protection, so a violent circle might be drawn around them. In Tallahassee in 1911, a front-page news report on the lynching of six black men, though duly noting the governor's promise to bring the perpetrators to justice, also speculated that the "details" of the original crime, the murder of a white man, were "harrowing to all white people" ("Avenging Mob" 1). In Chickasha, lynchings took place nearby into the 1920s, one of them of a woman and her son; and the Klan visited the Oklahoma College for Women campus with a stern warning that they were being watched. Philadelphia, Mississippi, where civil rights workers James Chaney, Michael Schwerner, and Andrew Goodman were killed in 1964, is approximately ninety miles from Columbus and Mississippi State College for Women. Superficially serene, these campuses lived on as beacons of culture in their largely rural communities. The two realities—the aesthetically pleasing and the truly ugly—were coexistent.

If the drama and conflict Kenneth Burke (*Grammar of Motives*) links to all action are held to the minimum in most of the public women's colleges, at some point in all of their histories there is drama and conflict, not always revealed by yearbook histories. In their earliest years, these schools had to struggle to define themselves and their mission as they made the transition from tentative educational experiments to full-blown, comprehensive public universities for women. In their later years, they faced drama once again as they transitioned to integrated and coeducational institutions, creating conflict for both college and community. For some the transition went smoothly. Florida State College for Women and North Carolina College for Women went coeducational with little incident—in part because coeducation promised women wider opportunities for higher education in the state system—but the relative ease of this transition also assisted the erasure of these institutions' early histories as women's colleges from public memory. In some locations, as the colleges changed in profile, what their traditions—and alumnae—symbolized as a marker of the past became ambiguous. At Texas Woman's University (TWU, formerly Texas State College for Women), plans to consolidate the school with the neighboring University of North Texas in the 1980s were actively opposed by TWU alumnae, students, and faculty, who stressed the school's historic and continuing importance to women, and its institutional excellence independent of its separatism (Sahlin 119–22). After a highly visible public battle, the institution retained its independence, name, and purpose; as of 2010, its mission statement still noted that the institution was "primarily for women."[4] At Mississippi University for Women (MUW, formerly Mississippi State College for Women), which has in contrast struggled to maintain enrollment and state support, a recent plan to change the school's name to a gender-neutral one, led by President Claudia Limbert (2002–10), eventually stalled in the legislature in 2010, though the tensions that inspired the plan remain. In 2006, when traditional alumnae wanted more power and notice, Limbert denied them and fired the alumnae association board and staff, leading to the organization's official disaffiliation from the university. Commenting on events, Limbert said, "In our planning efforts, we are not using a rearview mirror approach, but, with a glance now and then in our rearview mirror, we are fully focused and looking ahead through the windshield at our future" (qtd. in Tubb 6). More than a glance back to history here is portrayed as a potential danger. Nonetheless, one can see how this could be so in a college that now serves many African American students—approximately 37 percent of the current student body (Mississippi University for Women, "Fact Book" 4)—and where some observers refer to the old-guard alumnae as the "blue-haired mafia." At the same time, the former MUW Alumnae Association, reorganized as Mississippi's First Alumnae Association (MFAA), remains closely involved with the campus and an important source of support.[5] Responding to a Columbus *Dispatch* editorial calling for a name change to help the university survive, MFAA board member Lenore Griffin wrote, "Tradition has not killed Denton, TX, nor TWU. . . . It is NOT the name that is hurting the [school]!"

At the former Oklahoma College for Women, it also became difficult to bridge from the college that once was to the university that might exist today and in the future. In 1973, fourteen mostly new faculty did not have their contracts renewed after protesting what they saw as entrenched policies during a difficult transition to a coeducational liberal arts college. The new faculty later won a court case and were rehired or compensated; the school's name was changed from the Oklahoma College of Liberal Arts to the University of Science and Arts of Oklahoma. More sports were added to appease many local residents, who faced the influx of "hippies" in the late 1960s with horror. The school acronym became USA-OK to signal its patriotism and conservatism. The newly reconfigured university essentially ignored its past and its women's college alumnae until it began fundraising near its recent centennial. Today, however, it is a nationally rated public liberal arts college building on its illustrious past.

Looking Forward

This book ends with the beginning of World War II because the colleges, along with society, began to transform. As with the workplace in general, women gained more equality with men in coeducational institutions, with the men away. Many women's college campuses, meanwhile, offered space for training programs for troops, so that these colleges and communities became more comfortable seeing men around. Mixed dances and other activities, once forbidden, were increasingly frequent occurrences. Would the women of these southern states have been any better off without these public women's colleges? Would they have ultimately integrated into men's colleges in the South and won success? We know from our present vantage point that ultimate success is not yet in women's hands despite the large numbers of women students and faculty in coeducational institutions. Lynn D. Gordon's study of Progressive-era women's education sends a doubled message about women in either coed or women's colleges in that period: "Women students . . . found no ivory towers on their campuses. At coeducational colleges and universities, many male faculty, administrators, and students viewed women's higher education as an unwelcome threat to the social order. And at women's colleges, administrators proclaimed their own and their institutions' adherence to traditional gender roles" (*Gender and Higher Education* 189).

Nonetheless, Gordon notes that especially in the "second generation of college women," leadership by women faculty and a "lively student life" provided young women rich and broad experiences (189). Separate colleges and separate spheres of extracurricular activities in coeducational institutions provided a power base for women in both types of institutions. Women's colleges also became places where, with similar curricula and extracurricular activities like debate, "women learned to think and act like men" (190). At the southern public colleges for women, the explicit mission of educating state citizens for public and professional life kept such activities in the forefront and contributed to a rich rhetorical classroom and campus environment.

In general, composition instruction in the colleges followed the national (and coeducational) trajectory, as many of the women faculty were active in national professional organizations such as MLA and NCTE. At times, a particularly talented faculty member would innovate a startlingly local curriculum, such as at Mississippi, where Ardrey Shields McIlwaine shaped the writing course around his women students' experiences personally, locally, and nationally; or Florida, where Earl Vance had students interrogate with "critical eyes" life in their hometowns (McIlwaine, *Freshman English*; Vance, "Integrating" 319). The separation of distinct speech and journalism programs from English also seemed to follow national patterns, and if separate programs developed slowly in some colleges, the reasons may have been the small size of the institutions or underfunding by the state. In short, women probably received similar training in writing and speech as in other public colleges before World War II, although perhaps it was more intensive because of the cloistered nature of the campuses, ubiquity of speaking and writing experiences on campus inside and outside of class, and institutional emphasis on professional training. Nonetheless, the residual emphasis from the colleges' histories placed on language seems to have led to high standards and a premium on excellence in speaking and writing.

The legacy of the southern public women's colleges speaks to both the history of women's education and contemporary challenges in the teaching of rhetoric and writing. The close involvement of faculty and administrators with student lives and the extent to which speaking and writing permeated all facets of college life at these schools may not be replicable today. But the reasons for which these schools were established—to educate young women of modest economic means for public and professional roles in a rapidly changing society—remain a critical concern for contemporary instructors.

How do we balance liberal arts with professional training? How do we devise appropriate curricula for our local campus constituencies? How do we negotiate with publics with views on education at variance with our own? And how do we find room for instruction in the forms of reading, writing, *and* speaking our students will need? Though the histories of the public women's colleges do not provide simple answers to these questions, they do suggest the power of locally responsive curricula to meet student needs, the remarkable adaptability of students in responding to institutional ideologies, and the value of focused institutional missions, thus providing an important model of rhetorical success in the education of women.

APPENDIX

NOTES

BIBLIOGRAPHY

INDEX

Appendix: Name Changes of Southern Public Colleges for Women

The chart below traces the names of the public women's colleges, from their founding as largely normal or industrial colleges to their current status as coeducational universities.

State	As women's college	As fully coeducational
AL	1896–1965	1965–
	Ala. Girls' Indust. School (1896–1911) Ala. Girls' Tech. Inst. (1911–19) Ala. Tech. Inst. & Coll. for Women (1919–23) Alabama Coll. for Women (1923–56)*	Ala. Coll. (1956–69) U of Montevallo (1969–)[†]
FL	1905–47	1947–
	Fla. Female Coll. (1905–9) Fla. St. Coll. for Women (1909–47)	Fla. St. U (1947–)
GA	1889–1967	1967–
	Ga. Normal & Indust. Coll. (1889–1922) Ga. St. Coll. for Women (1922–61) Woman's Coll. of Ga. (1961–67)	Ga. Coll. 1967–96 Ga. Coll. & St. U (1996–)[†]
MS	1884–1982	1982–
	Miss. Indust. Inst. & Coll. (1884–1920) Mississippi St. Coll. for Women (1920–74) Miss U for Women (1974–82)	Miss. U for Women (1982–)[‡]
NC	1891–1963	1963–
	N. Car. St. Normal & Indust. School (1891–97) N. Car. St. Normal & Indust. Coll. (1897–1919) N. Car. Coll. for Women (1919–32) Woman's Coll. of N. Car. (1932–63)	U of N. Car. at Greensboro (1963–)
OK	1908–65	1965–
	Okla. Indust. Inst. & Coll. for Girls (1908–16) Okla. Coll. for Women (1916–65)	Okla. Coll. of Lib. Arts (1965–74)[†] U of Sci. & Arts of Okla. (1974–)
TX	1905–94	1994–
	Girls Indust. Coll. (1901–5) Coll. of Indust. Arts (1905–34) Tex. St. Coll. for Women (1934–57) Tex. Woman's U (1957–94)	Texas Woman's U (1994–)[‡]
SC	1891–1974	1974–
	S. Car. Indust. & Winthrop Normal Coll. (1891–93) Winthrop Normal & Indust. Coll. of S. Car. (1893–1920) Winthrop Coll. (1920–74)*	Winthrop Coll. (1974–92) Winthrop U (1992–)

* Alabama in 1923 was designated Alabama College, the State College for Women, though it was known variously as simply Alabama College or Alabama College for Women; we have used the latter term in the text. Winthrop in 1920 was designated Winthrop College, South Carolina College for Women, but was universally known as simply Winthrop College, the term we have used in the text.

[†] Became public liberal arts college: Oklahoma, 1965; Alabama (Montevallo), 1978; Georgia, 1996.

[‡] Texas and Mississippi have retained their names as coeducational institutions.

Notes

Introduction: Peculiar Institutions

1. As each of these schools went through several name changes, we use these designations throughout for ease of reference. Dates in parentheses are those of the state charters for each institution and typically used by the schools as their founding dates; in some cases, campuses opened a year or more after chartering (for a complete list of name changes of all the public women's colleges over time, see the appendix).

2. The last extensive examination was Milton Lee Orr's 1930 *The State-Supported Colleges for Women*, although Amy Thompson McCandless does treat them helpfully in her 1999 *The Past in the Present: Women's Higher Education in the Twentieth-Century American South*.

3. A proposed change to a gender-neutral name at Mississippi, led by president Claudia Limbert (2002–10), eventually stalled in the state legislature and as of writing appears to be on hold. When asked about the name change in December 2011, incoming president Jim Borsig stated, "I think the conversation is essential. It's not necessarily the most important thing to me at this moment" (qtd. in Young).

4. C. Vann Woodward has suggested that the South's experience of "frustration, failure, and defeat" are more in line with the general human condition than our national myths of prosperity, progress, and innocence (*Burden of Southern History* 19).

5. Kinard's dissertation in philology was on the rhetoric of Bishop Wulfstan's homilies.

6. In 1973, Liddell testified in favor of the ERA before a committee of the Florida House of Representatives. In answer to the argument that women could rely on their mates for support, she noted, "I've never had a husband—not mine nor anyone else's" (qtd. in Stern 50).

7. Black students had been segregated in coeducational normal and A&M colleges, and the newly created A&M system for white men in the South did not generally welcome women. This pattern held throughout the region, where Jim Crow laws dominated, and ideals for white southern women discouraged them from attending A&M schools for men even where they were nominally allowed.

8. See Giovanni Levi, "On Microhistory."

1. Making Modern Girls: The Ideals of the Southern Public Colleges for Women

1. Locals would have recognized the setting as the Grove, the 1830s family home of an antebellum Florida governor and a local landmark.

2. Marshall Field in Chicago banned the bob from its sales floor in 1921, and business and educational leaders frequently opined that they would not hire a young woman with one, dismissing the haircut as evidence of immodesty, frivolity, and vanity. The vociferous debates featured in news items and editorial pages of the day suggest that both detractors and defenders understood the haircut was as much a declaration of liberation as of style.

3. Though by the turn of the twentieth century, the "new woman" of America was a subject of national discourse (see Patterson), in the South, the new woman could not be easily separated from the new South. Beginning in the 1880s, new South

boosters began promoting economic development and a refashioned cultural identity for the region while still holding on to old South ideals; likewise, the ideal "new
woman of the South," as described by one Louisiana clubwoman, was "progressive,
while still holding to a safe conservatism" (Nobles 377). The new South era, roughly
concomitant with the Progressive era—and the establishment of the public women's
colleges—was a time of general optimism in the white South, before the economic
downturn of the Depression and the somewhat more somber self-reflection of the
Southern Renaissance and Civil Rights eras. The term "new South" was most closely
associated with *Atlanta Constitution* managing editor and part-owner Henry W.
Grady, who popularized it in speeches and essays; see in particular "The New South,"
first delivered in New York in 1886 (Grady 7–22).

4. Women across the South also worked early on in textile mills and entrepre-
neurial ventures in ways we are just beginning to understand. See Susanna Delfino
and Michele Gillespie's edited collection, *Neither Lady nor Slave: Working Women
of the Old South*, which includes chapters on black and Native American women as
well as white working women.

5. In an extended passage in chapter 46 of 1883's *Life on the Mississippi*, Twain
blames the "Sir Walter disease" for the continuing admixture of the medieval and the
modern in the contemporary South. "There, the genuine and wholesome civilization
of the nineteenth century is curiously confused and commingled with the Walter Scott
Middle-Age sham civilization, and so you have practical common sense, progressive
ideas, and progressive works, mixed up with the duel, the inflated speech, and the
jejune romanticism of an absurd past. . . . Sir Walter had so large a hand in making
Southern character . . . that he is in great measure responsible for the war" (375–76).

6. Censer argues that the "nondependence" ideal of "self-reliance and female capabil-
ity" (7) promulgated by many southern women in the 1870s and 1880s was increasingly
challenged by "revived notions of belledom" at the end of the century, particularly among
young elite women, for whom employment held less appeal as the region began to revive
than for "farmers' daughters" (279). It is perhaps not surprising that the class-conscious
students at the southern public women's colleges drew from both tropes.

7. This does not include Native American women, who were known openly to
be property owners and producers of goods by their own powers in the Southeast.
See the chapters by James Taylor Carson and Sarah H. Hill in Delfino and Gillespie.

8. These figures exclude Oklahoma (then the Oklahoma and Indian territories),
which did not achieve statehood until 1907 and was not included in the federal
census until 1890. In the seven remaining southern states where public women's
colleges were established, in 1860, of a combined white population of 2,891,600,
1,487,012 were men; in 1870, of 3,172,100, 1,573,928 were men (U.S. Bureau of the
Census, *Census 1860, 1870*).

9. Incomplete records make an accurate tallying of Confederate casualties difficult; "the figure of 258,000 Confederate military deaths commonly cited by historians
today can at best be regarded as an educated guess" (Faust, *Republic of Suffering*
257). Recently, J. David Hacker, analyzing census data, has argued that traditional
estimates undercount the total number of Union and Confederate deaths; see "A
Census-Based Count of the Civil War Dead."

10. Though the belle was thought to be naturally fascinating or bewitching by
virtue of being young, white, female, and southern, she also required training to
enhance her prospects (Farnham 127–28).

11. Yale College's 1828 *Reports on the Course of Instruction*, commonly known as the Yale Report, famously defended classics from the increasingly popular modern language study. Though the classical curriculum would retain its force in liberal arts colleges through the end of the century, it was increasingly supplanted by the elective system, modern languages and other emerging academic research subjects, and preprofessional training.

12. Andrea L. Turpin suggests that the weakening of southern women's institutions in the wake of the Civil War may have been one reason the founders of early northern private colleges for women "were more inclined to consider Northern models of successful women's education" (138).

13. Horowitz suggests that eventual tensions regarding Jewish students at Barnard were in part class based; in a letter to trustee Annie Nathan Meyer, dean of the college Virginia Gildersleeve complained that "the intense ambition of the Jews for education has brought to college girls from a lower social level than that of most of the non-Jewish students" (qtd. in Horowitz 259). Though instrumental in the founding of Barnard, Meyer's role was later downplayed in official histories, in part because of her Jewish background. See Gordon, "Annie Nathan Myer"; Horowitz (258–60).

14. In *A Feminist Legacy* (see in particular chapter 2), Suzanne Bordelon notes the overlooked influence on both Scott and Buck of Scott's elder sister, Harriet M. Scott, principal of the Detroit Normal Training School (now Wayne State University), with whom Buck collaborated on a pedagogical guide, *Organic Education* (Scott and Buck).

15. Where "domestic" activities did occur in early curricula at the Seven Sisters colleges, they tended to be downplayed or "leaned . . . toward the aesthetic rather than the practical" (Turpin 155–56).

16. This language in the Smith catalogue remained little altered from 1874 to 1903; thereafter the college offered that it was "not in any sense a technical or professional school, but is intended to give women a broad and liberal culture, and . . . develop and perfect the characteristics of a complete womanhood" (*Catalogue 1904–5* 11).

17. In 1880 only 41.4 percent of southern white children were in school compared to 60.6 percent in the non-South. This gap narrows to 61.8 vs. 67.1 percent by 1910 though never entirely closes during the period of our study (Collins and Margo 122).

18. One Florida State College for Women faculty member noted that during the Depression, families "who would normally have sent their daughters to Vassar and Wellesley" began discovering the value of FSCW (Herndon 5).

19. Winthrop enrolled 946 full-time college students, 1,086 in its summer school (split roughly between working teachers seeking credits or certification and local women taking practical domestic courses), and 359 children in its on-campus training school, for a total of 2,391 (*Report of the Board of Trustees 1918* 8).

20. Writing for the 1913 *A Cyclopedia of Education*, Kendric B. Babcock of the U.S. Bureau of Education noted that coeducation was "tolerated" in the South, "accepted" in the East, and "approved" in the West (675).

21. This figure rises to 37 percent if summer session students are included, the majority of whom were women (*Catalogue 1924–25* 234).

22. Florida never established a white A&M.

23. Flagships are the Universities of Mississippi (1848), Georgia (1785), North Carolina (1789), South Carolina (1801), Alabama (1831), Texas (1883), Florida (1853), and Oklahoma (1890). Of these, only Texas and Oklahoma were coed at their founding. A&M universities are Mississippi A&M, now State (1878); Georgia School of

Technology, now Georgia Tech (1885); North Carolina A&M, now State (1887); Clemson (1889); A&M of Alabama, now Auburn (1872); Texas A&M (1871); and Oklahoma A&M, now State (1890). Of these, only Oklahoma was coed at its founding. Women were admitted to Mississippi A&M beginning in 1882 but were excluded again in 1912. Black land-grant universities are Alcorn A&M in Mississippi, now Alcorn State (1871); Georgia State College, now Savannah State (1890); North Carolina A&T (1891); South Carolina A&M, now State (1896); Alabama A&M (1873); Prairie View A&M in Texas (1876); Florida A&M (1887); and Oklahoma Agricultural and Normal, now Langston (1897); all were founded as coed with the exception of Alcorn A&M, though prior to it becoming coed Mississippi had provided public education for black women in coeducational state-supported normal schools.

24. Reneau (1837–78) was educated at Holly Springs Female Institute, Peyton (1852–98) at Whitworth College, a Methodist women's school.

25. William Yates Atkinson, later governor (1894–98). During his campaign, an *Atlanta Constitution* reporter taken with his wife's accomplishments quipped, "Whether Colonel Atkinson ever becomes governor or not, one thing is certain, that Mrs. Atkinson deserves to be the wife of a governor" ("Hon. W. Y. Atkinson" 6).

26. These included Helen Stoddard, president of the state Women's Christian Temperance Union; Eleanor Brackenridge, president of the Woman's Club of San Antonio and a leader in the Texas Federation of Women's Clubs and state suffrage movement; and Isadore Callaway (better known by her nom de plume, Pauline Periwinkle), a popular columnist for the *Dallas Morning News* and a leader in the Texas Women's Press Association.

27. Educated at Vassar and Washington and Lee, Tutwiler became an advocate for vocational training for women after traveling and studying in Europe. In 1882, she became coprincipal at a private normal school in Livingston, Alabama, and when that school became state funded, she became its president until she retired and continued her reform work in education, prisons, and temperance. By the time the legislation to create the women's college passed, her influence was such that the first board of trustees elected her president, but she declined, perhaps because of her commitment to Livingston or her concerns that the new college would be underfunded (Pannell and Wyatt).

28. Winthrop traces its history to the Winthrop Training School, a city normal school founded in Columbia in 1886, but it was the 1891 act, by which the school was "adopted by the state and made the nucleus of the contemplated new institution" (*Catalogue 1903–4* 9), that established the school as a public women's college. The new school, the Winthrop Normal and Industrial College, opened in Rock Hill in 1895. Winthrop is named after Robert C. Winthrop, chair of the Peabody Education Fund, which provided the original funding to establish the training school.

29. Men's A&M colleges also emphasized their practical orientation. The act to establish Mississippi A&M noted, "The college is not to be in the strictest sense either literary, classical, or military; but, rather, it is to be a college in which the industrial classes shall be given a general education combined with such scientific and practical knowledge as will make them familiar with the nature of the objects and the forces with which they have to deal" (qtd. in Maynes 232).

30. Seven of the colleges were accredited by SACS, while Oklahoma was accredited by the North Central Association of Colleges and Secondary Schools, now the North Central Association of Colleges and Schools. In 1930, four white public colleges in

Mississippi, including the State College for Women, temporarily lost their SACS accreditation in response to a large-scale firing of faculty and administrators by the state system's board of trustees, led by appointees of Governor Theodore Bilbo. See Sansing, *Making Haste* (91–110).

31. Women would not equal their 1920 proportion until 1976; they exceeded men for the first time in 1979 and have steadily increased their enrollment since (National Center for Education Statistics, *Digest 2008* 277–78).

32. Sources for the above years are 1900 (U.S. Bureau of Education, *Report 1899–1900* 1944–53); 1945, 1960 (Harwarth, Maline, and DeBra 17); 1976 (National Center for Education Statistics, "Profile of Women's Colleges" 2–3); 2009 (National Center for Education Statistics, *Digest 2010* 357). It is of course difficult to determine with accuracy the exact number of women's colleges in the United States at any one time, as definitions and accounting methods are fluid.

33. The number of single-sex male institutions also declined during this period.

34. President Doak Campbell hoped that coeducation might end the funding disparity between the two campuses.

35. Enrollment figures in this section are taken from various years of the *World Almanac and Book of Facts*.

36. Its current mission is in some ways closest to the original mission of the women's colleges: "to provide students from throughout the state an affordable, geographically accessible, 'small college' public higher educational experience of high quality, with a strong emphasis on undergraduate liberal studies and with professional programs supported by a broad base of arts and sciences, designed for their intellectual and personal growth in the pursuit of meaningful employment and responsible, informed citizenship" (University of Montevallo, "Mission and Vision").

37. Coeducation was delayed for a year at Greensboro to allow a transition period, taking effect in 1964–65.

38. In siding with the university, the U.S. District Court decision cited both the U.S. Supreme Court's 1982 *Hogan* decision and 1996's *United States v. Virginia*, which ruled that the publicly supported Virginia Military Institute's exclusion of women was unconstitutional.

2. Effective Literacy: Writing Instruction and Student Writing

1. Thus, the belletristic rhetoric of the eighteenth century, with its emphasis on developing faculties of taste, is a precursor to the rhetoric of liberal culture in the early twentieth century, with its Arnoldian emphasis on modeling for students the "best" of written culture, and also to the expressivism associated with Peter Elbow in the late twentieth century, with its emphasis on personal expression and psychological development. Classical rhetoric, with its emphasis on public persuasion, is a precursor to the rhetoric of liberal public discourse of the early twentieth century, with its emphasis on the social uses of writing, and to the epistemic rhetoric of the late twentieth century, with its social constructivist understanding of knowledge making. The much maligned current-traditional rhetoric of the late nineteenth and early twentieth centuries, with its subjectivity-disciplining goal of transmitting hegemonic discourse norms and obsession with prescription, has its roots in eighteenth-century Scottish common sense realism; though not advocated by contemporary theorists, Berlin, Crowley, and others have noted its persistence in actual classroom practice.

2. In three articles in *College Composition and Communication* over roughly three decades—"Four Philosophies of Composition" (1979), "Composition Theory in the Eighties" (1990), and "Composition at the Turn of the Twenty-First Century (2005)—Fulkerson has traced the evolution of goals and practices in composition studies.

3. For an extended treatment of these themes, see Gold, "Remapping."

4. Before 1907, the National Education Association was named the National *Educational* Association.

5. Hanus, the first professor of education at Harvard (1891–1921), published widely on curricular development and reform. In a 1901 *Educational Review* article, "Preparation for College and Preparation for Life," he advocates for a blurring of the "artificial distinction" (152) between "useful knowledge" and "liberal culture" (150) in colleges and secondary schools.

6. Tucker, trained at Columbia, and originally a faculty member at the old Florida State College that had preceded the women's college, eventually left for the Brooklyn Polytechnic Institute (now the Polytechnic Institute of New York University).

7. At Georgia, the curriculum was also influenced by President Guy H. Wells (1934–53), who had studied under progressive educator James Heard Kilpatrick at Teachers College.

8. Better Speech Week briefly became a national phenomenon, where its iterations sometimes partook of both nationalist and nativist sentiment; a better speech pledge promoted by the Chicago Woman's Club has children promise to "say a good American 'yes' and 'no' in place of an Indian grunt 'um-hum' and 'nup-um' or a foreign 'ya' or 'yeh' and 'nope'" (Robbins 171; see also "National American Speech Week"). Though Crumpton did express concern with the "threatening influx of foreign expressions" into English, this does not appear to be a central motive in her work; in a 1919 essay, she attempts to strike a balance between linguistic descriptivists who suggest there is no single standard of American speech and overly zealous prescriptivists who might do "more harm than good" (Crumpton, "American Speech Week throughout the Nation" 279, 285).

9. Dodd appears to have been influenced by Linn, who considered himself fairly progressive on the teaching of grammar, allowing to pass uncorrected "even . . . split infinitives"; who emphasized "thought, not phrasing, organization, not detail"; and who encouraged students to find "something to say" by doing research ("What the University Expects" 99; *Essentials* vi, 3–4).

10. Though Chappell officially retired due to ill health in 1905, his successor, Marvin M. Parks, began serving as acting president in 1904; school materials sometimes exhibit discrepancies in these dates.

11. A member of the United Daughters of the Confederacy, Scott helped plan Milledgeville's Civil War centennial events and wrote a pageant on Georgia's secession for the city's 1958 sesquicentennial. Of her former student Flannery O'Connor, she said, "I read one of her books [*Wise Blood*], and Flannery could have done the world a big favor by killing off that odious main character on the first page instead of waiting to the end of the book. Flannery was a genius—warped, but a genius, all the same" (Schemmel 179).

12. Woolley's subtitle gives an accurate sense of the text's flavor: "A compendium of rules regarding good English, grammar, sentence structure, paragraphing, manuscript arrangement, punctuation, spelling, essay writing, and letter writing."

13. Though this principle has ancient roots, it was perhaps most powerfully articulated by the Swiss educational reformer Johann Heinrich Pestalozzi (1746–1827)—

"Either we lead the children through knowledge of names to that of things, or else through knowledge of things to that of names" (325)—a key influence on progressive American educational reformers such as John Dewey and William Heard Kilpatrick, both faculty members at Teachers College during Scott's matriculation there. Scott would have undoubtedly been familiar with Kilpatrick's concept of the "project method." In an influential 1918 article that crystallized progressive educational principles, Kilpatrick called for "making the purposeful act"—whole-hearted, meaningful activity within a social environment—"the typical unit of instruction" (7).

14. Mossman, an industrial education and project method advocate, is best known for *The Activity Concept* (1938).

15. A common conceit of nineteenth-century grammar instruction was that it strengthened the mental faculties.

16. McIlwaine moved to Southwestern College (now Rhodes) in Memphis, where he taught composition, literature, debate, and journalism, serving as faculty advisor for student publications, then to New York State Teachers College at Albany (now SUNY Albany), where an annual prize in poetry is still awarded in his honor. He was a popular teacher at both institutions. His 1939 *The Southern Poor-White* was long considered an important work of literary and social history.

17. Shaw (1847–1919) died soon thereafter; in 1921, a residence hall on the campus was named in her honor.

18. Edited by Rogers, Ruby V. Redinger, and Hiram C. Haydn II, the book appears to have had modest though short-lived success. (Only one edition was published, extant in 109 WorldCat libraries.) Rogers left NCCW for Tulane in 1945 but died that year.

19. For an extended treatment of student writing at Florida, see Gold, "Eve Did No Wrong."

3. Evolution of Expression: Speech Arts and Public Speaking

1. The title references a popular late-nineteenth-century elocution textbook by Charles Wesley Emerson that was used for decades at several of these colleges.

2. Mount Holyoke, an important model for the other Seven Sisters colleges, was founded as a seminary in 1837 and chartered as a college in 1888. The remaining colleges are Vassar (1861), Wellesley (1870), Smith (1871), Bryn Mawr (1885), Barnard (1889), and Radcliffe (1894, est. 1879 as the Harvard Annex).

3. Early on, Mount Holyoke had a department of rhetoric through which it offered English courses. For a time, Wellesley distinguished between offerings in English language and rhetoric and those in English literature. In their examination of early-twentieth-century meetings among writing instructors from the Seven Sisters schools, Lisa Mastrangelo and Barbara L'Eplattenier point to the complex reconfigurations of English language, literature, and composition at these schools over time.

4. Lindal Buchanan notes that an ongoing "regendering" of delivery had been taking place even before the Civil War, with women retooling methods of public presentation that had been developed by and for men, and Carolyn Eastman suggests that some conclusions regarding the limits on women's public speaking have been overdrawn (54; 237n5). The extent to which this holds for the early South is still to be ascertained.

5. Both Eastman and Kelley suggest that the public/private dilemma that undergirds much scholarly debate about women's speaking might be addressed through the

lens of "civil society," the vast middle range of social life—or publics—"centered on shared interests, purposes, and values . . . that [blur] the lines between state, family, market, and culture" (Eastman 12; see also Kelley 5).

6. On elocution, debate, and oratory at black colleges, see, for example, Kates on Hallie Quinn Brown's elocutionary instruction at Wilberforce University (53–74); Jarratt on rhetorical instruction at Atlanta, Fisk, and Howard Universities ("Classics and Counterpublics"); Gold on Melvin Tolson at Wiley College (*Rhetoric at the Margins* 14–62). Shirley Wilson Logan notes that elocutionary performances may have also served a role in communal literacy among African American communities (*Liberating Language* 126–27).

7. Between 1839 and 1844 in Boston, journalist and activist Margaret Fuller (1810–50) organized a series of discussion-based classes for women, which she termed "conversations." For a recent treatment, see Kristen Garrison's "To Supply This Deficiency."

8. Swedenborg's (1688–1772) Neoplatonist doctrine of correspondence postulated that the natural world could be read as a symbolic representation and manifestation of the spiritual. Eighteenth-century French language philosopher Abbé de Condillac put forth a similar system of correspondences in his "On the Art of Writing" for the Prince of Parma: "The passions have command over all the movements of the soul and body. . . . It is in vain for man to flatter himself that he can evade this domination: everything in him is the expression of feelings: a word, a gesture, a glance reveals them, and his soul is disclosed. It is in this manner that our body, in spite of us, retains a language that manifests even our most hidden thoughts" (578). Similar theories of the parallelism of mind and body were later valued by acting teachers such as Stanislavsky (see Ruyter 76–77).

9. According to Delsarte, these relationships manifest the unity of the divine. For example, the relationship of the notes in a major chord correspond to the Trinity; the tonic, or first note in the scale (God) generating the dominant or fifth note (the Son), with the mediant or third note (the Holy Ghost) proceeding from the first two (*Delsarte System of Oratory* 484–85).

10. Emerson's system could be as complex and baffling as Delsarte's. As Renshaw elaborates, "Emerson's theory of evolution was that the mind (and hence all art) develops in four stages or planes. Each plane consists of four steps. But each of these four steps is made up of the same four steps. A rough analogy can be made to a picture which contains a smaller representation of the same picture. As long as another picture can be discerned there is a repetition on a different scale of the first picture" (312).

11. In 1920–21, at UT, four faculty offered ten courses; at TSCW, six faculty offered thirteen distinct courses, not including independent study sections.

12. UT's School of Oratory was not completely opened up to women until 1921, and they were not permitted to participate in intercollegiate debates until 1943 (Regan 33–35).

13. As Olive McClintic Johnson, she published two well-received books of declamations for schoolchildren but made her reputation with western-themed literature.

14. Texas Fairmont, associated with the Presbyterian Church, closed in 1920. In her 1916 survey of southern women's colleges, Elizabeth Avery Colton, president of the Southern Association of College Women, classified it as an "imitation and nominal" college (23). Davis (or the president) may have been ashamed of this credential as it disappears from the catalogue after her first year.

15. For decades Te Ata performed and interpreted these Indian stories on the world stage, at the White House, and annually at Oklahoma College for Women. Videotapes of Te Ata's later performances reveal a formal elocutionary or theatrical style, in which she was no doubt trained by Davis.

16. As Mastrangelo and L'Eplattenier report, Vassar in 1906 had the same three divisions of English (140).

17. After resigning, Orr became president of the state suffrage association, speaking across the state until she had to quit in 1917 to care for her aging father. She later went to New York and maintained an active literary salon until her death at age 94.

18. Welty left to attend the University of Wisconsin, where she graduated in 1929.

19. Graff discusses early proponents of humanism and generalism in English such as Hiram Corson, a philologist who taught at Cornell from 1870 to 1903, a former popular lecturer famous for his elocutionary readings of great literature in the classroom (46–47). Robert McLean Cumnock, who began Northwestern's School of Oratory and Elocution, was similarly a "promoter of literary elocution." Cumnock's classes, "often readings in Scottish dialect or selections from the Bible and Shakespeare," drew a "predominantly female enrollment" (Graff 49).

20. The early impact of philology on English literature pedagogy seemed to be a focus on grammar study and English language history, especially Anglo-Saxon, and thus soon a historical orientation of literature study, from Beowulf and Chaucer to English literature by periods or major figures. Graff discusses the Teutonic national racial characteristics associated with this study (70). The German model did not encourage rhetoric study.

21. Published in 1888, Lockwood's Lessons was one of a number of textbooks written by women during this period (see Donawerth 126–45); like other works intended for the schools, it was also used in colleges. She also cowrote the 1901 Composition and Rhetoric for Higher Schools with Mary Alice Emerson, then dean of women and a professor of English at Carleton College.

22. Such close oversight of the private lives of faculty at these schools—usually by a patriarchal president—was a commonplace. Personnel files show that actions such as having a beer in Heidelberg on a study tour could get women faculty thrown out. Snell ended up at Henderson-Brown College in Arkansas (now Henderson State University), where she taught speech and drama, founding the college Masquers in 1925.

23. Dodd supported curricular changes in 1915 that gave students more freedom in selecting courses, allowing speech to find "an appropriate place in the curriculum," and in 1931, on his recommendation, speech, a de facto department aligned with English for most of the college's early history, was granted status as a major department (Dodd, "Florida State" 107–8).

24. In 1926, Buford, née Hollingsworth, married Florida Supreme Court justice Rivers Buford, making her perhaps "the first Supreme Court spouse to have a career while her husband served on the Court" (Buford 2). Judge Buford himself was widely regarded as a formidable orator.

25. At Texas and Florida, nearly the entire student body participated in literary societies in the schools' earliest years. Alabama's initially exclusive clubs changed to open groups during the Depression years.

26. Gaither also helped found the Civic League and the Student Government Association (Pieschel and Pieschel 59).

27. The flower rituals of graduation start early in the twentieth century, with Winthrop's daisy chain beginning in 1903. Pieschel and Pieschel illustrate the magnolia chain at Mississippi State College for Women (169–70) that started as a daisy chain in 1915 but became a magnolia chain the next year. Underclass young women wove the chain of flowers, which was carried onto the field at graduation, after which seniors rushed to pick a magnolia flower for good luck. A song by alumna Frances Jones Gaither accompanied the ritual.

4. Useful Careers: Professional Training for Women of the New South

1. The study was conducted in part to examine how women had fared during the Depression and to what extent they faced employment discrimination.

2. Campbell would later serve as president of Florida State College for Women and its later incarnation, Florida State University (1941–57).

3. This question was open ended, making classification somewhat subjective. But, by our count, we find that of 2,983 responses by the 1,508 women in the study, there were 614 mentions of various branches of home economics (including clothing, foods, hygiene, mothercraft, etc.) and 327 of English (including composition and British and American literature). Also popular were courses in various business subjects, art and music, speech (including expression, debate, and drama), and education.

4. Like other advocates of industrial education, Mayo's support was tinged with the paternalistic attitudes about race and class issues of his time: "Whether the white girl of the South is to 'lie off' and 'play lady,' while her colored sister 'toils and spins,' or take her part in the rising sphere of profitable industry . . . is to be decided by this movement for the training of the hand of the rising womanhood of the South" (281).

5. Lawrence A. Cremin credits the Philadelphia Centennial Exposition of 1876 with influencing such patterns of industrial education in the late nineteenth century (223).

6. Though courses in domestic education at various levels became increasingly common in both Europe and America from the 1870s on, dedicated trade schools for girls and women began in Europe; Leake lists the first as being established in 1865, the Bischoffsheim school, in Brussels (277), which became known for work in decorative arts. The Manhattan Trade School for Girls was the first in America, beginning in 1902. It taught dressmaking, millinery, sewing, cooking, and other related trades (281). By all measures, the southern public women's colleges helped pioneer vocational higher education for women in the United States.

7. Several of the early women's colleges, including Mississippi, Winthrop, and Alabama, claim they took their models from Europe. Alabama's early proponent of women's higher education, Julia Tutwiler, for example, studied in a combination normal and industrial school in Europe.

8. By 1910, membership in the General Federation of Women's Clubs numbered nearly one million, with forty-six state federations. It grew from the Sorosis Club founded by Jane Cunningham Croly in 1868 as a middle- and upper-class alternative to radical women's groups seeking suffrage, independence, and political power. GFWC members were often "domestic feminists," who believed in separate spheres but also in women extending their influence into neighborhoods and governments. They supported home economics for women's development but also as a way to solve the "servant problem" (see Powers 65–69).

9. South Carolina governor (1890–94) and U.S. senator (1895–1918) "Pitchfork Ben" Tillman was a controversial figure, notorious for his agrarian populism and

white supremacism. Described by communication scholar E. Culpepper Clark as the "archetype" of the modern southern demagogue (425), he was instrumental in the post-Reconstruction disenfranchisement of African Americans in South Carolina. See also Kantrowitz.

10. However, it was soon forgotten in at least one state, Oklahoma, where a dissertation on the history of industrial education published in 1952 makes no mention of the early days of Oklahoma College for Women; see Franklin.

11. It should be noted that trade education for young women had never received the backing or enthusiasm that did home economics from groups such as the General Federation of Women's Clubs (Powers 75).

12. Oklahoma was made a liberal arts college upon coeducation in 1965; Alabama continued as a comprehensive university from coeducation in 1956, through 1978, when it was redesignated a public liberal arts school offering a "small college" experience; Georgia continued as a comprehensive university from coeducation in 1967, through 1996, when it was redesignated the state's public liberal arts university. All are members of the Council of Public Liberal Arts Colleges.

13. The legislative act founding the school defined its purpose as follows:

> establishment and maintenance of a first-class industrial school for the education of white girls in the State of Alabama in industrial and scientific branches, at which said girls may acquire a thorough normal school education, together with a knowledge of kindergarten instruction and music; also a knowledge of telegraphy, stenography, photography and phonography, type-writing, printing, book-keeping, indoor carpentry, electrical construction, clay-modeling, architectural and mechanical drawing, sewing, dress-making, millinery, cooking, laundry, house, sign and fresco painting, home nursing, plumbing, and such other practical industries as, from time to time, to them may be suggested by experience or tend to promote the general object of said girls' industrial school, to-wit: fitting and preparing such girls for the practical industries of the age. (Alabama, *Acts of the General Assembly* 1004)

14. By the end of the century, Western Union "had run a direct line to the depot," giving the college direct telegraphic contact to the outer world (Griffith 50).

15. Although graduates of northern women's seminaries in the early nineteenth century worked as well, primarily as teachers, they did not tend to make it a career. Studying Mount Holyoke from 1837 to 1850, David F. Allmendinger Jr. finds that although graduates "taught in overwhelming proportions"—82.5 percent —"most used teaching as a temporary profession," with less than half teaching five years or more and only 6 percent making it a career for life. Of the 81 percent of graduates who married, "only 7 percent ever taught again" (40). Education, he concludes, did not so much change these women's expected life trajectories as delay it; these early students "saw only a wedge of a new female life career" (41) that women would later experience.

16. McIver's wife, Lula, would become an advocate of racial equality; see chapter 5 in this volume.

17. Winthrop, a descendent of the Puritan governor of Massachusetts John Winthrop, had served as a U.S. representative (1840–50), then a brief appointment as senator (1850–51). Opposed to slavery, he lost this seat, then a subsequent election for

governor, after which he left public service to engage in cultural projects. The Massachusetts-born Sears had served as secretary of the state board of education (1848–55) and president of Brown University (1855–67) before joining the Peabody fund. The Alabama-born Curry had served as a representative in the U.S. (1857–61) and the Confederate (1861–64) congresses, then after the war as a professor at Richmond College (1867–81), teaching law and philosophy; an advocate for rural education, he worked to establish graded public schools in the South.

18. Educator and reformer Catharine Beecher (1800–78) is perhaps best known for her 1841 *Treatise on Domestic Economy*, a comprehensive volume for American women explaining "every aspect of domestic life from the building of a house to the setting of a table." An immediately popular work, it was in its fourth printing by the summer of 1843 and "was reprinted nearly every year from 1841 to 1856" (Sklar 151). From the start, it was designed to be used in women's educational institutions.

19. A pioneer in food and water safety, Richards (1842–1911), née Swallow, studied astronomy and chemistry at Vassar, where she received a B.A. in 1870. Enrolling in MIT as a special student, she received a B.S. in chemistry in 1873—the institution's first degree to a woman—and an M.A. from Vassar that same year on the basis of a thesis and examination. She remained associated with MIT throughout her life, first in unpaid instructional positions, then, beginning in 1884, as an instructor in sanitary chemistry.

20. In 1969, Cornell's well-established College of Home Economics was officially redesignated the College of Human Ecology, a name since adopted by other institutions.

21. Richards later championed what she called "euthenics" (see her *Euthenics: The Science of Controllable Environment*). Meant by Richards as an environmental counterpoint to eugenics, "euthenics" as a branch of home economics found expression in the "better living" courses found at the public women's colleges and elsewhere.

22. U.S. senator Hoke Smith of Georgia and U.S. representative Asbury Francis "Frank" Lever of South Carolina sponsored the 1914 act.

23. A survey of 1,565 graduates working full time found that teachers averaged $1,264 a year and home demonstration agents $2,486; home economics workers overall, which included demonstration agents, Farm Service Agency supervisors, dieticians, and home service workers, averaged $1,833, with each subgroup earning more than the average teacher salary (Bentinck 94).

24. The "practice" house or home allowed students to practice homemaking, purchasing, cooking, cleaning, laundering, poultry raising, bookkeeping, and gardening.

25. In 1919, five years or so later than white home demonstration agents were hired at Winthrop, the first black women in South Carolina were hired in home demonstration service. Until 1928, they worked under white women at Winthrop and Clemson instead of for supervisors in the black land-grant college. But slowly over time, black women in South Carolina gained a share of funding and extension posts. In 1930, Marian B. Paul, a black home economist, was hired and rose to be state supervisor of black home demonstration workers before retiring in 1959. In the 1960s, integration of the state's home demonstration services in the wake of the Civil Rights Act erased the black structure and eliminated many jobs. See C. Harris.

26. By the 1950s, there was trouble because Clemson wanted the home economics agents transferred there. A woman on the Winthrop board of trustees, Christine

South Gee, was a former home economics demonstration agent, and she objected (Webb 159). Guards were used to prevent the transfer of files and offices to Clemson. Later, demonstration agents were transferred to Clemson, and both Clemson and Winthrop started graduate programs in home economics and shared the costs of the programs and research.

27. Walker and Frayser are featured today in a series of alumnae portraits on the Winthrop library wall.

28. In his history of Winthrop, *The Torch Is Passed*, Ross A. Webb suggests that Frayser's idea for a "New Deal for South Carolina" in 1912 was a stimulus for Roosevelt's New Deal in 1933.

29. Replicating early divisions within the emerging field, a distinction was initially drawn between domestic science (cookery, sanitation, household management) and domestic art (decoration, dressmaking, millinery, sewing).

30. According to the report, "Alabama was chosen for special study because it represents aspects of both an industrial and a rural section in the United States in which unskilled, manual labor is done largely by negroes. It therefore presents an interesting study in the types of occupations in which trained women of the section are engaged" (National Federation 40). The report also examines 142 unemployed women enrolled in emergency relief teacher training classes.

31. Forty-nine (15 percent) of the 318 women reported having suffered from "openly expressed discrimination because of sex" (National Federation 66).

5 The Absent Presence of Race

1. Not until C. Vann Woodward's 1955 *The Strange Career of Jim Crow* would white scholars begin to treat the racialized identity of the South as historically and consciously constructed, rather than organic and inevitable. Recent cultural shifts as well as black remigration to the South have further helped to break down this racialized identity.

2. Rebecca Bridges Watts has recently posited that the South's social order is shifting from being marked by what Kenneth Burke termed *division* to *identification* (Watts 16; see also Burke, *Rhetoric of Motives*), arguing that current debates about southern identity embodied in controversies over symbols such as the Confederate battle flag are indicative of "the diversity of voices" that now make up the "continuing conversation of what it means to be a Southerner" (3). Though her assessment may seem somewhat over-optimistic, the dismantling of legalized segregation has allowed southerners, both black and white, to find some common cultural ground in shared elements of their regional experience. While ambivalence about the South has long marked African American writing about the region, black residents of the South today are as likely to self-identify as southerners as their white counterparts. This deracializing of southern identity has been hard fought, and, of course, remains unfinished. As Larry J. Griffin, Ranae J. Evenson, and Ashley B. Thompson have pointed out, "the region's African Americans have always been indisputably southern, whatever the attributions of southern whites or the racially exclusive constructions of the South's collective identity" (8).

3. The American Missionary Association–sponsored Tougaloo (now Tougaloo College) received state appropriations through 1890; Holly Springs was closed by the state in 1904. A third black school, the land-grant Alcorn A&M College (1871, now Alcorn State University), was male only until 1895.

4. Sledd's article, "The Negro: Another View," had previously been responsible for him being forced to resign from a position at Emory.

5. Wrote the *Outlook* in 1933, "Mr. White's conception of the negro is that he is the greatest source of laughter in our nation, that he is funny to others albeit serious about himself. . . . His present volume should furnish many laughs to readers . . . who cherish the tradition of the 'old time Southern darky'" ("Dean White's Black Stories" 45). In 1937, White presented a copy of *Chocolate Drops from the South* to Eleanor Roosevelt, who recommended it in her "My Day" column to "anyone who wants a laugh a day" (52).

6. Lindeman would go on to have a distinguished career at the New York School of Social Work (later part of Columbia University) and would become a leader in adult education.

7. From 1909 to 1932, Jackson was head of the Department of History, becoming dean in 1915, then vice president and head of the new social science division in 1922. In 1932, he left for an administrative position at the University of North Carolina, then returned as president in 1934 until his retirement in 1950. Under the state university system, which consolidated in 1931, Jackson's official title was dean of administration, then later chancellor.

8. In the school's early years, the best of these were delivered by students at commencement. The practice ended in 1912.

9. Numerous campus documents from the eight colleges refer to the notable percentages of students who were fatherless or orphaned, were supporting themselves or helping to pay for their education, or lacked the funds to have attended another college.

10. Long was president of the junior class and the Thalian Literary Society.

11. The poem appears in Childs's *De Namin' ob de Twins*, which she dedicated to the United Daughters of the Confederacy. The book was popular enough to go through four editions through 1928.

12. Director D. W. Griffith's *Birth of a Nation*, based on Thomas Dixon's *The Clansman*, essentially rewrote Reconstruction, glorified the Klan, and justified white supremacy. In the wake of World War I, economic instability, trenchant racism, and fear of rising black assertiveness led to heightened mob violence against African American communities; at its worst, in what James Weldon Johnson called the "Red Summer" of 1919 (341), there were over two dozen separate events nationwide.

13. The others were Edna St. Vincent Millay, Sara Teasdale, and Vachel Lindsay (*Florida Flambeau* 18 May 1934 7).

14. The contest was judged by the sorority Chi Delta Pi, the English department's Literatae Club, and the club's sponsors, English faculty Caroline Laird and Margaret Elliott.

15. Bloodworth went on to become an English professor at the University of Florida.

Conclusion: A Continuing Legacy

1. Pieschel also notes that both William Faulkner's and Tennessee Williams's mothers attended Mississippi State College for Women at some point; Williams's mother "attended college, courted, married, and protected Tennessee Williams during the first three years of his life at Columbus," which was said to have an active cultural life (iii).

2. In her biography of Welty, Suzanne Marrs also reports that the daily prayer meetings in the post office lobby "drove her to distraction" (17).

3. Once in 1906, the kind-hearted Winthrop students gathered a train car of violets, putting them on ice to send to young women who worked in factories in New York City (Webb 73–74).

4. TWU's updated 2011 mission statement describes the university as "build[ing] on its long tradition as a public institution primarily for women by educating a diverse community of students to lead personally and professionally fulfilling lives."

5. As of writing, the MFAA is considering reuniting with the university's officially sanctioned alumni organization, the MUW Alumni Association.

Bibliography

Adams, Charles Francis, Edwin Lawrence Godkin, and Josiah Quincy. *Report of the Committee on Composition and Rhetoric to the Board of Overseers at Harvard College*. Cambridge: Harvard U, 1892.

Alabama [State of]. *Acts of the General Assembly of Alabama, Passed by the Session of 1892–93*. Montgomery: Brown Printing, 1893.

Alabama College for Women [a.k.a. Alabama Girls' Industrial School/Technical Institute; Alabama Technical Institute and College for Women]. *Catalogue.*

——. *Technala/Chiaroscuro* [yearbooks].

Allmendinger, David F., Jr. "Mount Holyoke Students Encounter the Need for Life-Planning, 1837–1850." *History of Education Quarterly* 19.1 (Spring 1979): 27–46.

American Council on Education. *American Universities and Colleges*. Ed. David Allan Robertson. New York: Scribner's, 1928.

Andrews, Elizabeth Gordon. *A Study in Personnel*. Bulletin of the Florida State College for Women 24.4 (Dec. 1931).

Apple, Rima D. "Liberal Arts or Vocational Training? Home Economics Education for Girls." Stage and Vincenti 79–95.

Applebee, Arthur N. *Tradition and Reform in the Teaching of English: A History*. Urbana, IL: National Council of Teachers of English, 1974.

Arnold, Aerol. "Propaganda for Democracy." Rev. of *Explorations in Living: A Record of the Democratic Spirit*, ed. by Winfield H. Rogers, Ruby V. Redinger, and Hiram C. Haydn. *College English* 3.4 (Jan. 1942): 424–25.

"An Avenging Mob Butchers Six Negroes." *Weekly True Democrat* [Tallahassee, FL] 26 May 1911: 1.

Babcock, Kendric C. "American State Universities." *A Cyclopedia of Education*. Vol. 5. Ed. Paul Monroe. New York: Macmillan, 1913. 673–80.

Bailey, Fred Arthur. "Free Speech at the University of Florida: The Enoch Marvin Banks Case." *Florida Historical Quarterly* 71.1 (July 1992): 1–17.

Banaji, Paige V. "Womanly Eloquence and Rhetorical Bodies: Regendering the Public Speaker through Physical Culture." Gold and Hobbs 154–76.

Banks, Enoch Marvin. "A Semi-Centennial View of Secession." *Independent* 9 Feb. 1911: 299–303.

Barry, John M. *Rising Tide: The Great Mississippi Flood of 1927 and How It Changed America*. New York: Simon and Schuster, 1997.

Beecher, Catharine. *A Treatise on Domestic Economy, for the Use of Young Ladies at Home and at School*. 1841. Rev. ed. Boston: T. H. Webb, 1843.

Bell, Allene. "Objectives for a Home Economics Education Program at Alabama College, Montevallo, Alabama." M.S. thesis. Iowa State U, 1929.

Bentinck, Catherine. "A Statistical Analysis of the Vocations and Earnings of 1669 Employed TSCW Alumnae, 1915–1939." M.A. thesis. Texas State College for Women, 1941.

Berlin, James A. *Rhetoric and Reality: Writing Instruction in American Colleges, 1900–1985*. Carbondale: Southern Illinois UP, 1987.

——. *Writing Instruction in Nineteenth-Century American Colleges*. Carbondale: Southern Illinois UP, 1984.

Birnbaum, Shira. "Making Southern Belles in Progressive Era Florida: Gender in the Formal and Hidden Curriculum of the Florida Female College." *Frontiers* 16.2/3 (1996): 218–46.

Bishir, Catherine W. "Landmarks of Power: Building a Southern Past, 1885–1915." *Southern Cultures* Inaugural Issue (1993): 5–45.

Bizzell, Patricia. "What Happens When Basic Writers Come to College?" *College Composition and Communication* 37.3 (Oct. 1986): 294–301.

———. "William Perry and Liberal Education." *College English* 46.5 (Sept. 1984): 447–54.

Bordelon, Suzanne. "Composing Women's Civic Identities during the Progressive Era: College Commencement Addresses as Overlooked Rhetorical Sites." *College Composition and Communication* 61.3 (Feb. 2010): 510–33.

———. *A Feminist Legacy: The Rhetoric and Pedagogy of Gertrude Buck*. Carbondale: Southern Illinois UP, 2007.

Brown, Charlotte Hawkins. Letter to Galen Stone. [1921?] Charlotte Hawkins Brown Papers, Harvard U.

Brundage, W. Fitzhugh. "White Women and the Politics of Historical Memory in the New South, 1880–1920." *Jumpin' Jim Crow: Southern Politics from Civil War to Civil Rights*. Ed. Jane Dailey, Glenda Elizabeth Gilmore, and Bryant Simon. Princeton: Princeton UP, 2000. 115–39.

Buchanan, Lindal. *Regendering Delivery: The Fifth Canon and Antebellum Women Rhetors*. Carbondale: Southern Illinois UP, 2005.

Buck, Gertrude, and Elisabeth Woodbridge. *A Course in Expository Writing*. New York: Holt, 1899.

Buford, Barbara. "Justice Rivers H. Buford." *Historia Juris* July 2002: 2.

Burke, Kenneth. *A Grammar of Motives*. 1945. Berkeley: U of California P, 1969.

———. *Permanence and Change: An Anatomy of Purpose*. 3rd ed. Berkeley: U of California P, 1984.

———. *A Rhetoric of Motives*. 1950. Berkeley: U of California P, 1969.

Burke, Peter, ed. *New Perspectives on Historical Writing*. 2nd ed. Pennsylvania State UP, 2001.

Campbell, Doak S. *Problems in the Education of College Women: A Study of Women Graduates of Southern Colleges*. Field Study No. 6. Nashville: George Peabody College for Teachers, 1933.

Campbell, JoAnn. "Controlling Voices: The Legacy of English A at Radcliffe College 1883–1917." *College Composition and Communication* 43.4 (Dec. 1992): 472–85.

———. "Freshman (sic) English: A 1901 Wellesley College 'Girl' Negotiates Authority." *Rhetoric Review* 15.1 (Fall 1996): 110–27.

———. "'A Real Vexation': Student Writing in Mount Holyoke's Culture of Service, 1837–1865." *College English* 59.7 (Nov. 1997): 767–88.

Campbell, Karlyn Kohrs. *Man Cannot Speak for Her: A Critical Study of Early Feminist Rhetoric*. [Vol. 1.] Westport, CT: Greenwood P, 1989.

Carnegie Foundation for the Advancement of Teaching. *Seventh Annual Report of the President and of the Treasurer*. Boston: Merrymount P, 1912.

Carr, Jean Ferguson, Stephen L. Carr, and Lucille M. Schultz. *Archives of Instruction: Nineteenth-Century Rhetorics, Readers, and Composition Books in the United States*. Carbondale: Southern Illinois UP, 2005.

Carson, James Taylor. "Dollars Never Fail to Melt Their Hearts: Native Women and the Market Revolution." Delfino and Gillespie 15–33.

Cash, W. [Wilbur] J. *The Mind of the South*. New York: Knopf, 1941.

Censer, Jane Turner. *The Reconstruction of White Southern Womanhood, 1865–1895*. Baton Rouge: Louisiana State UP, 2003.

Charney, Davida, John H. Newman, and Mike Palmquist. "'I'm Just No Good at Writing': Epistemological Style and Attitudes toward Writing." *Written Communication* 12.3 (July 1995): 298–329.

Chepesiuk, Ron, and Magdalena Chepesiuk, eds. *Winthrop University: Memories and Traditions, 1886–1945*. Charleston, SC: Arcadia P, 2000.

Childs, Mary Fairfax. *De Namin' ob de Twins: And other Sketches from the Cotton Land*. New York: B. W. Dodge, 1908.

Clark, E. Culpepper. "Pitchfork Ben Tillman and the Emergence of Southern Demagoguery." *Quarterly Journal of Speech* 69.4 (Nov. 1983): 423–33.

Clark, Gregory, and S. Michael Halloran, eds. *Oratorical Culture in Nineteenth-Century America: Transformations in the Theory and Practice of Rhetoric*. Carbondale: Southern Illinois UP, 1993.

Clark, J. Scott. *A Practical Rhetoric for Instruction in English Composition and Revision in Colleges and Intermediate Schools*. New York: Henry Holt, 1886.

Clifford, Geraldine Jonçich. "'Marry, Stitch, Die, or Do Worse': Educating Women for Work." *Work, Youth, and Schooling: Historical Perspectives on Vocationalism in American Education*. Ed. Harvey Kantor and David B. Tyack. Stanford, CA: Stanford UP, 1982. 223–68.

Cohen, Herman. *The History of Speech Communication: The Emergence of a Discipline, 1914–1945*. Annandale, VA: Speech Communication Association, 1994.

Collins, William J., and Robert A. Margo. "Historical Perspectives on Racial Differences in Schooling in the United States." *Handbook of the Economics of Education*. Vol. 1. Ed. Eric A. Hanushek and Finis Welch. Amsterdam: Elsevier, 2006. 107–54.

Colton, Elizabeth Avery. *The Various Types of Southern Colleges for Women*. Bulletin 2 of 1916 Publications of the Southern Association of College Women. Raleigh, NC: Edwards and Broughton, 1916.

"Comparative Expenses at Six Colleges." *Smith Alumnae Quarterly* 13.2 (Feb. 1922): 125.

Condillac [Abbé de], Étienne Bonnot. "De l'Art d'Écrire" [On the Art of Writing]. *Cours d'Etudes pour l'Instruction du Prince de Parme*. 1775. Pt. 3. *Oeuvres Philosophiques de Condillac*. Vol. 1. Ed. Georges Le Roy. Paris: Presses Universitaires de France, 1947. 517–611.

Connors, Robert J. *Composition-Rhetoric: Backgrounds, Theory, and Pedagogy*. Pittsburgh: U of Pittsburgh P, 1997.

Conradi, Edward. *Teacher and Student*. Bulletin of the Florida State College for Women 22.3 (Dec. 1929).

Conway, Kathryn M. "Woman Suffrage and the History of Rhetoric at the Seven Sisters Colleges, 1865–1919." Lunsford 203–26.

Cooper, Anna Julia. *A Voice from the South*. 1892. New York: Oxford UP, 1988.

Corbett, Edward P. J. "The Usefulness of Classical Rhetoric." *College Composition and Communication* 14.3 (Oct. 1963): 162–64.

———. "What Is Being Revived?" *College Composition and Communication* 18.3 (Oct. 1967): 166–72.

Cornell, Charlotte. "Survey of Graduate Alumnae of the Texas State College for Women, 1904 to 1921." M.A. thesis. Texas State College for Women, 1941.

Crane, Lillian A. Resignation letter. 1924. Louise Pettus Archives and Special Collections, Winthrop U.

Cremin, Lawrence A. *American Education: The Metropolitan Experience, 1876–1980.* New York: Harper and Row, 1988.

Crowley, Sharon. *Composition in the University: Historical and Polemical Essays.* Pittsburgh: U of Pittsburgh P, 1998.

———. *Methodical Memory: Invention in Current-Traditional Rhetoric.* Carbondale: Southern Illinois UP, 1990.

Crumpton, Claudia E. "American Speech Week throughout the Nation." *English Journal* 8.5 (May 1919): 279–86.

———. "Better Speech Week at Montevallo." *English Journal* 5.8 (Oct. 1916): 569–70.

Curl, Lottie Moring. "The History of the Georgia State College for Women." M.A. thesis. George Peabody College for Teachers, 1931.

Curry, Samuel Silas. *Foundations of Expression: Studies and Problems for Developing the Voice, Body, and Mind in Reading and Speaking.* Boston: Expression, 1907.

———. *The Province of Expression: A Search for Principles Underlying Adequate Methods of Developing Dramatic and Oratoric Delivery.* Boston: Expression, 1891.

Dean, Pamela. *Women on the Hill: A History of Women at the University of North Carolina.* Division of Student Affairs, U of North Carolina at Chapel Hill, 1987. Also available (27 June 2013) at <http://ia601501.us.archive.org/21/items/womenonhillhistooodean/womenonhillhistooodean.pdf>.

"Dean White's Black Stories." *Texas Outlook* 17.4 (Apr. 1933): 45.

Delfino, Susanna, and Michele Gillespie, eds. *Neither Lady nor Slave: Working Women of the Old South.* Chapel Hill: U of North Carolina P, 2002.

Delsarte System of Oratory, Including the Complete Works of M. L'Abbé Delaumosne and Mme. Angelique Arnaud (Pupils of Delsarte) with the Literary Remains of François Delsarte. 3rd. ed. New York: Edgar S. Werner, 1887.

Dennis, Leah. "Guide to Errors." Rev. of *Harbrace Handbook of English,* by John C. Hodges. *South Atlantic Bulletin* 7.2 (Oct. 1941): 16–17.

———. "The Progressive Tense: Frequency of Its Use in English." *PMLA* 55.3 (Sept. 1940): 855–65.

Dodd, William G. "Florida State College for Women: Notes on the Formative Years." 1958–59. Unpublished MS. Special Collections and Archives, Florida State U Library.

———. "Old Times I Remember . . . in the Big Bend." *Tallahassee Democrat* [1962?]: n. pag. Special Collections and Archives, Florida State U Library.

———. *Some Objects and Problems in Teaching English.* Bulletin of the Florida State College for Women 7.4 (Dec. 1914).

Donahue, Patricia, and Gretchen Flesher Moon, eds. *Local Histories: Reading the Archives of Composition.* Pittsburgh: U of Pittsburgh P, 2007.

Donawerth, Jane. *Conversational Rhetoric: The Rise and Fall of a Women's Tradition, 1600–1900.* Carbondale: Southern Illinois UP, 2012.

DuBois, W. E. B. *The Souls of Black Folk.* 1903. Ed. Henry Louis Gates Jr. and Terri Hume Oliver. New York: Norton, 1999.

Eastman, Carolyn. *A Nation of Speechifiers: Making an American Public after the Revolution.* Chicago: U of Chicago P, 2009.

Elbow, Peter. *Writing without Teachers.* New York: Oxford UP, 1973.

Eldred, Janet Carey, and Peter Mortensen. *Imagining Rhetoric: Composing Women of the Early United States.* Pittsburgh: U of Pittsburgh P, 2002.

Emerson, Charles Wesley. *Evolution of Expression: A Compilation of Selections Illustrating the Four Stages of Development in Art as Applied to Oratory.* 4 vols. Rev. ed. Boston: Emerson College, 1910.

——. *The Sixteen Perfective Laws of Art Applied to Oratory.* 4 vols. Boston: Emerson College, 1910–13.

Emerson, Michael O., Rachel Tolbert Kimbro, and George Yancey. "Contact Theory Extended: The Effects of Prior Racial Contact on Current Social Ties." *Social Science Quarterly* 83.3 (Sept. 2002): 745–61.

Enoch, Jessica. *Refiguring Rhetorical Education: Women Teaching African American, Native American, and Chicano/a Students, 1865–1911.* Carbondale: Southern Illinois UP, 2008.

Farnham, Christie Anne. *The Education of the Southern Belle: Higher Education and Student Socialization in the Antebellum South.* New York: New York UP, 1994.

Faust, Drew Gilpin. *Mothers of Invention: Women of the Slaveholding South in the American Civil War.* Chapel Hill: U of North Carolina P, 1996.

——. *This Republic of Suffering: Death and the American Civil War.* New York: Alfred A. Knopf, 2008.

Fisher, Berenice M. *Industrial Education: American Ideals and Institutions.* Madison: U of Wisconsin P, 1967.

Fitzgerald, Kathryn. "The Platteville Papers: Inscribing Frontier Ideology and Culture in a Nineteenth-Century Writing Assignment." *College English* 64.3 (Jan. 2002): 273–301.

Florida [State of]. *Report of the Board of Control of the State Educational Institutions of Florida, 1909–1910.* Tallahassee: T. J. Appleyard, State Printer, 1911.

Florida State College for Women [a.k.a. Florida Female College]. *Alumnae News.* Nov. 1931.

——. *Catalogue.*

——. *Flastacowo* [yearbook].

——. *Florida Flambeau* [student newspaper].

——. *Talisman/Distaff* [student literary journal].

Foucault, Michel. *The Order of Things: An Archeology of the Human Sciences.* New York: Pantheon, 1970.

Fox-Genovese, Elizabeth. *Within the Plantation Household: Black and White Women of the Old South.* Chapel Hill: U of North Carolina P, 1988.

Franklin, Marion E. "A History of Industrial Education in Oklahoma up to 1950." Diss. U of Oklahoma, 1952.

Fulkerson, Richard. "Composition at the Turn of the Twenty-First Century." *College Composition and Communication* 56.4 (June 2005): 654–87.

——. "Composition Theory in the Eighties: Axiological Consensus and Paradigmatic Diversity." *College Composition and Communication* 41.4 (Dec. 1990): 409–29.

——. "Four Philosophies of Composition." *College Composition and Communication* 30.4 (Dec. 1979): 343–48.

Fulton, Robert I., and Thomas C. Trueblood. *Practical Elements of Elocution: Designed as a Text-Book for the Guidance of Teachers and Students of Expression.* 3rd ed. Boston: Ginn, 1893.

Gaddis, John Lewis. *The Landscape of History: How Historians Map the Past*. New York: Oxford UP, 2002.

Garbus, Julia. "Service-Learning, 1902." *College English* 64.5 (May 2002): 547–65.

Garbus, Julie [Julia]. "Vida Scudder in the Classroom and in the Archives." Donahue and Moon 77–93.

Garrison, Kristen. "'To Supply This Deficiency': Margaret Fuller's Boston Conversations as Hybrid Rhetorical Practice." Gold and Hobbs 96–115.

Gehrke, Pat J. *The Ethics and Politics of Speech: Communication and Rhetoric in the Twentieth Century*. Carbondale: Southern Illinois UP, 2009.

Genung, John F. *Outlines of Rhetoric: Embodied in Rules, Illustrative Examples, and a Progressive Course of Prose Composition*. Boston: Ginn, 1893.

Georgia [State of]. *Acts and Resolutions of the General Assembly of the State of Georgia, 1888–1889*. Vol. 2. Atlanta: W. J. Campbell, 1889.

———. *Forty-First Annual Report of the Department of Education to the General Assembly of the State of Georgia for the School Year Ending December 31, 1912*. Atlanta: Chas. P. Byrd, 1913.

Georgia State College for Women [a.k.a. Georgia Normal and Industrial College]. *Catalogue*.

Gere, Anne Ruggles. *Intimate Practices: Literacy and Cultural Work in U.S. Women's Clubs, 1880–1920*. Urbana: U of Illinois P, 1997.

Gilmore, Glenda Elizabeth. *Gender and Jim Crow: Women and the Politics of White Supremacy in North Carolina, 1896–1920*. Chapel Hill: U of North Carolina P, 1996.

Glenn, Cheryl, and Jessica Enoch. "Invigorating Historiographic Practices in Rhetoric and Composition Studies." Ramsey, Sharer, L'Eplattenier, and Mastrangelo 11–27.

Gold, David. "'Eve Did No Wrong': Effective Literacy at a Public College for Women." *College Composition and Communication* 61.2 (Dec. 2009): W177–96.

———. "Remapping Revisionist Historiography." *College Composition and Communication* 64.1 (Sept. 2012): 15–34.

———. *Rhetoric at the Margins: Revising the History of Writing Instruction in American Colleges, 1873–1947*. Carbondale: Southern Illinois UP, 2008.

Gold, David, and Catherine L. Hobbs, eds. *Rhetoric, History, and Women's Oratorical Education: American Women Learn to Speak*. New York: Routledge, 2013.

Gordon, Lynn D. "Annie Nathan Meyer and Barnard College: Mission and Identity in Women's Higher Education, 1889–1950." *History of Education Quarterly* 26.4 (Winter 1986): 503–22.

———. *Gender and Higher Education in the Progressive Era*. New Haven: Yale UP, 1990.

Grady, Henry W. *The Complete Orations and Speeches of Henry W. Grady*. Ed. Edwin DuBois Shurter. New York: Hinds, Noble, and Eldredge, 1910.

Graff, Gerald. *Professing Literature: An Institutional History*. Chicago: U of Chicago P, 1987.

Green, Elna C. *Southern Strategies: Southern Women and the Woman Suffrage Question*. Chapel Hill: U of North Carolina P, 1997.

Griffin, Larry J., Ranae J. Evenson, and Ashley B. Thompson. "Southerners All?" *Southern Cultures* 11.1 (Spring 2005): 6–25.

Griffin, Lenore. Reader Comments, "Stay the Course on Name Change." *Dispatch* [Columbus, MS] 21 Oct. 2009. 26 Mar. 2011 <http://www.cdispatch.com/opinions/article.asp?aid=3420&sort=p>.

Griffith, Lucille. *Alabama College, 1896–1969*. Montevallo: Alabama College, 1969.

Guba, Egon G. "The Alternative Paradigm Dialog." *The Paradigm Dialog*. Ed. Egon G. Guba. Newbury Park, CA: SAGE, 1990. 17–27.

Hacker, J. David. "A Census-Based Count of the Civil War Dead." *Civil War History* 57.4 (Dec. 2011): 307–48.

Hackney, Sheldon. *Magnolias without Moonlight: The American South from Regional Confederacy to National Integration*. New Brunswick, NJ: Transaction, 2005.

Hair, William Ivy, James C. Bonner, and Edward B. Dawson. *A History of Georgia College*. Milledgeville: Georgia College, 1979.

Hanus, Paul H. "Preparation for College and Preparation for Life." *Educational Review* 21.2 (Feb. 1901): 140–52.

Harris, Carmen. "Grace under Pressure: The Black Home Extension Service in South Carolina, 1919–1966." Stage and Vincenti 203–28.

Harris, Robin O. *The First One Hundred Years: Georgia College Alumni Association*. Milledgeville: Georgia College, 1995.

Harwarth, Irene, Mindi Maline, and Elizabeth DeBra. *Women's Colleges in the United States: Histories, Issues, and Challenges*. U.S. Department of Education. Washington, DC: GPO, 1997.

Hawk, Byron. *A Counter-History of Composition: Toward Methodologies of Complexity*. Pittsburgh: U of Pittsburgh P, 2007.

Herndon, Sarah. Interview with Robin Sellers. 9 Nov. 1989. Reichelt Oral History Program Collection, Florida State U.

Herrick, Robert, and Lindsay Todd Damon. *Composition and Rhetoric for Schools*. Chicago: Scott, Foresman, 1899.

Hill, Adams Sherman. *The Principles of Rhetoric and Their Application*. New York: Harper, 1878.

Hill, David J. *The Science of Rhetoric: An Introduction to the Laws of Effective Discourse*. New York: Sheldon, 1877.

Hill, Sarah H. "Made by the Hands of Indians: Cherokee Women and Trade." Delfino and Gillespie 34–54.

Hobbs, Catherine, ed. *Nineteenth-Century Women Learn to Write*. Charlottesville: UP of Virginia, 1995.

Hobbs, Dan S. "The History of the University of Science and Arts of Oklahoma." 2007. Unpublished MS provided by author.

Hodges, John C. *Harbrace Handbook of English*. New York: Harcourt, Brace, 1941.

Hollis, Karyn L. *Liberating Voices: Writing at the Bryn Mawr Summer School for Women Workers*. Carbondale: Southern Illinois UP, 2004.

"Hon. W. Y. Atkinson." *Atlanta Constitution* 17 Sept. 1893: 6.

Horner, Winifred Bryan. *Nineteenth-Century Scottish Rhetoric: The American Connection*. Carbondale: Southern Illinois UP, 1993.

Horowitz, Helen Lefkowitz. *Alma Mater: Design and Experience in the Women's Colleges from Their Nineteenth-Century Beginnings to the 1930s*. 2nd ed. Amherst: U of Massachusetts P, 1993.

Howell, Wilbur Samuel. "English Backgrounds of Rhetoric." Wallace 3–47.

Hubbard, Louis H. *Recollections of a Texas Educator*. Salado, TX: Author, 1964.

Hunt, Mary Alice. Interview with Robin Sellers. 2 Dec. 1993. Reichelt Oral History Program Collection, Florida State U.

"Increase in Faculty Pay and Student Tuition." *National School Digest* 41.2 (Oct. 1921): 73–74.

Jackson, Connie Vann. Interview with Catherine Hobbs. 13 Jan. 2011.

Jackson, Walter Clinton. *A Boys' Life of Booker T. Washington.* New York: Macmillan, 1922.

Jarratt, Susan C. "Classics and Counterpublics in Nineteenth-Century Historically Black Colleges." *College English* 72.2 (Nov. 2009): 134–59.

———. *Rereading the Sophists: Classical Rhetoric Refigured.* Carbondale: Southern Illinois UP, 1991.

Johnson, James Weldon. *Along This Way: The Autobiography of James Weldon Johnson.* 1933. New York: Da Capo, 2000.

Johnson, Joan Marie. "'Drill into Us . . . the Rebel Tradition': The Contest over Southern Identity in Black and White Women's Clubs, South Carolina, 1898–1930." *Journal of Southern History* 66.3 (Aug. 2000): 525–62.

———. *Southern Ladies, New Women: Race, Region, and Clubwomen in South Carolina, 1890–1930.* Gainesville: UP of Florida, 2004.

Johnson, Nan. *Gender and Rhetorical Space in American Life, 1866–1910.* Carbondale: Southern Illinois UP, 2002.

———. *Nineteenth-Century Rhetoric in North America.* Carbondale: Southern Illinois UP, 1991.

Kantrowitz, Stephen David. *Ben Tillman and the Reconstruction of White Supremacy.* Chapel Hill: U of North Carolina P, 2000.

Kates, Susan. *Activist Rhetorics and American Higher Education, 1885–1937.* Carbondale: Southern Illinois UP, 2001.

Keith, William. "On the Origins of Speech as a Discipline: James A. Winans and Public Speaking as Practical Democracy." *Rhetoric Society Quarterly* 38.3 (Summer 2008): 239–58.

Kelley, Mary. *Learning to Stand and Speak: Women, Education, and Public Life in America's Republic.* Chapel Hill: U of North Carolina P, 2006.

Kerber, Linda K. "Separate Spheres, Female Worlds, Woman's Place: The Rhetoric of Women's History." *Journal of American History* 75.1 (June 1988): 9–39.

Kilpatrick, William Heard. "The Project Method: The Use of the Purposeful Act in the Educative Process." *Teachers College Record* 19.4 (Sept. 1918): 319–34. Rpt. *The Project Method.* New York: Teachers College, Columbia U, 1920.

Kinard, James Pickney. *A Study of Wulfstan's Homilies: Their Style and Sources.* Baltimore: John Murphy, 1897.

Kirsch, Gesa E., and Liz Rohan, eds. *Beyond the Archives: Research as a Lived Process.* Carbondale: Southern Illinois UP, 2008.

Kliebard, Herbert M. *Schooled to Work: Vocationalism and the American Curriculum, 1876–1946.* New York: Teachers College P, 1999.

Kohn, Sheldon Scott. "The Literary and Intellectual Impact of Mississippi's Industrial Institute and College, 1884–1920." Diss. Georgia State U, 2007.

Lake Placid Conference on Home Economics. *Proceedings of the Fourth Annual Conference.* Lake Placid, 16–20 Sept. 1902, N.p.: Lake Placid, NY, 1902.

"Launching of College Was Big News Here: How Denton Record 'Covered' Opening." *Denton Record-Chronicle* 5 Nov. 1952, sec. 2: 1–10.

Leake, Albert H. *The Vocational Education of Girls and Women.* New York: Macmillan, 1918.

Lebsock, Suzanne. *The Free Women of Petersburg: Status and Culture in a Southern Town, 1784–1860*. New York: Norton, 1984.

Leloudis, James L. *Schooling the New South: Pedagogy, Self, and Society in North Carolina, 1880–1920*. Chapel Hill: U of North Carolina P, 1996.

———. "School Reform in the New South: The Woman's Association for the Betterment of Public School Houses in North Carolina, 1902–1919." *Journal of American History* 69.4 (Mar. 1983): 886–909.

L'Eplattenier, Barbara. E. "An Argument for Archival Research Methods: Thinking Beyond Methodology." *College English* 72.1 (Sept. 2009): 67–79.

Levi, Giovanni. "On Microhistory." P. Burke 97–119.

Lewis, Edwin Herbert. *A Second Manual of Composition: Designed for Use in Secondary Schools*. New York, Macmillan, 1900.

Linn, James Weber. *The Essentials of English Composition*. New York: Scribner's, 1912.

———. "What the University Expects of High-School Students in English." *School Review* 19.2 (Feb. 1911): 96–102.

Lockwood, Sara E. Husted. *Lessons in English, Adapted to the Study of American Classics: A Text-Book for High Schools and Academies*. Boston: Ginn, 1888.

Lockwood, Sara E. H., and Mary Alice Emerson. *Composition and Rhetoric for Higher Schools*. Boston: Ginn, 1901.

Logan, Shirley Wilson. *Liberating Language: Sites of Rhetorical Education in Nineteenth-Century Black America*. Carbondale: Southern Illinois UP, 2008.

———. *"We Are Coming": The Persuasive Discourse of Nineteenth-Century Black Women*. Carbondale: Southern Illinois UP, 1999.

Lunsford, Andrea A., ed. *Reclaiming Rhetorica: Women in the Rhetorical Tradition*. Pittsburgh: U of Pittsburgh P, 1995.

Marrs, Suzanne. *Eudora Welty: A Biography*. Orlando, FL: Harcourt, 2005.

Masters, Thomas M. *Practicing Writing: The Postwar Discourse of Freshman English*. Pittsburgh: U of Pittsburgh P, 2004.

Mastrangelo, Lisa S. "Learning from the Past: Rhetoric, Composition, and Debate at Mount Holyoke College." *Rhetoric Review* 18.1 (Fall 1999): 46–64.

Mastrangelo, Lisa, and Barbara L'Eplattenier. "'Is It the Pleasure of This Conference to Have Another?' Women's Colleges Meeting and Talking about Writing in the Progressive Era." *Historical Studies of Writing Program Administration: Individuals, Communities, and the Formation of a Discipline*. Ed. Barbara L'Eplattenier and Lisa Mastrangelo. West Lafayette, IN: Parlor P, 2004. 117–43.

Mattingly, Carol. *Appropriate[ing] Dress: Women's Rhetorical Style in Nineteenth-Century America*. Carbondale: Southern Illinois UP, 2002.

———. *Well-Tempered Women: Nineteenth-Century Temperance Rhetoric*. Carbondale: Southern Illinois UP, 1998.

Maynes, Edward. *History of Education in Mississippi*. Contributions to American Educational History no. 24. Washington, DC: GPO, 1899.

Mayo, Armory Dwight. *Southern Women in the Recent Educational Movement in the South*. 1892. Ed. Dan T. Carter and Amy Friedlander. Baton Rouge: Louisiana State UP, 1978.

McCandless, Amy Thompson. *The Past in the Present: Women's Higher Education in the Twentieth-Century American South*. Tuscaloosa: U of Alabama P, 1999.

———. "'Separate but Equal' Case Law and the Higher Education of Women in the Twenty-First-Century South." *Southern Women at the Millennium:*

A Historical Perspective. Ed. Melissa Walker, Jeanette R. Dunn, and Joe P. Dunn. Columbia: U of Missouri P, 2003.

McCosh, James. *The Laws of Discursive Thought: Being a Text-Book of Formal Logic.* New York: Robert Carter and Brothers, 1870.

McIlwaine, A. S. [Ardrey Shields]. *Freshman English Manual: Mississippi State College for Women, 1930–31.* Mississippi U for Women Library.

——. *The Southern Poor-White from Lubberland to Tobacco Road.* Norman: U of Oklahoma P, 1939.

McIver, Charles D. "The Education of the White Country Girl." *University of Tennessee Record* no. 6 (Nov. 1901): 354–58.

Miller, Thomas P. *The Evolution of College English: Literacy Studies from the Puritans to the Postmoderns.* Pittsburgh: U of Pittsburgh P, 2011.

——. *The Formation of College English: Rhetoric and Belles Lettres in the British Cultural Provinces.* Pittsburgh: U of Pittsburgh P, 1997.

Mississippi State College for Women [a.k.a. Mississippi Industrial Institute and College]. *Alumnae Yearbook, Columbus, Mississippi—Alumni Day, April 10, 1918.* College bulletin 10.6 (July 1918).

——. *Catalogue.*

——. *Meh Lady* [yearbook].

——. *The Spectator* [student newspaper].

Mississippi University for Women. *Mississippi University for Women Fact Book 2010–2011.* Office of Institutional Research, Mississippi University for Women. 2011.

Moon, Gretchen Flesher. "Locating Composition History." Donahue and Moon 1–13.

Mossman, Lois Coffey. *The Activity Concept: An Interpretation.* New York: Macmillan, 1938.

Mountford, Roxanne. *The Gendered Pulpit: Preaching in American Protestant Spaces.* Carbondale: Southern Illinois UP, 2003.

Munslow, Alun. *Deconstructing History.* 2nd ed. New York: Routledge, 2006.

"National American Speech Week." *Literary Digest* 71.5 (29 Oct. 1921): 36.

National Center for Education Statistics. *Digest of Education Statistics 2001.* Washington, DC: U.S. Department of Education, 2002.

——. *Digest of Education Statistics 2008.* Washington, DC: U.S. Department of Education, 2009.

——. *Digest of Education Statistics 2010.* Washington, DC: U.S. Department of Education, 2011.

——. "Profile of Women's Colleges: Enrollment Statistics." 1979. ERIC document no. ED178021. 15 July 2009 <http://www.eric.ed.gov:80/ERICDocs/data/ericdocs2sql/content_storage_01/0000019b/80/32/f3/2a.pdf>.

National Educational Association. *Report of the Committee of Ten on Secondary School Studies, with the Reports of the Conferences Arranged by the Committee.* American Book Co.: New York, 1894.

National Federation of Business and Professional Women's Clubs with Alabama Federation and Alabama College. *A Study of Employability of Women in Alabama, 1929–1935.* Alabama College for Women bulletin 29.1 (July 1936).

Newcomer, Mabel. *A Century of Higher Education for American Women.* New York: Harper, 1959.

Newman, Louise Michele. *White Women's Rights: The Racial Origins of Feminism in the United States.* New York: Oxford UP, 1999.

Nobles, Katharine. "Club Life in the South." *Arena* 6, no. 33 (Aug. 1892): 376–78.

North Carolina College for Women [a.k.a. North Carolina State Normal and Industrial School/College]. *Catalogue.*

———. *Decennial* [yearbook]. 1902.

———. *A Manual of Instructions for English 101–102.* 1942–43. Special Collections and University Archives, U of North Carolina at Greensboro Library.

———. *A Manual of Instructions for Freshman English.* 1930–31. Special Collections and University Archives, U of North Carolina at Greensboro Library.

———. *Representative Essays.* 1905–11. Special Collections and University Archives, U of North Carolina at Greensboro Library.

———. *State Normal Magazine/Coraddi* [student literary journal].

Norton, Mary Beth. *Separated by Their Sex: Women in Public and Private in the Colonial Atlantic World.* Ithaca, NY: Cornell UP, 2011.

Oklahoma [State of]. *State of Oklahoma Session Laws of 1907–1908.* Guthrie: Oklahoma Printing, 1908.

Oklahoma College for Women [a.k.a. Oklahoma Industrial Institute and College for Girls]. *Argus* [yearbook].

———. *Catalogue.*

———. *Trend* [student newspaper].

Orr, M. L. [Milton Lee]. "Curriculum Revision at Alabama College." *Journal of Higher Education* 6.4 (Apr. 1935): 179–84.

———. *The State-Supported Colleges for Women.* Nashville: George Peabody College for Teachers, 1930.

Paine, Charles. *The Resistant Writer: Rhetoric as Immunity, 1850 to the Present.* Albany: State U of New York P, 1999.

Pannell, Anne Gary, and Dorothea E. Wyatt. *Julia S. Tutwiler and Social Progress in Alabama.* Tuscaloosa: U of Alabama P, 1961.

Patterson, Martha H., ed. *The American New Woman Revisited: A Reader, 1894–1930.* New Brunswick, NJ: Rutgers UP, 2008.

Perelman, Chaim, and Lucie Olbrechts-Tyteca. *The New Rhetoric: A Treatise on Argumentation.* Trans. John Wilkinson and Purcell Weaver. Notre Dame, IN: U of Notre Dame P, 1969.

Perry, William G., Jr. *Forms of Intellectual and Ethical Development in the College Years: A Scheme.* New York: Holt, 1970.

Pestalozzi, Johann Heinrich. *How Gertrude Teaches Her Children: An Attempt to Help Mothers to Teach Their Own Children and an Account of the Method.* 1801. Trans. Lucy E. Holland and Frances C. Turner. Ed. Ebenezer Cooke. Syracuse, NY: Bardeen, 1898.

Peterson's College Planner: Student Edition. Peterson's. Accessed 5 July 2009 <http://www.petersons.com/college_home.asp?path=ug.home>.

Pettigrew, Thomas F. "Intergroup Contact Theory." *Annual Review of Psychology* 49 (1998): 65–85.

Phillips, Ulrich B. "The Central Theme of Southern History." *American Historical Review* 34.1 (Oct. 1928): 30–43.

Pieschel, Bridget Smith, and Stephen Robert Pieschel. *Loyal Daughters: One Hundred Years at Mississippi University for Women, 1888–1984.* Jackson: UP of Mississippi, 1984.

Pieschel, Steve [Stephen Robert]. "A Centennial Review of MUW's Literary Connections: William Faulkner, Tennessee Williams, and Eudora Welty." Unpublished MS. Sept. 1983. Provided by Bridget Pieschel.

Porterfield, Amanda. *Mary Lyon and the Mount Holyoke Missionaries*. New York: Oxford UP, 1997.

Powers, Jane Bernard. *The 'Girl Question' in Education: Vocational Education for Young Women in the Progressive Era*. London: Falmer P, 1992.

"Program, Leaman Literary Society, Feb. 12, 1913." University Archives, University of Science and Arts of Oklahoma Library.

Rable, George C. *Civil Wars: Women and the Crisis of Southern Nationalism*. Urbana: U of Illinois P, 1989.

Ramsey, Alexis E., Wendy B. Sharer, Barbara L'Eplattenier, and Lisa S. Mastrangelo, eds. *Working in the Archives: Practical Research Methods for Rhetoric and Composition*. Carbondale: Southern Illinois UP, 2010.

Regan, Alison Elizabeth. "Promises, Problems, and Politics: The History of Rhetoric, English Studies, and Writing Instruction at the University of Texas at Austin, 1883–1994." Diss. U of Texas at Austin, 1996.

Renshaw, Edyth. "Five Private Schools of Speech." Wallace 301–25.

Rev. of *The Negro and His Songs*, by Howard W. Odum and Guy B. Johnson. *Journal of Negro History* 10.4 (Oct. 1925): 775–76.

Richards, Ellen H. *Euthenics: The Science of Controllable Environment: A Plea for Better Living Conditions as a First Step toward Higher Human Efficiency*. Boston: Whitcomb and Barrows, 1910.

Robbins, Katharine Knowles. "The Work of the American Speech Committee of the Chicago Woman's Club, and Notes upon Its School Survey." *English Journal* 7.3 (Mar. 1918): 163–76.

Rogers, Winfield H., Ruby V. Redinger, and Hiram C. Haydn II, eds. *Explorations in Living: A Record of the Democratic Spirit*. New York: Reynal and Hitchcock, 1941.

Roosevelt, Eleanor. *Eleanor Roosevelt's My Day: Her Acclaimed Columns, 1936–1945*. Ed. Rochelle Chadakoff. New York: Pharos, 1989.

Rothermel, Beth Ann. "'Our Life's Work': Rhetorical Preparation and Teacher Training at a Massachusetts State Normal School, 1839–1929." Donahue and Moon 134–58.

———. "A Sphere of Noble Action: Gender, Rhetoric, and Influence at a Nineteenth-Century Massachusetts State Normal School." *Rhetoric Society Quarterly* 33.1 (Winter 2003): 35–64.

Royster, Jacqueline Jones. *Traces of a Stream: Literacy and Social Change among African American Women*. Pittsburgh: U of Pittsburgh P, 2000.

Royster, Jacqueline Jones, and Gesa E. Kirsch. *Feminist Rhetorical Practices: New Horizons for Rhetoric, Composition, and Literacy Studies*. Carbondale: Southern Illinois UP, 2012.

Russell, Andrew L. "'Rough Consensus and Running Code' and the Internet-OSI Standards War." *IEEE Annals of the History of Computing* 28.3 (July–Sept. 2006): 48–61.

Ruyter, Nancy Lee Chalfa. *The Cultivation of Body and Mind in Nineteenth-Century American Delsartism*. Westport, CT: Greenwood P, 1999.

Ryan, Abram J. *Father Ryan's Poems*. Mobile, AL: J. L. Rapier, 1879.

Sahlin, Claire L. "Texas Woman's University: Threats to Institutional Autonomy and Conflict over the Admission of Men." *Challenged by Coeducation: Women's Colleges since the 1960s*. Ed. Leslie Miller-Bernal and Susan L. Poulson. Nashville: Vanderbilt UP, 2006. 108–44.

Sánchez, Raúl. *The Function of Theory in Composition Studies*. Albany: State U of New York P, 2005.

Sansing, David G. *Making Haste Slowly: The Troubled History of Higher Education in Mississippi*. Jackson: UP of Mississippi, 1990.

———. *The University of Mississippi: A Sesquicentennial History*. Jackson: UP of Mississippi, 1999.

Schemmel, William. *Georgia Curiosities: Quirky Characters, Roadside Oddities and Other Offbeat Stuff*. 3rd ed. Guilford, CT: Globe Pequot, 2011.

Schultz, Lucille M. *The Young Composers: Composition's Beginnings in Nineteenth-Century Schools*. Carbondale: Southern Illinois UP, 1999.

Scott, Anne Firor. *The Southern Lady: From Pedestal to Politics, 1830–1930*. Chicago: U of Chicago P, 1970.

Scott, Fred Newton, and Joseph Villiers Denney. *Composition-Rhetoric: Designed for Use in Secondary Schools*. Boston: Allyn and Bacon, 1897.

———. *Elementary English Composition*. Boston: Allyn and Bacon, 1900.

Scott, Harriet M., and Gertrude Buck. *Organic Education: A Manual for Teachers in Primary and Grammar Grades*. Ann Arbor: Sheehan, 1897.

Scott, Katherine Kirkwood. "Creative Composition." 1935. Unpublished MS. Special Collections, Georgia College and State U Library.

———. "Inductive Teaching of English." *Georgia Education Journal* 23.3 (Nov. 1930): 19–21.

———. "My Emerged Opinions." 1940. Unpublished MS. Special Collections, Georgia College and State U Library.

Sellers, Robin Jeanne. *Femina Perfecta: The Genesis of Florida State University*. Tallahassee: Florida State U Foundation, 1995.

Sharer, Wendy B. *Vote and Voice: Women's Organizations and Political Literacy, 1915–1930*. Carbondale: Southern Illinois UP, 2004.

Shaver, Claude L. "Steele MacKaye and the Delsartian Tradition." Wallace 202–18.

Simmons, Sue Carter. "Radcliffe Responses to Harvard Rhetoric: 'An Absurdly Stiff Way of Thinking.'" C. Hobbs 264–92.

Sklar, Kathryn Kish. *Catharine Beecher: A Study in American Domesticity*. New Haven: Yale UP, 1973.

Slattery, Patrick J. "Applying Intellectual Development Theory to Composition." *Journal of Basic Writing* 9.2 (Fall 1990): 54–65.

———. "The Argumentative, Multiple-Source Paper: College Students Reading, Thinking, and Writing about Divergent Points of View." *Journal of Teaching Writing* 10.2 (Fall/Winter 1991): 181–99.

Sledd, Andrew. "The Negro: Another View." *Atlantic Monthly* July 1902: 65–73.

Smith College. *Catalogue*.

Smith-Rosenberg, Carroll. *Disorderly Conduct: Visions of Gender in Victorian America*. New York: Alfred A. Knopf, 1985.

South Carolina [State of]. *Acts and Joint Resolutions of the General Assembly of the State of South Carolina, Passed at the Regular Session of 1891*. Columbia: James H. Woodrow, State Printer, 1892.

Southwick, Jessie Eldridge. *The Emerson Philosophy of Expression; an Application to Character Education*. Boston: Expression, 1930.

———. *Expressive Voice Culture, Including the Emerson System*. Boston: Expression, 1929.

Stage, Sarah. "Introduction: Home Economics: What's in a Name?" Stage and Vin-
    centi 1–13.
Stage, Sarah, and Virginia B. Vincenti, eds. *Rethinking Home Economics: Women
    and the History of a Profession.* Ithaca, NY: Cornell UP, 1997.
Stebbins, Genevieve. *Delsarte System of Expression.* 1885. 6th ed. New York: Edgar
    S. Werner, 1902.
Steckel, Minnie L. *The Alabama Business Woman as Citizen.* Alabama Federation
    of Business and Professional Women's Clubs with Alabama College. College
    bulletin 30.1 (July 1937).
Stern, Maxine, ed. *FSU Voices: An Informal History of 150 Years.* Tallahassee: Florida
    State U, 2002.
Stevenson, Hazel Allison. "Facing the Problem in Upperclass English." *College English*
    13.1 (Oct. 1951): 32–37.
Stewart, Donald C. "Rediscovering Fred Newton Scott." *College English* 40.5 (Jan.
    1979): 539–47.
———. "The Status of Composition and Rhetoric in American Colleges, 1880–1902:
    An MLA Perspective." *College English* 47.7 (Nov. 1985): 734–46.
Student at Oklahoma College for Women. Interview with Catherine Hobbs. 9 Aug.
    2007.
Suter, Lisa. "The Arguments They Wore: The Role of the Neoclassical Toga in Amer-
    ican Delsartism." Gold and Hobbs 134–53.
Texas State College for Women [a.k.a. Girls Industrial College; College of Industrial
    Arts]. *Catalogue.*
———. *Daedalian* [student literary journal].
Texas Woman's University. "University Mission Statement" [passed 19 Feb. 2010]. Re-
    gents Policies, Texas Woman's University. 16 Aug. 2010. 26 Dec. 2011 <https://
    www.twu.edu/regents/university-mission-statement.asp>.
———. "University Mission Statement" [passed 3 June 2011]. Regents Policies, Texas
    Woman's University. 9 Dec. 2011. 26 Dec. 2011 <https://www.twu.edu/re-
    gents/p-university-mission-statement.asp>.
Thompson, Holland. *The New South: A Chronicle of Social and Industrial Evolution.*
    New Haven: Yale UP, 1919.
Thomson, Elizabeth. Interview with Robin Sellers. 30 Aug. 1990. Reichelt Oral His-
    tory Program Collection, Florida State U.
Threlkeld, Hilda [printed as "Thelkeld"]. "What the South Expects of the Education
    of Its College Women." *Proceedings of the Twenty-Fourth Annual Meeting,
    Southern Association of Colleges for Women.* Louisville, 1 Dec. 1947. 35–40.
Touchton, Judith G., and Lynne Davis. *Fact Book on Women in Higher Education.*
    American Council on Education. New York: Macmillan, 1991.
Trelease, Allen W. *Making North Carolina Literate: The University of North Carolina
    at Greensboro, from Normal School to Metropolitan University.* Durham:
    Carolina Academic P, 2004.
Tubb, Laura. "Limbert Looks Back, and Ahead." *Spectator* [Mississippi U for Women]
    23 Mar. 2006: 1+.
Tucker, S. [Samuel] M. "The Relation of the Southern College to the Public School"
    [including discussion]. *Journal of Proceedings and Addresses of the Sixteenth
    Annual Meeting.* Southern Educational Association. Nashville, 23–25 Nov.
    1905. Chattanooga: Southern Educational Review, 1905. 125–38.

Turpin, Andrea L. "The Ideological Origins of the Women's College: Religion, Class, and Curriculum in the Educational Visions of Catharine Beecher and Mary Lyon." *History of Education Quarterly* 50.2 (May 2010): 133–58.

Twain, Mark. *Life on the Mississippi.* 1883. New York: Harper, 1917.

University of Montevallo. "Mission and Vision." UM at a Glance, University of Montevallo. 2013. 9 Sept. 2013. <http://www.montevallo.edu/about-um /um-at-a-glance/mission-vision/>.

University of South Carolina. *Catalogue.* 1924–25.

U.S. Bureau of the Census. *Eighth Census of the United States, 1860.* Population. Washington, DC: GPO, 1864.

———. *Historical Statistics of the United States: Colonial Times to 1970.* pt. 1. Washington, DC: GPO, 1975.

———. *Ninth Census of the United States, 1870.* Vol. 1. *Population.* Washington, DC: GPO, 1872.

———. *Thirteenth Census of the United States, 1910.* Vol. 2. *Population.* Washington, DC: GPO, 1913.

U.S. Bureau of Education. *Biennial Survey of Education in the United States, 1916–18.* Washington, DC: GPO, 1921.

———. *Report of the Commissioner of Education, 1899–1900.* Vol. 2. Washington, DC: GPO, 1901.

———. *Report of the Commissioner of Education, 1906.* Vol. 1. Washington, DC: GPO, 1907.

Vance, Earl L. "Freedom of the Press for Whom?" *Virginia Quarterly Review* 21.3 (Summer 1945): 340–54.

———. "Integrating Freshman Composition." *English Journal* [college ed.] 26.4 (Apr. 1937): 318–23.

———. "Training for Journalism Teachers." *English Journal* 19.9 (Nov. 1930): 738–44.

Vaughan, A. W. "What's Wrong with Us English Teachers?" *English Journal* 28.2, pt. 2 (Feb. 1939): 28–29.

Vaughn-Roberson, Courtney Ann. "Having a Purpose in Life: Western Women Teachers in the Twentieth Century." *The Teacher's Voice: A Social History of Teaching in Twentieth-Century America.* Ed. Richard J. Altenbaugh. London: Falmer P, 1992. 12–25.

Veysey, Laurence R. *The Emergence of the American University.* Chicago: U of Chicago P, 1965.

"A Vital Question." *Atlanta Constitution* 25 Aug. 1889: 15.

Vorse, Mary Heaton. *Strike!* 1930. Urbana: U of Illinois P, 1991.

Waddy, Virginia. *Elements of Composition and Rhetoric.* New York: American Book Co., 1889.

Wagner, Joanne. "'Intelligent Members or Restless Disturbers': Women's Rhetorical Styles, 1880–1920." Lunsford 185–202.

Wallace, Karl R., ed. *History of Speech Education in America: Background Studies.* New York: Appleton-Century-Crofts, 1954.

Washington, Robert E. *The Ideologies of African American Literature: From the Harlem Renaissance to the Black Nationalist Revolt.* Lanham, MD: Rowman and Littlefield, 2001.

Watts, Rebecca Bridges. *Contemporary Southern Identity: Community through Controversy.* Jackson: UP of Mississippi, 2008.

Webb, Ross A. *The Torch Is Passed: A History of Winthrop University.* Mansfield, OH: Bookmasters, 2002.

Wells, Ida B. *Southern Horrors and Other Writings: The Anti-Lynching Campaign of Ida B. Wells, 1892–1900.* Ed. Jacqueline Jones Royster. Boston: Bedford, 1997.

Welty, Eudora. *Losing Battles.* New York: Random House, 1970.

———. *One Writer's Beginnings.* 1983. New York: Warner, 1985.

Wendell, Barrett. *English Composition: Eight Lectures Given at the Lowell Institute.* New York: Scribner's, 1891.

White, Deborah Gray. *Too Heavy a Load: Black Women in Defense of Themselves, 1894–1994.* New York: Norton, 1999.

White, Edmund Valentine. *Chocolate Drops from the South: A Book of Negro Humor and Philosophy.* Austin: E. L. Steck, 1932.

———. *Lengthening Shadows, or, From Country School to College Campus.* Denton, TX: Author, 1948.

———. *Senegambian Sizzles: Negro Stories.* Dallas: Banks Upshaw, 1945.

White, Hayden. *Metahistory: The Historical Imagination in Nineteenth-Century Europe.* Baltimore: Johns Hopkins UP, 1973.

White, Newman Ivey, and Walter Clinton Jackson, eds. *An Anthology of Verse by American Negroes.* Durham, NC: Trinity College P, 1924.

Whites, LeeAnn. *The Civil War as a Crisis in Gender: Augusta, Georgia, 1860–1890.* Athens: U of Georgia P, 1995.

Winthrop College [a.k.a. South Carolina Industrial and Winthrop Normal College; Winthrop Normal and Industrial College of South Carolina]. *Catalogue.*

———. *Report of the Board of Trustees of the Winthrop Normal and Industrial College of South Carolina to the General Assembly of South Carolina, 1902.* Collected in *Reports and Resolutions of the General Assembly of the State of South Carolina, 1903.* Vol. 1. Columbia: The State Co., State Printers, 1903.

———. *Report of the Board of Trustees of the Winthrop Normal and Industrial College of South Carolina to the General Assembly, 1918.* Columbia: Gonzales and Bryan, 1919.

———. *Report of the Board of Trustees of the Winthrop Normal and Industrial College of South Carolina to the General Assembly, 1919.* Columbia: Gonzales and Bryan, 1920.

———. *Tatler* [yearbook].

Woodward, C. Vann. *The Burden of Southern History.* 3rd ed. Baton Rouge: U of Louisiana P, 1993.

———. *The Strange Career of Jim Crow.* 1955. Commemorative ed. New York: Oxford UP, 2002.

Woolley, Edwin C. *Handbook of Composition.* Boston: Heath, 1907.

World Almanac and Book of Facts. New York: Press Publishing. Various years.

Wynn, William T. *An English Grammar.* 1927. Rev. ed. Macon, GA: J. W. Burke, 1930.

Yale College. *Reports on the Course of Instruction in Yale College; by a Committee of the Corporation and the Academical Faculty.* New Haven: Hezekiah Howe, 1828.

Young, Nerissa. "The Borsig Era Begins." *Dispatch* (Columbus, MS) 3 Dec. 2011. 20 Dec. 2011 <http://www.cdispatch.com/news/article.asp?aid=14340>.

Index

The letter *t* following a page number indicates a table.

David Gold, an associate professor of English at the University of Michigan, is the author of *Rhetoric at the Margins: Revising the History of Writing Instruction in American Colleges, 1873–1947* (Southern Illinois University Press, 2008), winner of the 2010 Conference on College Composition and Communication Outstanding Book Award.

Catherine L. Hobbs, a professor of English at the University of Oklahoma, is the editor of *Nineteenth-Century Women Learn to Write* (1995) and the author of *Rhetoric on the Margins of Modernity. Vico, Condillac, Monboddo* (Southern Illinois University Press, 2002) and *The Elements of Autobiography and Life Narratives* (2005).

They previously collaborated on an edited collection, *Rhetoric, History, and Women's Oratorical Education: American Women Learn to Speak* (2013).

Studies in Rhetorics and Feminisms

Studies in Rhetorics and Feminisms seeks to address the interdisciplinarity that rhetorics and feminisms represent. Rhetorical and feminist scholars want to connect rhetorical inquiry with contemporary academic and social concerns, exploring rhetoric's relevance to current issues of opportunity and diversity. This interdisciplinarity has already begun to transform the rhetorical tradition as we have known it (upper-class, agonistic, public, and male) into regendered, inclusionary rhetorics (democratic, dialogic, collaborative, cultural, and private). Our intellectual advancements depend on such ongoing transformation.

Rhetoric, whether ancient, contemporary, or futuristic, always inscribes the relation of language and power at a particular moment, indicating who may speak, who may listen, and what can be said. The only way we can displace the traditional rhetoric of masculine-only, public performance is to replace it with rhetorics that are recognized as being better suited to our present needs. We must understand more fully the rhetorics of the non-Western tradition, of women, of a variety of cultural and ethnic groups. Therefore, Studies in Rhetorics and Feminisms espouses a theoretical position of openness and expansion, a place for rhetorics to grow and thrive in a symbiotic relationship with all that feminisms have to offer, particularly when these two fields intersect with philosophical, sociological, religious, psychological, pedagogical, and literary issues.

The series seeks scholarly works that both examine and extend rhetoric, works that span the sexes, disciplines, cultures, ethnicities, and sociocultural practices as they intersect with the rhetorical tradition. After all, the recent resurgence of rhetorical studies has been not so much a discovery of new rhetorics as a recognition of existing rhetorical activities and practices, of our newfound ability and willingness to listen to previously untold stories.

The series editors seek both high-quality traditional and cutting-edge scholarly work that extends the significant relationship between rhetoric and feminism within various genres, cultural contexts, historical periods, methodologies, theoretical positions, and methods of delivery (e.g., film and hypertext to elocution and preaching).

Queries and submissions:

Professor Cheryl Glenn, Editor
    E-mail: cjg6@psu.edu
Professor Shirley Wilson Logan, Editor
    E-mail: slogan@umd.edu

Studies in Rhetorics and Feminisms

Department of English
142 South Burrowes Bldg.
Penn State University
University Park, PA 16802-6200